MONEY TO WORK II
FUNDING FOR VISUAL ARTISTS

Edited by Helen M. Brunner
and Donald H. Russell
with Grant E. Samuelsen

ART RESOURCES INTERNATIONAL
WASHINGTON, DC
Published with support from the National Endowment for the Arts

Additional copies of this book are available for
$15.20, postpaid, from:

Art Resources International
5813 Nevada Avenue, NW
Washington, DC 20015-2544
Telephone: 202-363-6806

Editors: Helen M. Brunner and Donald H. Russell
Research and Editorial Associate: Grant E. Samuelsen
Editorial Assistance: Wilfred R. Brunner, Eva Gross, Lynn A. McCary
Cover Design: Scott Severson, Signal Communications, Bethesda, MD

This project was funded by the National Endowment for the Arts, a federal agency.

Printed in the United States of America
First edition, April, 1992

Library of Congress Cataloging in Publication Data:

Money to work II: funding for visual artists / edited by Helen M. Brunner and Donald H. Russell. --Rev. and expanded ed., 1st ed.
320 p. 22 x 14 cm.
Includes bibliographic references and index.
ISBN 0-929665-01-5 $11.95
1. Art–United States–Scholarships, fellowships, etc. - Directories. I. Brunner, Helen M. II. Russell, Donald H. III Art Resources International.
N347.M63 1992
707'.9'73–dc20 92-6549

Contents

Preface

The National Endowment for the Arts Visual Arts Program is pleased to be able to support *Money to Work II.* Building on the success of the first edition, published in 1988, this publication gives visual artists access to an even wider range of public and private funding sources for their work.

Since the Endowment was established as an independent agency of the federal government in 1965, support for visual artists through non-project fellowships has remained the Visual Arts Program's first priority. Through a highly competitive peer panel review process, approximately $5 million is awarded to 500 artists in every two-year funding cycle in the disciplines of painting, sculpture, crafts, photography, works on paper, and new genres. In addition to national fellowships, the Endowment has initiated an expanding network of regional fellowships, which provides over $500,000 in awards to about 100 artists through regionally administered programs throughout the country.

The concept of fellowships that simply "buy time with no strings attached" has been a difficult funding policy for some granting agencies to embrace. However, during the past decade, many new sources of support for visual artists have developed. The majority of state arts agencies and a growing number of private foundations recognize the primary need of visual artists to have an unencumbered block of time to concentrate on the development of their work. We are pleased that this new edition of *Money to Work* also offers information on other kinds of support, such as residencies, project grants, public art commissions, and travel grants.

Most artists do not earn their livelihood from the sale of their work. Most earn a living from other employment and therefore seek funding and recognition from other sources in order to more fully concentrate on creating new work. Visual artists' contributions to the health and vitality of America's culture are becoming more recognized. We hope this guide to sources of support for your work will help to encourage your endeavors.

We welcome your comments and suggestions.

Michael Faubion
Assistant Director
Visual Arts Program
National Endowment for the Arts

Introduction

An Assessment of Support for Visual Artists

This book presents information on funding sources serving individual visual artists. These sources include federal, state, and local arts agencies, private foundations, and non-profit arts organizations. The book is designed to familiarize artists and arts administrators with the field, so that existing resources can be utilized effectively and new and improved resources can be developed. Visual artists have very distinct needs from performing and literary artists, yet it was not until the first edition of *Money to Work* in 1988 that a single book was dedicated to fellowship sources for visual artists. The new edition has been expanded to include project grants, residencies, travel grants, and public art commissions, as well as updated information on fellowship programs.

During the past several years, the arts community has been subjected to intense political scrutiny in addition to being plagued by an economic recession. In this climate, there is legitimate cause for concern about the levels of continued funding for living artists, especially for those who are emerging and under-recognized or whose work has political content or uses non-traditional forms. Government support for the arts, and even rights of free expression, are in serious jeopardy. The result could be substantially decreased art support and growing self-censorship among artists. It is critical that artists become active in preserving and strengthening the principles that have driven arts support for the past twenty-five years. The degree of scrutiny of contemporary art, brought on by recent controversies, offers an unprecedented opportunity for artists and arts administrators to advocate for public's understanding about the constructive role artists play in our society.

The purpose of this book is to make basic information about funding sources available and to give artists a sense of familiarity and even "ownership" of existing support structures. Too often, funding agencies are perceived as inhuman bureaucracies that mysteriously distribute funds. This is a dangerous stereotype. It is important to remember that these organizations exist to support artists' needs, not as a form of welfare or job assistance, but through recognition and economic compensation for artists' greatly undervalued contribution to cultural progress.

Until very recently, funding for artists has grown steadily, although rarely can funders award more than 10% of applicants seeking unrestricted grants. Funders have dedicated themselves to making the process as even-handed and fair as possible by using the peer panel review process, which is a standard procedure used throughout the academic and scientific communities to make decisions. How peer panels are implemented varies among funders, but generally between three and twelve individuals from the arts community (artists, critics, curators, historians) are brought together to review materials and make funding decisions. The process is not perfect and remains subject to criticisms that only friends or "sanctioned" artists receive funds. But over the years, the process has been greatly improved by instituting one-time only service for panelists, by carefully balancing panel diversity and demographics, and by instituting waiting periods for reapplication by former grant recipients. While these changes have improved artists' attitudes about the process, it remains vulnerable in the current political debate about arts funding because of the perceived insularity of the arts community. In response to such criticisms, funders may be pressured to use panelists from outside the arts community, a development that will erode the peerage that makes the process so responsive to artists.

Regardless of how fair the peer panel process is, it serves no purpose without substantial funding, and the strongest argument for increased funding is based on the level of demand from artists. It is therefore of vital importance that all artists apply for funding on a regular basis. Unfortunately, there is evidence that it can take an artist at least five years of judicious applications before actually receiving a grant. This may mean as many as ten to fifteen rejections. While no artist likes to be rejected, especially repeatedly, a clear understanding of the process and balanced expectations are extremely important to stay active in the process. Funders have made the application process as straightforward as possible. Panels change, competition varies, and funding priorities may shift from year to year. The artist's main task is to keep track of funding opportunities, target the most appropriate sources, and prepare high quality, coherent and visually compelling documentation of their work. It is dangerously easy to procrastinate or let misconceptions get in the way of applying for funding, but artists must accept the terms of operating within the process to achieve better service of their needs and the needs of other artists.

Donald H. Russell
Washington, 1992

Visual Artists Funding - A Statistical Overview

The following tables, based on information gathered in 1991, provide data on the number of funding sources, the number of applicants and recipients, the percentage of applicants that actually receive funds, and the dollar amounts awarded. Travel grants have been combined either with residencies or project grants, depending on which was the most appropriate. Public art funders were not included in the following tables because of the fluctuating nature of their funding.

Source	# of Sources	Applicants/Recipients	% funded	Dollars
Unrestricted Fellowships				
National	23	14,013/1,304	9%	$8,930,000
Regional	9	5,852/144	2.5%	1,090,000
State and Local	72	13,818/1,177	8.5%	7,477,500
Sub-total	104	33,683/2,625	7.8%	17,497,500
Project Grants				
National	17	2,001/239	8.3%	839,000
Regional	12	3,656/154	4.2%	640,750
State and Local	47	2,565/612	23.8%	1,525,500
Sub-total	76	8,222/1,005	12%	3,005,250
Residencies				
National	55	11,039/1,098	10%	1,569,700
Regional	4	385/70	18%	244,800
State and Local	5	400/195	48.7%	96,000
Sub-total	64	11,824/1,363	11.5%	1,910,500
Awards by Nomination Only				
Combined	16	n.a./85	n.a.	1,067,250
Grand Total	**260**	**53,729/5,078**	**9.5%**	**$23,480,500**

How to Use This Book

Funding sources included in this book provide awards of $500 or more, maintain open applications and do not require artists to pay participation fees. The book combines unrestricted fellowships, residencies, project grants, travel grants, and public art commissions into three sections based on geographic eligibility. Based on artistic medium and other restrictions, artists may apply to appropriate sources in the National Section, the Regional Section, and State and Local Section.

The Geographic/Media Index on p.300 will target the most suitable sources, although it is a good idea to review the entire book to understand the field more fully. If you do not find a listing for a particular grant, check the Alphabetical Index on p. 309 for a cross-reference, since it may be administered by another funding source. In some cases, a single funder will have additional programs appearing in different geographic eligibility sections of the book. Other restrictions may apply, so please read the organzation's entry carefully.

Artists' organizations have been included only if they maintain an open applications process for projects offering a honorarium of $500 or more. Additional artists' organizations that pay honoraria to exhibitiong artists are listed in , the *NAAO Directory of Artists Organizations* (see Bibliography, p. 297).

A separate listing of grants awarded "by nomination only" is included on p. 281 to show the amount of support these funding sources provide to the field. Remember that these organizations do not accept unsolicited applications.

Information about public art funders is difficult to compile because their activities fluctuate based on the number of commissions available at any given time. Sources that offer commissions on a regular basis are integrated with the other funding sources. A supplementary list of additional public art sources is included on p. 291. Contact these organizations to receive commission announcements.

This book is the result of considerable research using existing reference works, data base searches, and widely disseminated requests for funding information. Over 1,200 potential funding sources were sent a questionnaire about their programs. Of the questionnaires returned, 244 were within the stated criteria. There may be other sources that we did not locate, and we would appreciate hearing about them so they can be included in later editions.

Please contact funding sources to receive complete guidelines and application information before applying. Remember that funders may change their criteria or methods, or even cease offering funds. We apologize for any inconvenience that this may cause, but every effort has been made to provide accurate information.

We welcome your response to the book and wish you the best of luck in finding support for your work.

NATIONAL SOURCES

Since funding organizations may change their policies, procedures, and award amounts, artists should always obtain current information and application guidelines directly from the funding sources before submitting material for award consideration. Exact deadlines are not included for this reason. For current information on new sources of support, contact appropriate state arts councils, regional arts organizations, and sources of information listed in the Bibliography and Resource Organizations section.

ACTS INSTITUTE
PO Box 10153
Kansas City , MO 64111
816-753-0208

AWARD

Title: Cash Grant Program For Colony Residents
Purpose: The program is open to artists who have been accepted at a colony but require financial assistance that the colony is unable to provide. Applicants must have applied for but denied funding from the NEA and their state and local arts councils to be eligible for funding. ACTS cash grants should be a "last resort" option.
Categories of Support: Artists' Books, Crafts, Drawing, New Genres, Painting, Photography, Printmaking, Public Art, Sculpture
Type of Support: Residency Fee Waiver
Year Established: Information not provided
Duration of Funding: n/a
Customary Month or Season of Deadline: n/a
Total Number of Applicants: Information not provided
Total Number of Recipients: Information not provided
Funding Amount: Varies with situation

APPLICATION PROCEDURE

Requirements: Write ACTS Institute for current application procedure.
Restrictions: n/a
Time Between Application Deadline and Award Notification: n/a
Reapplication by Former Recipients: n/a

SELECTION PROCESS

Method: n/a
Criteria: n/a

OTHER INFORMATION

Publications: n/a
Activities: n/a

EDWARD F. ALBEE FOUNDATION

14 Harrison Street
New York, NY 10013
212-226-2020

<u>AWARD</u>

Title: Residency
Purpose: Provides one month residencies at the William Flanagan Memorial Creative Persons Center ("The Barn") in Montauk, Long Island.
Categories of Support: Drawing, New Genres, Painting, Sculpture
Type of Support: Residency
Year Established: Information not provided
Duration of Funding: One month
Customary Month or Season of Deadline: April
Total Number of Applicants: Information not provided
Total Number of Recipients: Up to six per season
Funding Amount: Housing and studio for duration of residency

<u>APPLICATION PROCEDURE</u>

Requirements: Application form, resume, slides, project description/statement, two letters of recommendation
Restrictions: None
Time Between Application Deadline and Award Notification: One month
Reapplication by Former Recipients: Allowed immediately

<u>SELECTION PROCESS</u>

Method: Staff Members
Criteria: Quality of work is the primary criterion.

<u>OTHER INFORMATION</u>

Publications: Program Guidelines
Activities: n/a

ALTERNATIVE WORKSITE/BEMIS FOUNDATION ("The Bemis")

614 South 11th Street
Omaha, NE 68102
402-341-7130
Ree Shonlali, Executive Director
Joan Batson, Executive Assistant

AWARD

Title: Artist Residency
Purpose: Support for visual artists by providing large studios, living accomodations, work-related equipment (especially large-scale ceramic sculpture), and a monthly stipend of $200.
Categories of Support: Drawing, New Genres, Painting, Photography, Printmaking, Public Art, Sculpture
Type of Support: Residency
Year Established: 1985
Duration of Funding: Three - six months
Customary Month or Season of Deadline: March
Total Number of Applicants: 267
Total Number of Recipients: 26
Funding Amount: $200 stipend, studio and housing for duration of residency.

APPLICATION PROCEDURE

Requirements: Application form, resume, slides
Restrictions: None
Time Between Application Deadline and Award Notification: Two months
Reapplication by Former Recipients: Allowed immediately

SELECTION PROCESS

Method: Peer Panel
Criteria: Quality of work is the primary criterion. Other factors include: resume, appropriateness to guidelines, and project description.

OTHER INFORMATION

Publications: Program Guidelines
Activities: Occasional exhibition of recipient's work, slide registry

AMERICAN ACADEMY IN ROME

41 East 65th Street
New York, NY 10021-6508
212-517-4200
Adele Chatfield-Taylor, President
Buff Kauelman, Director of Programs

AWARD

Title: Rome Prize
Purpose: Provides room and board, studio, stipend, and travel allowance for outstanding visual artists to live, work, and research in Rome.
Categories of Support: Artists' Books, Drawing, New Genres, Painting, Photography, Printmaking, Public Art, Sculpture
Type of Support: Residency
Year Established: 1894
Duration of Funding: One year
Customary Month or Season of Deadline: November
Total Number of Applicants: 1000+
Total Number of Recipients: 4
Funding Amount: Room and board, studio, travel expenses, supplies and living stipend for duration of residency.

APPLICATION PROCEDURE

Requirements: Application form, slides, project description/statement, references
Restrictions: Applicant may not be currently enrolled in a degree-granting program. US citizenship
Time Between Application Deadline and Award Notification: Five months
Reapplication by Former Recipients: Not allowed

SELECTION PROCESS

Method: Peer Panel, Board Members
Criteria: Quality of work is the primary criterion. Project description is also considered.

OTHER INFORMATION

Publications: Program Guidelines
Activities: Exhibition of recipient's work in Rome, lecture series, concerts, and tours during residency.

AMERICAN MUSEUM OF WILDLIFE ART (AMWA)
3303 North Service Drive
Red Wing, MN 55066
612-388-0755
Byron G. Webster, Executive Director

AWARD

Title: The Gromme Grant
Purpose: To encourage and assist the artistic talent of an ever-growing number of artists who specialize in the field of wildlife and sporting art.
Categories of Support: Drawing, Painting, Printmaking, Sculpture
Type of Support: Unrestricted
Year Established: 1988
Duration of Funding: One year
Customary Month or Season of Deadline: February
Total Number of Applicants: 200
Total Number of Recipients: 1
Funding Amount: $3,000

APPLICATION PROCEDURE

Requirements: Application form, resume, slides, project description/statement
Restrictions: US citizenship
Time Between Application Deadline and Award Notification: One month
Reapplication by Former Recipients: Allowed after five years

SELECTION PROCESS

Method: Peer Panel, Staff Members
Criteria: Quality of work is the primary criterion. Other factors include: financial need, resume, and appropriateness to guidelines.

OTHER INFORMATION

Publications: Program Guidelines
Activities: Exhibition of recipient's work

AMERICAN-SCANDINAVIAN FOUNDATION

127 East 73rd Street
New York, NY 10021
212-879-9779
Lena Biorck Kaplan, Executive Director

AWARD

Title: Fellowships and Grants
Purpose: To support advanced study or research, in all fields, in the Scandinavian countries.
Categories of Support: Crafts, Drawing, Painting, Photography, Printmaking, Public Art, Sculpture
Type of Support: Unrestricted
Year Established: 1911
Duration of Funding: One year
Customary Month or Season of Deadline: November
Total Number of Applicants: 150
Total Number of Recipients: 45
Funding Amount: $2,500-15,000

APPLICATION PROCEDURE

Requirements: Application form, slides, resume, project description, letter or statement confirming availability of needed resources in Sandinavia.
Restrictions: U.S. citizenship
Time Between Application Deadline and Award Notification: Six months
Reapplication by Former Recipients: Allowed after one year

SELECTION PROCESS

Method: Peer Panel, Staff Members, Board Members
Criteria: Quality of work is the primary criterion. Other factors include: financial need, resume, project description, and appropriateness to guidelines.

OTHER INFORMATION

Publications: Program Guidelines, Annual Report
Activities: Information not provided

ANDERSON RANCH ARTS CENTER (ARAC)
PO Box 5598
Snowmass Village, CO 81615
303-923-3181
Brad Miller, Director

AWARD

Title: Assistantship
Purpose: To assist workshop instructors, program directors, and workshop participants during our summer workshop program which provides assistants the opportunity to work with many of the country's leading artists.
Categories of Support: Crafts, Drawing, New Genres, Painting, Photography, Printmaking, Sculpture
Type of Support: Residency
Year Established: Information not provided
Duration of Funding: Three months
Customary Month or Season of Deadline: March
Total Number of Applicants: 100
Total Number of Recipients: 12
Funding Amount: $3,000-3,300

APPLICATION PROCEDURE

Requirements: Application form, resume, slides, project description/statement, three references
Restrictions: None
Time Between Application Deadline and Award Notification: One month
Reapplication by Former Recipients: Allowed immediately

SELECTION PROCESS

Method: Staff Members
Criteria: Quality of work is the primary criterion. Resume is also considered.

OTHER INFORMATION

Publications: Program Guidelines
Activities: Exhibition of recipient's work

ART IN GENERAL

79 Walker Street
New York, NY 10013
212-219-0473
Holly Block, Executive Director

AWARD

Title: Artists' Honoraria
Purpose: To provide artists' fees for projects exhibited in the Art in General Space.
Categories of Support: Artists' Books, Drawing, New Genres, Painting, Photography, Printmaking, Public Art, Sculpture
Type of Support: Honoraria
Year Established: 1988
Duration of Funding: Five weeks
Customary Month or Season of Deadline: November
Total Number of Applicants: 600
Total Number of Recipients: 55
Funding Amount: $150-1,000

APPLICATION PROCEDURE

Requirements: Resume, project description/statement, slides
Restrictions: Applicant may not be currently enrolled in a degree-granting program.
Time Between Application Deadline and Award Notification: Five months
Reapplication by Former Recipients: Allowed after three years

SELECTION PROCESS

Method: Peer Panel, Staff Members
Criteria: Quality of work is the primary criterion. Other factors include: ethnic background, geographic representation, appropriateness to guidelines, project description, and economic need.

OTHER INFORMATION

Publications: Program Guidelines, Exhibition Brochures
Activities: Exhibition of recipient's work

ART IN PUBLIC PLACES COMMITTEE OF WEST PALM BEACH
P.O. Box 3366
West Palm Beach, FL 33402
407-659-8077
Sheryl Snyder, Program Director

AWARD
Title: 1% For Art Program
Purpose: Commission works of art for new or renovated city buildings.
Categories of Support: Public Art
Type of Support: Public Art Commission
Year Established: 1990
Duration of Funding: Varies with project
Customary Month or Season of Deadline: January
Total Number of Applicants: Information not provided
Total Number of Recipients: Information not provided
Funding Amount: Up to $150,000

APPLICATION PROCEDURE
Requirements: Resume, slides, project description
Restrictions: None
Time Between Application Deadline and Award Notification: Varies with project
Reapplication by Former Recipients: Information not provided

SELECTION PROCESS
Method: Board Members
Criteria: Quality of work is the primary criterion. Other factors include: resume, appropriateness to guidelines, and project description.

OTHER INFORMATION
Publications: Program Guidelines, Exhibition Catalogues of former recipients
Activities: Exhibition of recipient's work

ART MATTERS

131 West 24th Street
New York, NY 10011
212-929-7190
Alexander Gray, Program Coordinator

AWARD

Title: Grants to Individuals
Purpose: Fellowships to artists whose work deas with provocative contemporary issues in the arts. High priority is given to work dealing with social and political issues.
Categories of Support: Artists' Books, Crafts, Drawing, New Genres, Painting, Photography, Printmaking, Sculpture
Type of Support: Unrestricted
Year Established: 1985
Duration of Funding: One year
Customary Month or Season of Deadline: Fall and Spring
Total Number of Applicants: 91
Total Number of Recipients: 41
Funding Amount: $1,000-5,000

APPLICATION PROCEDURE

Requirements: Application form, slides, project description/statement, project budget
Restrictions: None
Time Between Application Deadline and Award Notification: Two months
Reapplication by Former Recipients: Allowed after one year

SELECTION PROCESS

Method: Peer Panel, Board Members
Criteria: Quality of work is the primary criterion. Other factors include: financial need, project description, geographic representation, and ethnic background.

OTHER INFORMATION

Publications: Program Guidelines
Activities: Information not provided

ARTPARK
Box 371
Lewiston, NY 14092
716-745-3377 (October-March)
716-754-9001 (April-September)
David Midland, Executive Director
Joan McDonough, Project Director

AWARD

Title: Residency
Purpose: Project artists use any media to create outdoor works which remain on site throughout the season.
Categories of Support: New Genres, Sculpture
Type of Support: Residency
Year Established: 1974
Duration of Funding: One year
Customary Month or Season of Deadline: September
Total Number of Applicants: 250
Total Number of Recipients: 6
Funding Amount: $500-35,000

APPLICATION PROCEDURE

Requirements: Application form, resume, slides
Restrictions: None
Time Between Application Deadline and Award Notification: Six months
Reapplication by Former Recipients: Allowed immediately

SELECTION PROCESS

Method: Guest Curator
Criteria: Quality of work is the primary criterion. Appropriateness to guidelines is also considered.

OTHER INFORMATION

Publications: Program Guidelines, exhibition catalogues of former recipients
Activities: n/a

ARTS INTERNATIONAL

Cintas Foundation Fellowship
809 United Nations Plaza
New York, NY 10017
212-984-5370
William B. Warren, Executive Director
Vanessa Palmer, Associate Program Officer

AWARD

Title: Cintas Fellowship
Purpose: To foster and encourage the development and recognition of talented creative artists in the fields of architecture, music composition, literature, and the visual arts.
Categories of Support: Artists' Books, Crafts, Drawing, New Genres, Painting, Photography, Printmaking, Sculpture
Type of Support: Unrestricted
Year Established: 1964
Duration of Funding: One year
Customary Month or Season of Deadline: March
Total Number of Applicants: 38
Total Number of Recipients: 7
Funding Amount: $7,500

APPLICATION PROCEDURE

Requirements: Application form, resume, slides, sample of original work, project description/statement, cover letter
Restrictions: Applicant must be of Cuban lineage.
Time Between Application Deadline and Award Notification: Five months
Reapplication by Former Recipients: Allowed immediately

SELECTION PROCESS

Method: Peer Panel
Criteria: Ethnic background is the primary criterion. Quality of work is also considered.

OTHER INFORMATION

Publications: Program Guidelines
Activities: See additional entries for this organization (*Arts International*)

ARTS INTERNATIONAL
Kade Collaborative Works Program
Institute for International Education
809 United Nations Plaza
New York, NY 10017-3580
212-984-5370
Vanessa Palmer, Program Officer

AWARD
Title: Kade Collaborative Works Program
Purpose: To encourage collaborative projects involving US, French, and German artists which expand understanding and expression and enrich the flow of ideas and practices.
Categories of Support: Artists' Books, Crafts, Drawing, New Genres, Painting, Photography, Printmaking, Public Art, Sculpture
Type of Support: Project Grant
Year Established: 1991
Duration of Funding: One year
Customary Month or Season of Deadline: Continuing
Total Number of Applicants: n/a (new program)
Total Number of Recipients: n/a (new program)
Funding Amount: $1,500-5,000

APPLICATION PROCEDURE
Requirements: Resume, project description/statement, slides
Restrictions: US, French, or German citizenship
Time Between Application Deadline and Award Notification: One to three months
Reapplication by Former Recipients: Information not provided

SELECTION PROCESS
Method: Peer Panel
Criteria: Quality of work and the project description are the primary criteria.

OTHER INFORMATION
Publications: Program Guidelines
Activities: See other entries for this organization.

ARTS INTERNATIONAL

Lila Wallace-Reader's Digest International Artists
Institute of International Education
809 United Nations Plaza
New York, NY 10017
212-984-5330

AWARD

Title: Lila Wallace-Reader's Digest International Artists
Purpose: Three-to-six month overseas residencies. Encourages connections between artists form the US and artists from around the world.
Categories of Support: Artists' Books, Crafts, Drawing, New Genres, Painting, Photography, Printmaking, Public Art, Sculpture, Video
Type of Support: Residency
Year Established: 1946
Duration of Funding: Three - six months
Customary Month or Season of Deadline: January
Total Number of Applicants: Information not provided
Total Number of Recipients: Information not provided
Funding Amount: $7,500-15,000 plus transportation, room and board, studio, insurance, additional funds depending on project

APPLICATION PROCEDURE

Requirements: Application form, biography, slides, project description/statement, additional supporting documentation as requested
Restrictions: U.S. citizenship or permanent residency
Time Between Application Deadline and Award Notification: Four months
Reapplication by Former Recipients: Not allowed

SELECTION PROCESS

Method: Panel Review—subject to approval by institution in host country
Criteria: Quality of work is the primary criterion. Project description and the applicant's history of participation in the community are also considered.

OTHER INFORMATION

Publications: Program Guidelines
Activities: Artist-initiated community activites upon completion of the residency.

ARTS INTERNATIONAL

Travel Grants Pilot
Institute of International Education
809 United Nations Plaza
New York, NY 10017
212-984-5370

AWARD

Title: Travel Grants Pilot
Purpose: The program is designed to enable artists to travel overseas to interact with their colleagues, to observe significant artistic developments in their fields, and to engage in other activites that will enrich their work.
Categories of Support: Artists' Books, Crafts, Drawing, New Genres, Painting, Photography, Printmaking, Public Art, Sculpture
Type of Support: Travel Grant
Year Established: 1992
Duration of Funding: Varies with project
Customary Month or Season of Deadline: February and May
Total Number of Applicants: n/a
Total Number of Recipients: n/a
Funding Amount: $500-2,500 average—$5,000 maximum

APPLICATION PROCEDURE

Requirements: Application form, resume, slides, project description/statement, project budget, background information on intended foreign host
Restrictions: Applicant may not be currently enrolled in a degree-granting program. U.S. citizenship. No funding for single-person exhibitions.
Time Between Application Deadline and Award Notification: Two months
Reapplication by Former Recipients: Information not provided

SELECTION PROCESS

Method: Peer Panel Review
Criteria: Quality of work is the primary criterion. Other factors include: feasibility of project, contribution of international experience to the applicant's professional career, and availability of needed resources in the intended host country.

OTHER INFORMATION

Publications: Program Guidelines
Activities: See additional entries for this organization

ASSOCIATION FOR VISUAL ARTISTS (AVA)

615 Lindsay Street
Chattanooga, TN 37403
615-265-4282
Peggy Wood, Executive Director

AWARD

Title: Artist-in-Residence Program
Purpose: To bring artists (regional and national) to Chattanooga to work in the public arena and exhibit their work. Twelve artists are selected every summer.
Categories of Support: Artists' Books, Crafts, Drawing, New Genres, Painting, Photography, Printmaking, Public Art, Sculpture
Type of Support: Residency
Year Established: 1988
Duration of Funding: Three months
Customary Month or Season of Deadline: April
Total Number of Applicants: 150
Total Number of Recipients: 12
Funding Amount: $600/week stipend, travel expenses, room and board

APPLICATION PROCEDURE

Requirements: Application form, resume, slides, project description/statement
Restrictions: None
Time Between Application Deadline and Award Notification: One month
Reapplication by Former Recipients: Allowed after one year

SELECTION PROCESS

Method: Peer Panel, Staff Members, Board Members
Criteria: Quality of work is the primary criterion. Other factors include: project description, geographic representation, and appropriateness to guidelines.

OTHER INFORMATION

Publications: Program Guidelines, Newsletter
Activities: Exhibition and public presentation by recipient, slide registry

BALTIMORE CLAYWORKS
5706 Smith Avenue
Baltimore, MD 21209
301-578-1919
Deborah Bedwell, Executive Director

AWARD

Title: Lormina Salter Residency Fellowship
Purpose: To encourage career development for emerging ceramic artists whose work is of the highest quality.
Categories of Support: Ceramics
Type of Support: Residency
Year Established: 1989
Duration of Funding: One year
Customary Month or Season of Deadline: June
Total Number of Applicants: 24
Total Number of Recipients: 1
Funding Amount: $3,200

APPLICATION PROCEDURE

Requirements: Application form, resume, slides, project description/statement
Restrictions: None
Time Between Application Deadline and Award Notification: One month
Reapplication by Former Recipients: Not allowed

SELECTION PROCESS

Method: Peer panel
Criteria: Quality of work is the primary criterion. Other factors include: resume, appropriateness to guidelines, and ethnic background.

OTHER INFORMATION

Publications: Program Guidelines
Activities: Exhibition of recipient's work

BEAVERTON ARTS COMMISSION (BAC)
P.O. Box 4755
Beaverton, OR 97076
503-526-2288
Jayne Scott, Executive Director

AWARD
Title: 1% For Art
Purpose: Commission works of art for public buildings.
Categories of Support: Painting, Photography, Printmaking, Public Art, Sculpture
Type of Support: Public Art Commission
Year Established: 1985
Duration of Funding: One year
Customary Month or Season of Deadline: Projects announced as they become available
Total Number of Applicants: 200
Total Number of Recipients: 7
Funding Amount: $3,000-60,000

APPLICATION PROCEDURE
Requirements: Application form, resume, slides, sample of original work dependent on media
Restrictions: None
Time Between Application Deadline and Award Notification: Three months
Reapplication by Former Recipients: Information not provided

SELECTION PROCESS
Method: Peer Panel
Criteria: Quality of work is the primary criterion. Other factors include: appropriateness to guidelines, project description, and resume.

OTHER INFORMATION
Publications: Program Guidelines, Annual Report
Activities: Exhibition of recipient's work

BLUE MOUNTAIN CENTER (BMC)

Blue Mountain Lake, NY 12812
518-352-7391
Harriet Barlow, Executive Director

AWARD

Title: Blue Mountain Center Residency
Purpose: To provide a peaceful and comfortable setting in which artists and writers may work.
Categories of Support: Artists' Books, Drawing, New Genres, Painting, Photography, Printmaking, Public Art, Sculpture
Type of Support: Residency
Year Established: 1981
Duration of Funding: One month
Customary Month or Season of Deadline: February
Total Number of Applicants: Information not provided
Total Number of Recipients: Information not provided
Funding Amount: Studio, room and board for duration of residency.

APPLICATION PROCEDURE

Requirements: Resume, slides, sample of original work, project description/ statement
Restrictions: None
Time Between Application Deadline and Award Notification: One month
Reapplication by Former Recipients: Allowed immediately

SELECTION PROCESS

Method: Peer Panel
Criteria: Quality of work is the primary criterion.

OTHER INFORMATION

Publications: Program Guidelines
Activities: In-house exhibition of recipient's work

BRANDYWINE WORKSHOP

1520-22 Kater Street
Philadelphia, PA 19146
215-546-3657
James Dupree, Artistic Director
Jennifer Desnouee, Assistant Artistic Director

AWARD

Title: Visiting Artist Program
Purpose: Promotes interest and talent in fine art offset printmaking. Brandywine operates a fine art offset facility and while this is the focus of the Visiting Artist Program, all disciplines are encouraged to apply.
Categories of Support: Artists' Books, Crafts, Drawing, New Genres, Painting, Photography, Printmaking, Sculpture
Type of Support: Residency
Year Established: 1975
Duration of Funding: One week
Customary Month or Season of Deadline: May
Total Number of Applicants: 75
Total Number of Recipients: 24
Funding Amount: $300 stipend, living and travel expenses, offset printing materials and facilites.

APPLICATION PROCEDURE

Requirements: Application form, resume, slides, project description/statement
Restrictions: Applicant may not be currently enrolled in a degree-granting program.
Time Between Application Deadline and Award Notification: One month
Reapplication by Former Recipients: Allowed after one year

SELECTION PROCESS

Method: Peer Panel
Criteria: Quality of work is the primary criterion. Other factors include: financial need, resume, and project description.

OTHER INFORMATION

Publications: Program Guidelines, Annual Report
Activities: Exhibition of recipient's work

BRITISH SCHOOL AT ROME
Regent's College
Inner Circle, Regent's Park
London, NW 1 4NS
England
071- 4877603
Ann Marie Tighe, General Seretary

<u>**AWARD**</u>
Title: Abbey Major Scholarship
Purpose: To allow a painter to research and work in Rome.
Categories of Support: Painting
Type of Support: Residency
Year Established: Information not provided.
Duration of Funding: Nine months
Customary Month or Season of Deadline: December
Total Number of Applicants: 120
Total Number of Recipients: 1
Funding Amount: £4,000 (approx.$7,050) plus room and board

<u>**APPLICATION PROCEDURE**</u>
Requirements: Application form, slides, sample of original work, project description/statement
Restrictions:US citizenship
Time Between Application Deadline and Award Notification: Two months
Reapplication by Former Recipients: Allowed immediately

<u>**SELECTION PROCESS**</u>
Method: Board Members
Criteria: Quality of work is the primary criterion.

<u>**OTHER INFORMATION**</u>
Publications: Program Guidelines
Activities: Exhibition of recipient's work

BRONX COUNCIL ON THE ARTS (BCA)

1738 Hone Avenue
Bronx, NY 10461
212-931-9500
Bill Aquado, Executive Director
Fred Wilson, Curator

AWARD

Title: Scholarship Studio Program
Purpose: To provide free studio space and a materials stipend to visual artists for periods ranging from two to nine months.
Categories of Support: Artists' Books, Crafts, Drawing, Painting, Photography, New Genres, Printmaking, Public Art, Sculpture
Type of Support: Residency
Year Established: 1987
Duration of Funding: Two to nine months
Customary Month orSeason of Deadline: January
Total Number of Applicants: 40
Total Number of Recipients: 4
Funding Amount: $100-500/month materials stipend and studio space for duration of residency

APPLICATION PROCEDURE

Requirements: Application form, resume, project description/statement, slides
Restrictions: Applicant must be 18 years of age or older and not currently enrolled in a degree-granting program.
Time Between Application Deadline and Award Notification: Six months
Reapplication by Former Recipients: Not allowed

SELECTION PROCESS

Method: Peer panel
Criteria: Quality of work is the primary criterion. Project description/statement and ethnic background are also considered.

OTHER INFORMATION

Publications: Program Guidelines, exhibition catalogues of former recipients
Activities: Exhibition of recipient's work

MARY INGRAHAM BUNTING INSTITUTE OF RADCLIFFE COLLEGE

34 Concord Avenue
Cambridge, MA 02138
617-495-8212
Florence C. Ladd, Executive Director
Chiho Tokita, Fellowships Coordinator

AWARD

Title: Bunting Fellowship
Purpose: To support women scholars, researchers, scientists, writers, performing and visual artists of exceptional promise and demonstrated achievement.
Categories of Support: Crafts, Drawing, New Genres, Painting, Photography, Printmaking, Public Art, Sculpture
Type of Support: Unrestricted
Year Established: Information not provided
Duration of Funding: One year
Customary Month or Season of Deadline: October
Total Number of Applicants: 126
Total Number of Recipients: 1
Funding Amount: $28,500

APPLICATION PROCEDURE

Requirements: Application form, resume, slides, project description/statement
Restrictions: Applicant may not be currently enrolled in a degree-granting program.
Time Between Application Deadline and Award Notification: Information not provided
Reapplication by Former Recipients: Allowed after five years

SELECTION PROCESS

Method: Peer Panel
Criteria: Quality of work is the primary criterion. Financial need and resume are also considered.

OTHER INFORMATION

Publications: Program Guidelines
Activities: Exhibition of recipient's work

CALIFORNIA ARTS COUNCIL

2411 Alhambra Blvd
Saramento, CA 95817
916-739-3186
Kathi Stockdale, Acting Executive Director
Scott Heckes, Administrator, Art in Public Buildings

AWARD

Title: Art in Public Buildings Commission
Purpose: To increase public access to art and afford opportunities to artists through the placement of art in public, state buildings.
Categories of Support: Crafts, Painting, Photography, Public Art, Sculpture
Type of Support: Public Art Commission
Year Established: 1976
Duration of Funding: Varies with project (up to three years)
Customary Month or Season of Deadline: October
Total Number of Applicants: 450
Total Number of Recipients: 3
Funding Amount: $5,000-30,000

APPLICATION PROCEDURE

Requirements: Application form, resume, slides, project description/statement
Restrictions: None
Time Between Application Deadline and Award Notification: Eight months
Reapplication by Former Recipients: Allowed after three years

SELECTION PROCESS

Method: Staff Members, Board Members
Criteria: Quality of work is the primary criterion. Resume and appropriateness to guidelines are also considered.

OTHER INFORMATION

Publications: Program Guidelines
Activities: See additional entries for this organization. Exhibition of recipient's work, slide registry.

CAPP STREET PROJECT/AVT
270 14th Street
San Francisco, CA 94103
415-626-7747
Alan Millar, Executive Director
Susan Miller, Program Director

AWARD
Title: Artist-in-Residence
Purpose: To provide an opportunity for multi-disciplinary artists to create and present new installations in San Francisco.
Categories of support: New Genres, Public Art, Sculpture
Type of support: Residency
Year established: 1983
Duration of funding: Three months
Customary Month or Season of Deadline: Fall
Total Number of Applicants: 40
Total Number of Recipients: 4
Funding Amount: Up to $10,000 fabrication/production expenses plus $4,500 stipend

APPLICATION PROCEDURE
Requirements: Application form, resume, project description/statement, slides
Restrictions: Preliminary submissions are open, fall applications by invitation only.
Time Between Application Deadline and Award Notification: Six weeks
Reapplication by Former Recipients: Not allowed

SELECTION PROCESS
Method: Peer panel, staff members
Criteria: Quality of work is the primary criterion. Other factors include: project description/statement, resume, appropriateness to guidelines, ethnic background, and geographic representation.

OTHER INFORMATION
Publications: Program Guidelines
Activities: Exhibition of recipient's work

CAPP STREET PROJECT/AVT

270 14th Street
San Francisco, CA 94103
415-626-7747
Alan Millar, Executive Director
Susan Miller, Program Director

AWARD

Title: Temporary Off-Site Installations
Purpose: To facilitate the creation and presentation of new public installations in the San Francisco Bay area. One site-specific installation is created each year with Capp Street Project acting as a facilitator for additional fundraising, fabrication, and site-negotiation.
Categories of Support: Public Art, Sculpture, New Genres
Type of Support: Project Grant
Year Established: 1990
Duration of Funding: Varies with project
Customary Month or Season of Deadline: Fall
Total Number of Applicants: 40
Total Number of Recipients: 1
Funding Amount: Up to $12,000 fabrication/production expenses plus $5,500 stipend/honoraria

APPLICATION PROCEDURE

Requirements: Application form, resume, slides, project description/statement
Restrictions: Preliminary submissions are open. Final submissions in the Fall are by invitation only.
Time Between Application Deadline and Award Notification: Six weeks
Reapplication by Former Recipients: Not allowed

SELECTION PROCESS

Method: Peer Panel , Staff Members
Criteria: Quality of work is the primary criterion. Other factors include: project description, resume, geographic representation, and ethnic background.

OTHER INFORMATION

Publications: Program Guidelines
Activities: See additional entries for this organization.

CENTRUM RESIDENCY PROGRAM

Fort Warden State Park
PO Box 1158
Port Townsend, WA 98368
206-385-3102
Sarah Muirhead, Progam Coordinator

AWARD

Title: Centrum Artists-in-Residence Program
Purpose: To provide a quiet, isolated environment in which artists may focus on their work.
Categories of Support: Printmaking
Type of Support: Residency
Year Established: 1982
Duration of Funding: One month
Customary Month or Season of Deadline: April and October
Total Number of Applicants: 100
Total Number of Recipients: 5
Funding Amount: $75/week stipend, housing and studio during residency

APPLICATION PROCEDURE

Requirements: Application form, resume, slides, project description/statement
Restrictions: None
Time Between Application Deadline and Award Notification: Information not provided
Reapplication by Former Recipients: Allowed after one year

SELECTION PROCESS

Method: Peer Panel
Criteria: Quality of work is the primary criterion. Project description is also considered.

OTHER INFORMATION

Publications: Program Guidelines
Activities: Information not provided

CITY OF KENT ARTS COMMISSION

220 4th Avenue South
Kent, WA 98032
206-859-3991
Patrice Thorell, Executive Director
Liz Carpenter, Visual Arts Coordinator

AWARD

Title: City Art Program
Purpose: City funded public art program, $2 per capita annually
Categories of Support: Public Art
Type of Support: Public Art Commission
Year Established: 1986
Duration of Funding: Varies with project
Customary Month or Season of Deadline: Varies with project
Total Number of Applicants: Information not provided
Total Number of Recipients: Varies with number of projects
Funding Amount: $100-50,000

APPLICATION PROCEDURE

Requirements: Resume, slides, project description/statement
Restrictions: None
Time Between Application Deadline and Award Notification: Varies with project
Reapplication by Former Recipients: May vary with project

SELECTION PROCESS

Method: Peer Panel, Staff Members, Board Members
Criteria: Quality of work is the primary criterion. Resume and project description are also considered.

OTHER INFORMATION

Publications: Program Guidelines
Activities: Exhibition of recipient's work

COMMUNITY REDEVELOPMENT AGENCY OF THE CITY OF LOS ANGELES (CRA-LA)

354 South Spring Street, 7th Floor
Los Angeles, CA 90013-1258
213-977-1771
Mickey Gustin, Arts Planner
Julie Silliman, Associate Arts Planner

AWARD

Title: Public Art Program
Purpose: The mission of the CRA is to eliminate blight and revitalize the city through development in designated areas. Since 1985, the CRA has required most developments in its redevelopment areas to obligate 1% of development costs to public art.
Categories of Support: Public Art
Type of Support: Public Art Commission
Year Established: 1985
Duration of Funding: Varies with project
Customary Month or Season of Deadline: Information not provided
Total Number of Applicants: Information not provided
Total Number of Recipients: Information not provided
Funding Amount: $5000-1,000,000

APPLICATION PROCEDURE

Requirements: Resume, slides, project description/statement
Restrictions: Varies with project. Regional residency often required.
Time Between Application Deadline and Award Notification: Varies with project
Reapplication by Former Recipients: Varies with project

SELECTION PROCESS

Method: Peer Panel (if CRA funded), consultant/developer selection (if privately funded)
Criteria: Quality of work is the primary criterion. Appropriateness to site is also considered.

OTHER INFORMATION

Publications: Program Guidelines/Brochure
Activities: Exhibition of recipient's work

CREATIVE GLASS CENTER OF AMERICA (CGCA)

P.O. Box 646
Millville, NJ 08332-0646
609-825-6800 ext. 2733
Susan Whitehouse, Managing Director

AWARD

Title: Artists' Fellowships
Purpose: To provide artists working in glass the support necessary to develop individual ideas and talents and to establish a body of work, regardless of personal or financial limitations.
Categories of Support: Crafts, Sculpture (glass only)
Type of Support: Residency
Year Established: 1983
Duration of Funding: Three to four months
Customary Month or Season of Deadline: September
Total Number of Applicants: 100
Total Number of Recipients: 14
Funding Amount: $500/month stipend plus studio, housing, and glassmaking supplies and materials

APPLICATION PROCEDURE

Requirements: Application form, resume, slides, project description/statement, references
Restrictions: Applicant must be 21 years of age or older
Time Between Application Deadline and Award Notification: Six weeks
Reapplication by Former Recipients: Information not provided

SELECTION PROCESS

Method: Peer Panel
Criteria: Quality of work is the primary criterion.

OTHER INFORMATION

Publications: Program Guidelines, Annual Report, exhibition catalogues of former recipients, auction catalogues
Activities: Biennial conference on contemporary glass, benefit auction

CREATIVE TIME INC.

66 West Broadway
New York, NY 10007
212-619-1955
Cee Scott Brown, Executive Director

AWARD

Title: Creative Time Citywide Project Series
Purpose: To enable visual and performing artists and architects to realize public projects throughout New York City at sites of their choice.
Categories of Support: Photography, New Genres, Public Art, Sculpture
Type of Support: Project Grant
Year Established: 1989
Duration of Funding: Varies with project
Customary Month or Season of Deadline: Continuing
Total Number of Applicants: 95
Total Number of Recipients: 15-20
Funding Amount: $500-10,000

APPLICATION PROCEDURE

Requirements: Application form, resume, project description/statement, slides, project budget
Restrictions: Applicant may not be currently enrolled in a degree-granting program.
Time Between Application Deadline and Award Notification: Immediate
Reapplication by Former Recipients: Allowed after one year

SELECTION PROCESS

Method: Peer panel
Criteria: Quality of work is the primary criterion. Other factors include: ethnic background, appropriateness to guidelines, and project description.

OTHER INFORMATION

Publications: Program Guidelines, Annual Report, exhibition catalogues of former recipients
Activities: n/a

DJERASSI FOUNDATION

Resident Artist Program
2325 Bear Gulch Road
Woodside, CA 94062
415-851-8395

AWARD

Title: Resident Artists Program
Purpose: "Undisturbed time to pursue one's art is a gift rarely given."
Categories of Support: Artists' Books, Crafts, Drawing, New Genres, Painting, Photography, Printmaking, Sculpture
Type of Support: Residency
Year Established: Information not provided
Duration of Funding: Two to six months
Customary Month or Season of Deadline: March
Total Number of Applicants: Information not provided
Total Number of Recipients: 20
Funding Amount: Studio, room and board for duration of residency

APPLICATION PROCEDURE

Requirements: Application form, slides, references, project description/statement
Restrictions: None
Time Between Application Deadline and Award Notification: Three months
Reapplication by Former Recipients: Allowed immediately

SELECTION PROCESS

Method: Selection committee.
Criteria: Quality of work is the primary criterion. Project description is also considered.

OTHER INFORMATION

Publications: Program Guidelines
Activities: Information not provided

ALDEN B. DOW CREATIVITY CENTER

Northwood Institute
Midland, MI 48640-2398
517-832-4478
Carol B. Coppage, Director

AWARD

Title: Northwood Institute/Alden B. Dow Creativity Center Fellowship
Purpose: The Center offers four fellowships each summer for individuals in any field or profession who wish to pursue an innovative project or creative idea.
Categories of Support: Artists' Books, Crafts, Drawing, New Genres, Painting, Photography, Printmaking, Public Art, Sculpture
Type of Support: Residency
Year Established: 1979
Duration of Funding: Ten weeks
Customary Month or Season of Deadline: December
Total Number of Applicants: 150
Total Number of Recipients: 4
Funding Amount: $500 stipend, room and board, studio space, travel expenses, possible project expenses

APPLICATION PROCEDURE

Requirements: Application form, resume, slides, interview
Restrictions: None
Time Between Application Deadline and Award Notification: Four months
Reapplication by Former Recipients: Allowed immediately

SELECTION PROCESS

Method: Peer Panel, Board Members
Criteria: Quality of work is the primary criterion. Resume and project description are also considered.

OTHER INFORMATION

Publications: Program Guidelines, summary of past fellows' work
Activities: Local presentation of work completed during residency

DUTCHESS COUNTY ARTS COUNCIL

39 Market Street
Poughkeepsie, NY 12601
914-454-3222
Sherre Wesley, Executive Director

AWARD

Title: Dutchess Arts Fund (DAF) Project Grants
Purpose: Grants for projects taking place in Dutchess County (NY). All individuals must apply through a sponsoring Dutchess County non-profit organization.
Categories of Support: Artists' Books, Crafts, Drawing, New Genres, Painting, Photography, Printmaking, Public Art, Sculpture
Type of Support: Project Grant
Year Established: 1979
Duration of Funding: Varies with project
Customary Month or Season of Deadline: September
Total Number of Applicants: Information not provided
Total Number of Recipients: Information not provided
Funding Amount: Up to $5,000

APPLICATION PROCEDURE

Requirements: Application form, resume, slides, project description/statement, support material from sponsoring organization
Restrictions: Applicant must be 18 years of age or older and not ccurrently enrolled in a degree-granting program. Funded project must *take place* in Dutchess County (NY).
Time Between Application Deadline and Award Notification: Varies with project
Reapplication by Former Recipients: Allowed immediately

SELECTION PROCESS

Method: Peer Panel Review, Board Members
Criteria: Quality of work is the primary criterion. Project description and appropriateness to guidelines are also considered.

OTHER INFORMATION

Publications: Program Guidelines
Activities: See additional entries for this organization. Grant Application Workshops.

EXPLORATORIUM

3601 Lyon Street
San Francisco, CA 94123
415-563-7337
Goery Delacote, Executive Director
Peter Richards, Director, Arts Programs

AWARD

Title: Artist-in-Residence at the Exploratorium
Purpose: Though the exploratorium is best known as a science museum, the museum has used the perceptions of both artists and scientists to establish notions of how we see, know, and understand the world around us. Artists' works convey a sense of the unity between nature and culture which encompasses both art and science.
Categories of Support: New Genres
Type of Support: Residency
Year Established: 1974
Duration of Funding: Varies with project
Customary Month or Season of Deadline: Continuing
Total Number of Applicants: Information not provided
Total Number of Recipients: 4
Funding Amount: $5,000-15,000

APPLICATION PROCEDURE

Requirements: Resume, slides, project description/statement
Restrictions: None
Time Between Application Deadline and Award Notification: Varies with project
Reapplication by Former Recipients: Information not provided

SELECTION PROCESS

Method: Staff members
Criteria: Quality of work is the primary criterion.

OTHER INFORMATION

Publications: Program Guidelines, museum information
Activities: Exhibition of recipient's work

FINE ARTS WORK CENTER IN PROVINCETOWN (FAWC)

24 Pearl Street
PO Box 565
Provincetown, MA 02657
508-487-9960
Susan Slocum, Visual Arts Coordinator
Richard Baker, Visual Arts Coordinator

AWARD

Title: Visual Arts Fellowship/Residency
Purpose: The center aims to aid emerging talents of outstanding promise who have completed their formal training and are already working on their own.
Categories of Support: Artists' Books, Drawing, New Genres, Painting, Photography, Printmaking, Sculpture
Type of Support: Residency
Year Established: 1968
Duration of Funding: Eight months
Customary Month or Season of Deadline: January
Total Number of Applicants: 337
Total Number of Recipients: 10
Funding Amount: $450/month stipend, housing and studio for duration of residency

APPLICATION PROCEDURE

Requirements: Application form, resume, slides, sample of original work
Restrictions: Applicant may not be currently enrolled in a degree-granting program.
Time Between Application Deadline and Award Notification: Three months
Reapplication by Former Recipients: Allowed immediately (once)

SELECTION PROCESS

Method: Peer Panel
Criteria: Quality of work is the primary criterion.

OTHER INFORMATION

Publications: Program Guidelines
Activities: Exhibition of recipient's work

FLORIDA STATE ARTS COUNCIL

The Capital, Division of Cultural Affairs
Tallahassee, FL 32399
904-487-2980
Ms. Peyton C. Fearington, Executive Director
Blair Sands, Arts Administrator

AWARD

Title: Art in State Buildings Program
Purpose: To acquire artwork for all state buildings which provide public access.
Categories of Support: Public Art
Type of Support: Public Art Commission
Year Established: 1979
Duration of Funding: n/a
Customary Month or Season of Deadline: Continuing
Total Number of Applicants: Information not provided
Total Number of Recipients: Information not provided
Funding Amount: $500-100,000

APPLICATION PROCEDURE

Requirements: Resume, slides, project description/statement
Restrictions: None
Time Between Application Deadline and Award Notification: Varies with project
Reapplication by Former Recipients: Not allowed

SELECTION PROCESS

Method: Peer Panel Review, Staff Members, Board Members
Criteria: Quality of work is the primary criterion. Other factors include: financial need, resume, geographic representation, ethnic background, and project description.

OTHER INFORMATION

Publications: Program Guidelines, Annual Report, exhibition catalogues of former recipients
Activities: See additional entries for this organization. Exhibition of recipient's work, subsidized museum purchase of recipient's work

RICHARD A. FLORSHEIM ART FUND

University of South Florida
PO Box 3033
Tampa, FL 33620-3033
813-949-6886
August L. Freundlich, President

AWARD

Title: Individaul Artist Grant
Purpose: To assist professional artists whose previous recognition may have been eclipsed by changes in fashion. Partial funding of museum exhibitions and purchases, monographs or books.
Categories of Support: Artists' Books, Crafts, Drawing, New Genres, Painting, Photography, Printmaking, Public Art, Sculpture
Type of Support: Project Grant
Year Established: 1985
Duration of Funding: Varies with project
Customary Month or Season of Deadline: October and March
Total Number of Applicants: 80
Total Number of Recipients: 8
Funding Amount: Up to $20,000

APPLICATION PROCEDURE

Requirements: Application form, resume, slides, project description/statement, financial statement, letters of recommendation suggested
Restrictions: Preference to applicants 55 and older.
Time Between Application Deadline and Award Notification: Six weeks
Reapplication by Former Recipients: Allowed immediately

SELECTION PROCESS

Method: Staff Members, Board Members
Criteria: Quality of work is the primary criterion. Other factors include: resume, project description, and appropriatenesss to guidelines.

OTHER INFORMATION

Publications: Program Guidelines
Activities: Exhibition of recipient's work, subsidized museum purchase of recipient's work

FRANKLIN FURNACE ARCHIVE, INC.

112 Franklin Street
New York, NY 10013
212-925-4671
Martha Wilson, Executive Director
Blanche, Program Director

AWARD

Title: Fund For Performance Art
Purpose: Grants to established performers to present work in New York State.
Categories of Support: New Genres
Type of Support: Project Grant
Year Established: 1982
Duration of Funding: One year
Customary Month or Season of Deadline: February
Total Number of Applicants: 200
Total Number of Recipients: 10
Funding Amount: $2,000- 5,000

APPLICATION PROCEDURE

Requirements: Application form, resume, slides, other documentation depending on medium, project description/statement
Restrictions: None
Time Between Application and Award Announcement: Three months
Reapplication by Former Recipients: Allowed after one year

SELECTION PROCESS

Method: Peer Panel
Criteria: Quality of work is the primary criterion.

OTHER INFORMATION

Publications: Program Guidelines
Activities: See additional entries for this organization.

FRANKLIN FURNACE ARCHIVE, INC.

112 Franklin Street
New York, NY 10013
212-925-4671
Martha Wilson, Executive Director
Blanche, Program Director

AWARD

Title: Franklin Furnace Emerging Artists
Purpose: Grants to emerging artists for performance art and exhibitions at Franklin Furnace.
Categories of Support: New Genres
Type of Support: Project Grant
Year Established: 1976
Duration of Funding: One year
Customary Month or Season of Deadline: April
Total Number of Applicants: 450
Total Number of Recipients: 28
Funding Amount: $1,000

APPLICATION PROCEDURE

Requirements: Application form, resume, slides, other documentation depending on medium, project description/statement
Restrictions: None
Time Between Application Deadline and Award Notification: Three months
Reapplication by Former Recipients: Allowed after one year

SELECTION PROCESS

Method: Peer Panel
Criteria: Quality of work is the primary criterion.

OTHER INFORMATION

Publications: Program Guidelines
Activities: See additional entries for this organization.

FRIENDS OF PHOTOGRAPHY
250 4th Street
San Francisco, CA 94103
415-495-7000
Ron Egherman, Executive Director
Debra Heimerdinger, Award Administrator

AWARD

Title: Ruttenberg Foundation Award/Ferguson Award
Purpose: To recognize emerging artists who have begun to establish a record of contributions to the creative photography field and who show promise of continuing that record. *Ruttenberg Foundation Award* is a purchase award, *Ferguson Award* is a direct cash grant.
Categories of Support: Photography
Type of Support: Unrestricted
Year Established: Ruttenberg Foundation 1982/Ferguson Award 1972
Duration of Funding: One year
Customary Month or Season of Deadline: September
Total Number of Applicants: Information not provided
Total Number of Recipients: One each for Ruttenberg and Ferguson Awards
Funding Amount: Ruttenberg: $2,000 purchase/Ferguson: $2,000 cash

APPLICATION PROCEDURE

Requirements: Application form, resume, slides, project description/statement
Restrictions: None
Time Between Application Deadline and Award Notification: One month
Reapplication by Former Recipients: Not allowed

SELECTION PROCESS

Method: One juror for each award
Criteria: Quality of work is the primary criterion. Other factors include: resume, appropriateness to guidelines, and project description.

OTHER INFORMATION

Publications: Program Guidelines
Activities: Exhibition of recipient's work, subsidized museum purchase of recipient's work (Ruttenberg Award)

GENERAL SERVICES ADMINISTRATION (GSA)

GSA/Art-in-Architecture Program, PGA
18th and F Streets, NW
Washington, DC 20405
202-501-1219
Dale M. Lanzone, Director, Arts and Historic Preservation
Susan Harrison, Chief, Art in Architecture

AWARD

Title: Art-in-Architecture Commissions
Purpose: To acquire works of living artists for the public benefit.
Categories of Support: Drawing, Painting, Photography, Printmaking, Public Art, Sculpture
Type of Support: Public Art Commission/Purchase
Year Established: 1963
Duration of Funding: Varies with project
Customary Month or Season of Deadline: Continuing
Total Number of Applicants: Information not provided
Total Number of Recipients: Information not provided
Funding Amount: $15,000-3,000,000

APPLICATION PROCEDURE

Requirements: Application form, slides
Restrictions: None
Time Between Application Deadline and Award Notification: Three to four months
Reapplication by Former Recipients: Allowed immediately

SELECTION PROCESS

Method: Peer Panel, Staff Members, Board Members
Criteria: Quality of work is the primary criterion.

OTHER INFORMATION

Publications: Program Guidelines, Annual Report
Activities: Exhibition of recipient's work, slide registry

GLASSELL SCHOOL OF ART
5101 Montrose Boulevard
Houston, TX 77006
713-639-7500
Daniel Gorski, Executive Director
Joseph Havel, Associate Director

AWARD
Title: The Core Program
Purpose: To provide talented young artists with a stimulating work environment between formal school training and professional life.
Categories of Support: Drawing, Painting, Photography, Printmaking, New Genres, Sculpture
Type of Support: Residency
Year Established: 1982
Duration of Funding: One to two years
Customary Month or Season of Deadline: April
Total Number of Applicants: 150
Total Number of Recipients: 7
Funding Amount: Studio plus $400/month stipend

APPLICATION PROCEDURE
Requirements: Application form, resume, project description/statement, slides
Restrictions: None
Time Between Application Deadline and Award Announcement: One month
Reapplication by Former Recipients: Not allowed

SELECTION PROCESS
Method: Board members
Criteria: Quality of work is the primary criterion. Resume and project description/ statement are also considered.

OTHER INFORMATION
Publications: Program Guidelines, exhibition catalogues of recipients
Activities: Exhibition of recipient's work

ADOLPH AND ESTHER GOTTLIEB FOUNDATION

380 West Broadway
New York, NY 10012
212-226-0581
Sanford Hirsh, Executive Director

AWARD

Title: Individual Support Grant
Purpose: To provide funds for general support to mature, creative painters and sculptors who are in current financial need. An artist must be able to demonstrate active involvement in a mature phase of his or her art for at least 20 years. Awarded annually.
Categories of Support: Drawing, Painting, Printmaking, Sculpture
Type of Support: Unrestricted
Year Established: 1985
Duration of Funding: One year
Customary Month or Season of Deadline: December
Total Number of Applicants: 500
Total Number of Recipients: 10
Funding Amount: $20,000

APPLICATION PROCEDURE

Requirements: First-party written request for information, application form, slides, project description/statement, financial statement
Restrictions: Applicant may not be currently enrolled in a degree-granting program.
Time Between Application Deadline and Award Notification: Three months
Reapplication by Former Recipients: Allowed after one year

SELECTION PROCESS

Method: Peer Panel
Criteria: Quality of work is the primary criterion. Financial need and resume are also considered.

OTHER INFORMATION

Publications: Program Guidelines
Activities: See additional entries for this organization.

ADOLPH AND ESTHER GOTTLIEB FOUNDATION

380 West Broadway
New York, NY 10012
212-226-0581
Sanford Hirsch, Executive Director

AWARD

Title: Emergency Grant
Purpose: Financial assistance to mature, creative painters and sculptors who are beset by a current emergency situation, such as fire, flood, medical, or other unexpected, catastrophic events. Artists must demonstrate at least 10 years in mature phase of work.
Categories of Support: Drawing, Painting, Printmaking,Sculpture
Type of Support: Emergency Grant
Year Established: 1985
Duration of Funding: Varies with nature of emergency
Customary Month or Season of Deadline: Continuing
Total Number of Applicants: 86
Total Number of Recipients: 24
Funding Amount: $10,000

APPLICATION PROCEDURE

Requirements: Application form, resume, professional referenes, documentation of emergeny situation
Restrictions: Applicant may not be currently enrolled in a degree-granting program.
Time Between Application Deadline and Award Notification: Six weeks
Reapplication by Former Recipients: Allowed immediately. Applicants may not reapply for same emergency.

SELECTION PROCESS

Method: Board Members
Criteria: Nature of emergency is the primary criterion.

OTHER INFORMATION

Publications: Program Guidelines
Activities: See additional entries for this organization.

GREENSHIELDS FOUNDATION
1814 Sherbrooke Street, West, Suite 1
Montreal, Quebec
Canada
H3H 1E4
514-937-9225

AWARD

Title: Elizabeth Greenshields Foundation Grant
Purpose: To aid talented young figurative/representational artists in the early stages of their careers.
Categories of Support: Drawing, Painting, Printmaking, Sculpture
Type of Support: Unrestricted
Year Established: 1955
Duration of Funding: One year
Customary Month or Season of Deadline: Continuing
Total Number of Applicants: 650
Total Number of Recipients: 45
Funding Amount: $10,000 (Canadian)

APPLICATION PROCEDURE

Requirements: Application form, slides
Restrictions: Applicant must be under 31 years of age. Work must be representational or figurative—no abstract or non-representational art.
Time Between Application Deadline and Award Notification: Three to four months
Reapplication by Former Recipients: Allowed after one year

SELECTION PROCESS

Method: Board Members
Criteria: Quality of work is the primary criterion. Other factors include: financial need, project description, and appropriateness to guidelines.

OTHER INFORMATION

Publications: Program Guidelines
Activities: Information not provided

GUGGENHEIM FOUNDATION

90 Park Avenue
New York, NY 11216
212-687-4470
Joel Conarroe, President

AWARD

Title: Guggenheim Fellowship
Purpose: To improve the quality of education and practice of the arts and related professions. Fellows engage in any field of knowledge and creation in any of the arts, under the freest possible conditions, based upon past accomplishment and future promise, irrespective of race, creed or gender.
Categories of Support: Artists' Books, Crafts, Drawing, New Genres, Painting, Photography, Printmaking, Sculpture
Type of Support: Unrestricted
Year Established: 1925
Duration of Funding: Six months to one year
Customary Month or Season of Deadline: October
Total Number of Applicants: 3092 (all disciplines)
Total Number of Recipients: 23 (visual arts)
Funding Amount: $26,500 average

APPLICATION PROCEDURE

Requirements: Application form, resume, slides, sample of original work, project description/statement
Restrictions: None
Time Between Application Deadline and Award Notification: Six months
Reapplication by Former Recipients: Information not provided

SELECTION PROCESS

Method: Peer Panel, Standing Committee
Criteria: Quality of work is the primary criterion.

OTHER INFORMATION

Publications: Program Guidelines, Annual Report
Activities: Information not provided

INSTITUT DES HAUTES ETUDES EN ARTS PLASTIQUES (IHEAP)

75 Rue du Temple
75003 Paris
France
1-48-87-05-00
Pontus Hulten, Executive Director
Annick Boisnard, Administrative Director

AWARD

Title: One Year Interdisciplinary Research Program for Artists in Paris
Purpose: Each session is devoted to a specific area of inquiry—seminars with internationally known professionals in different disciplines who are invited for each session. Applicants should be working artists in any media, 20-30 years old, and speak French.
Categories of Support: Artists' Books, Drawing, New Genres, Painting, Photography, Printmaking, Public Art, Sculpture
Type of Support: Unrestricted
Year Established: 1988
Duration of Funding: One year
Customary Month or Season of Deadline: August
Total Number of Applicants: 250
Total Number of Recipients: 20
Funding Amount: ff24,000 (approx. $4,400) for artists living in the Paris region-
ff27,000 (approx. $4,900)for artists living outside the Paris region

APPLICATION PROCEDURE

Requirements: Resume, slides
Restrictions: Applicant must be 20-30 years of age and must speak French.
Time Between Application Deadline and Award Notification: Two months
Reapplication by Former Recipients: Allowed immediately (once)

SELECTION PROCESS

Method: Board Members
Criteria: Quality of work is the primary criterion.

OTHER INFORMATION

Publications: Program Guidelines, exhibition catalogues of former recipients
Activities: Information not provided

INSTITUTE OF INTERNATIONAL EDUCATION

US Student Program Division/Fulbright Program
809 United Nations Plaza
New York, NY 10017
212-984-5330

AWARD

Title: Fulbright Grant
Purpose: To enable the government of the US to increase mutual understanding between the people of the US and other countries.
Categories of Support: Artists' Books, Crafts, Drawing, New Genres, Painting, Photography, Printmaking, Public Art, Sculpture
Type of Support: Unrestricted
Year Established: 1961
Duration of Funding: Varies with program and host country.
Customary Month or Season of Deadline: October
Total Number of Applicants: 3,333 (all categories)
Total Number of Recipients: 669 (all categories)
Funding Amount: Varies with project

APPLICATION PROCEDURE

Requirements: Application form, visual documentation and support materials suitable for medium/program, four years professional experience or academic study, and language proficiency for host country.
Restrictions: US citizenship. Applicant may not be employed by or be an immediate family member of an employee of the US Information Agency.
Time Between Application Deadline and Award Notification: Nine months
Reapplication by Former Recipients: Not allowed. Former recipients of a Fulbright Travel Grant may reapply once for full funding.

SELECTION PROCESS

Method: Screening Committee, approval by institution in host country
Criteria: Quality of work is the primary criterion. Other factors include: geographic representation, project description, language proficiency, appropriateness to guidelines, and veteran status.

OTHER INFORMATION::

Publications: Program Guidelines, *Financial Resources for International Study, Academic Year Abroad 1991/92, Basic Facts on Foreign Study, Vacation Study Abroad, Teaching Abroad, Open Doors*
Activities: Varies with program in host country.

INTERSECTION FOR THE ARTS

446 Valencia Street
San Francisco, CA 94103
415-626-2787
Frances Phillips, Executive Director
Linda Wilson, Gallery Director

AWARD

Title: Artists' Honoraria
Purpose: To present excellent, diverse work by mid-career artists. Applicants are discouraged from making general, unsolicited applications. Potential applicants may apply for inclusion in the announcement mailing list or may watch for entry announcements.
Categories of Support: Drawing, Painting, Photography, Public Art, Sculpture, New Genres
Type of Support: Honoraria
Year Established: 1985
Duration of Funding: Information not provided
Customary Month or Season of Deadline: November
Total Number of Applicants: Information not provided
Total Number of Recipients: 8
Funding Amount: $300-500

APPLICATION PROCEDURE

Requirements: Resume, project description/statement, slides
Restrictions: None
Time Between Application Deadline and Award Notification: Two months
Reapplication by Former Recipients: Allowed immediately

SELECTION PROCESS

Method: Peer panel
Criteria: Quality of work is the primary criterion. Other factors include: resume, project description, and appropriateness to guidelines.

OTHER INFORMATION

Publications: Calls for entries published in *Artweek*
Activites: Exhibition of recipient's work

IOWA ARTS COUNCIL (IAC)

Department of Cultural Affairs
Capitol Complex
1223 East Court
Des Moines, IA 50319
515-281-4006
Natalie A. Hala, Executive Director
Bruce Williams, Director of Creative Artists and Visual Arts

AWARD

Title: Art in State Buildings Program
Purpose: The program was enacted in 1979 to ensure that fine arts play an important and integral role in state construction projects.
Categories of Support: Crafts, Drawing, Painting, Photography, Printmaking, Public Art, Sculpture
Type of Support: Public Art Commission
Year Established: 1979
Duration of Funding: Varies with project
Customary Month or Season of Deadline: Varies with project
Total Number of Applicants: Information not provided
Total Number of Recipients: Information not provided
Funding Amount: Varies with project

APPLICATION PROCEDURE

Requirements: Application form, resume, slides, project description/statement
Restrictions: Applicant must be 18 years of age or older and not currently enrolled in a degree-granting program. US citizenship
Time Between Application Deadline and Award Notification: Varies with project
Reapplication by Former Recipients: Allowed immediately

SELECTION PROCESS

Method: Peer Panel
Criteria: Quality of work is the primary criterion. Resume and project description are also considered.

OTHER INFORMATION

Publications: Program Guidelines
Activities: See additional entries for this organization. Exhibition of recipient's work.

JAPAN FOUNDATION

142 West 57th Street, 6th Floor
New York, NY 10019
212-949-6360
Ei'ichi Hamanishi, Executive Director
Isao Tsujimoto, Deputy Director

AWARD

Title: Artists' Fellowship Program
Purpose: This program is designed to provide artists and specialists in the arts with the opportunity to pursue creative projects in Japan and to exchange opinions with Japanese specialists.
Categories of Support: Artists' Books, Crafts, Drawing, New Genres, Painting, Photography, Printmaking, Sculpture
Type of Support: Travel Grant/Residency
Year Established: 1972
Duration of Funding: One to six months
Customary Month or Season of Deadline: December
Total Number of Applicants: Information not provided
Total Number of Recipients: 10
Funding Amount: Travel and related expenses, housing, studio, 430,000 ¥/month (approx. $3,300) stipend

APPLICATION PROCEDURE

Requirements: Application form, slides, project description/statement
Restrictions: None
Time Between Application Deadline and Award Notification: Five months
Reapplication by Former Recipients: Allowed immediately

SELECTION PROCESS

Method: Board Members
Criteria: Quality of work is the primary criterion. Appropriateness to guidelines and project description/statement are also considered.

OTHER INFORMATION

Publications: Program Guidelines, Annual Report
Activities: Information not provided

KALANI HONUA OCEANSIDE RETREAT

RR 2, PO Box 4500
Pahoa-Kamaili, HI 96778
808-965-7828
Richard Koob, Artistic Director

AWARD

Title: Artist-in-Residence Program
Purpose: To provide artists with an inspiring and comfortable retreat for personal and artistic growth.
Categories of Support: Artists' Books, Crafts, Drawing, New Genres, Painting, Photography, Printmaking, Public Art, Sculpture
Type of Support: Residency
Year Established: 1980
Duration of Funding: Variable
Customary Month or Season of Deadline: Continuing
Total Number of Applicants: 40
Total Number of Recipients: 36
Funding Amount: Housing and studio for duration of residency

APPLICATION PROCEDURE

Requirements: Application form, slides, sample of original work
Restrictions: None
Time Between Application Deadline and Award Notification: Two weeks
Reapplication by Former Recipients: Allowed immediately

SELECTION PROCESS

Method: Peer Panel, Staff Members, Board Members
Criteria: Quality of work is the primary criterion.

OTHER INFORMATION

Publications: Program Guidelines, Annual Report
Activities: Informal open studio presentations

JOHN MICHAEL KOHLER ARTS CENTER (JMKAC)

PO Box 489
Sheboygan, WI 53081-0489
414-458-6144
Ruth DeYoung Kohler, Executive Director
Ellen Clark, Arts/Industry Coordinator

AWARD

Title: Arts/Industry Program
Purpose: To provide visual artists with an opportunity to gain access to industrial materials, technologies, and facilities so that they may develop new ways of thinking and working and create new bodies of work not possible in their own studios.
Categories of Support: Artists' Books, Crafts, Drawing, Painting, Photography, Printmaking, Public Art, Sculpture, New Genres
Type of Support: Residency
Year Established: 1974
Duration of Funding: Two to six months
Customary Month or Season of Deadline: August
Total Number of Applicants: 175
Total Number of Recipients: 14-22
Funding Amount: $4,000-30,000

APPLICATION PROCEDURE

Requirements: Resume, project description/statement, slides, references
Restrictions: Applicant must be 18 years of age or older.
Time Between Application Deadline and Award Notification: Three months
Reapplication by Former Recipients: Allowed immediately

SELECTION PROCESS

Method: Staff members
Criteria: Quality of work is the primary criterion. Project description and appropriateness to guidelines are also considered.

OTHER INFORMATION

Publications: Program Guidelines, exhibition catalogues of some recipients
Activities: Exhibition of recipient's work

LA NAPOULE ART FOUNDATION

11 East 73rd Street, Suite 1-C
New York, NY 10021
212-628-2996
Barbara Bratone, Executive Director

AWARD

Title: La Napoule Residency
Purpose: The purpose of La Napoule Art Foundation is to promote international understanding through cultural exchange. The offices of the organization are in the United States and it owns and maintains the Chateau La Napoule on the Cote d'Azur in France as the location for its programs.
Categories of Support: Crafts, Drawing, Painting, New Genres, Photography, Printmaking, Sculpture
Type of Support: Residency
Year Established: 1984
Duration of Funding: Two - three months
Customary Month or Season of Deadline: Information not provided
Total Number of Applicants: Information not provided
Total Number of Recipients: Information not provided
Funding Amount: $1,000 plus transportation, room and board, studio, and materials stipend.

APPLICATION PROCEDURE

Requirements: Application through: National Endowment for the Arts/Visual Arts Program; Artists Trust, Seattle, Washington; Atlantic Center for the Arts, Florida: North Carolina Arts Council; or Ohio Arts Council. Other partnerships pending.
Restrictions: U.S. Citizenship
Time Between Application Deadline and Award Announcement: Information not provided
Reapplication by Former Recipients: Information not provided

SELECTION PROCESS

Method: Varies with sponsoring organization, subject to committee approval in France.
Criteria: Quality of work is the primary criterion.

OTHER INFORMATION

Publications: Program Guidelines
Activities: n/a

LAKESIDE STUDIO

Lakeside Group
600 North McClurg Court, Suite 1302A
Chicago, IL 60611
312-787-6858
Cynthia Quick, Director

AWARD

Title: Artist-in-Residence Program
Purpose: To provide an alternative workplace where recognized visual artists may pursue new ideas in a peaceful environment away from the constraints of everyday living.
Categories of Support: Painting, Photography, Printmaking, Ceramics, Sculpture
Type of Support: Residency
Year Established: 1968
Duration of Funding: Five months
Customary Month or Season of Deadline: February
Total Number of Applicants: 50
Total Number of Recipients: 25
Funding Amount: Room, studio, technical assistance and supplies for duration of residency

APPLICATION PROCEDURE

Requirements: Application form, resume, slides, project description/statement, project budget.
Restrictions: None
Time Between Application Deadline and Award Notification: Six weeks
Reapplication by Former Recipients: Allowed immediately

SELECTION PROCESS

Method: Staff Members, Board Members
Criteria: Quality of work is the primary criterion. Resume and project description are also considered.

OTHER INFORMATION

Publications: Program Guidelines
Activities: Exhibition of recipient's work

DOROTHEA LANGE-PAUL TAYLOR PRIZE

Center for Documentary Studies
Duke University
Snow Building, #511
331 West Main Street
Durham, NC 27701
919-687-0487
Iris Tillman Hill, Executive Director
Darnell Arnold, Specialist for Programs

AWARD

Title: Dorothea Lange-Paul Taylor Prize
Purpose: The prize promotes collaboration between photographers and writers. Funds are intended for fieldwork in the formative stages of a project.
Categories of Support: Photography/Writer collaboration
Type of Support: Project Grant
Year Established: 1991
Duration of Funding: One year
Customary Month or Season of Deadline: December
Total Number of Applicants: 100
Total Number of Recipients: 1
Funding Amount: Up to $10,000

APPLICATION PROCEDURE

Requirements: Application form, resume, slides, project description/statement, project budget
Restrictions: Applicant may not be currently receiving other monies from the Center for Documentary Studies.
Time Between Application Deadline and Award Notification: Five months
Reapplication by Former Recipients: Allowed immediately

SELECTION PROCESS

Method: Peer Panel
Criteria: Quality of work is the primary criterion. Project description is also considered.

OTHER INFORMATION

Publications: Brochure
Activities: Public presentation by award recipients

LIGHTWORK
316 Waverly Avenue
Syracuse, NY 13210
315-443-1300
Jeffrey Hoone, Executive Director

AWARD

Title: Artist-in-Residence
Purpose: To support artists working in photography, computers, and related arts.
Categories of Support: Photography, New Genres
Type of Support: Residency
Year Established: 1976
Duration of Funding: One month
Customary Month or Season of Deadline: Continuing
Total Number of Applicants: 250
Total Number of Recipients: 15
Funding Amount: $1,200 plus housing, facilities/equipment access

APPLICATION PROCEDURE

Requirements: Resume, project description/statement, slides
Restrictions: None
Time Between Application Deadline and Award Notification: Information not provided
Reapplication by Former Recipients: Not allowed

SELECTION PROCESS

Method: Staff members
Criteria: Quality of work is the primary criterion. Other factors include: project description, ethnic background, economic need, geographic representation, resume, and appropriateness to guidelines.

OTHER INFORMATION

Publications: Program guidelines, exhibition catalogues of former recipients, *Contact Sheet*
Activities: Exhibition of recipient's work

LOS ANGELES COUNTY TRANSPORTATION COMMISSION (LACTC-A-R-T)

403 West 8th Street, #500
Los Angeles, CA 90014
213-626-0370
Jessica Cusick, Public Art Administrator

AWARD

Title: Public Art Program
Purpose: To create works of art throughout the new Los Angeles rail system in order to create unique visual identity for each station and contribute to community identity and pride. Goal of the program is an integrated art/design team. One project each year is open to national competition with the remainder limited to California artists only.
Categories of Support: Public Art
Type of Support: Public Art Commission
Year Established: 1989
Duration of Funding: Varies with project
Customary Month or Season of Deadline: Continuing
Total Number of Applicants: 500
Total Number of Recipients: 40 (1 national recipient)
Funding Amount: $60,000-300,000

APPLICATION PROCEDURE

Requirements: Application form, resume, slides
Restrictions: One project open to national artists each year. All others open to residents of California only.
Time Between Application Deadline and Award Notification: Varies with project
Reapplication by Former Recipients: Allowed after five years

SELECTION PROCESS

Method: Peer Panel
Criteria: Quality of work is the primary criterion. Appropriateness to guidelines is also considered.

OTHER INFORMATION

Publications: Program Guidelines
Activities: Exhibition of recipient's work, slide registry

LOUISVILLE VISUAL ART ASSOCIATION (LVAA)

3005 Upper River Road
Louisville, KY 40207
502-896-2146
John P. Begley, Executive Director
Al Gorman, Exhibitions Coordinator

AWARD

Title: Annual Installation Exhibition
Purpose: Site-specific installation opportunity. Projects activate historic landmark structures with contemporary, experimental installations.
Categories of Support: Experimental Installation, New Genres
Type of Support: Honoraria
Year Established: 1984
Duration of Funding: Varies with project
Customary Month or Season of Deadline: Continuing
Total Number of Applicants: 50
Total Number of Recipients: 1
Funding Amount: $1,500

APPLICATION PROCEDURE

Requirements: Resume, slides, project description/statement, letter of interest
Restrictions: Applicant may not be currently enrolled in a degree-granting program.
Time Between Applicartion Deadline and Award Notification: Three months
Reapplication by Former Recipients: Not allowed

SELECTION PROCESS

Method: Staff members, board approval
Criteria: Quality of work is the primary criterion. Project description is also considered.

OTHER INFORMATION

Publications: Information not provided
Activities: Exhibition of recipient's work

LOWER EAST SIDE PRINTSHOP INC.

59-61 East 4th Street
New York, NY 10003
212-673-5390
Maria Mingalone, Executive Director

AWARD

Title: Individual Artists Special Editions Program
Purpose: To enable artists to produce a unique, small, print-related project such as small editions, artists' books, monoprints, or installation.
Categories of Support: Artists' Books, Printmaking, Experimental Installation
Type of Support: Project Grant
Year Established: 1986
Duration of Funding: Varies with project
Customary Month or Season of Deadline: Spring
Total Number of Applicants: 50
Total Number of Recipients: 10
Funding Amount: $500 average

APPLICATION PROCEDURE

Requirements: Resume, Project Description/Statement, Slides, Financial Statement
Restrictions: None
Time Between Application Deadline and Award Notification: Four months
Reapplication by Former Recipients: Allowed after two years

SELECTION PROCESS

Method: Peer panel, Staff Members
Criteria: Quality of work is the primary criterion. Other factors include: resume, project description, and appropriateness to guidelines.

OTHER INFORMATION

Publications: Program Guidelines
Activities: Exhibition of recipient's work

MACDOWELL COLONY

100 High Street
Peterborough, NH 03458
603-924-3886
Mary Carswell, Executive Director
Shirley Bewley, Admissions Director

AWARD

Title: Artist Residencies
Purpose: To provide time and space for the individual pursuit of art.
Categories of Support: Artists' Books, Drawing, New Genres, Painting, Photography, Printmaking, Public Art, Sculpture
Type of Support: Residency
Year Established: 1907
Duration of Funding: Two months
Customary Month or Season of Deadline: January, April, and September
Total Number of Applicants: 148
Total Number of Recipients: 50
Funding Amount: Residency fee waivers, limited travel assistance possible

APPLICATION PROCEDURE

Requirements: Application form, slides, project description/statement
Restrictions: None
Time Between Application Deadline and Award Notification: Six weeks
Reapplication by Former Recipients: Allowed after one year

SELECTION PROCESS

Method: Peer Panel
Criteria: Quality of work is the primary criterion.

OTHER INFORMATION

Publications: Program Guidelines, Annual Report
Activities: Information not provided

METRO-DADE ART IN PUBLIC PLACES

Metro-Dade Center
111 NW First Street, Suite 610
Miami, FL 33128
305-375-5362
Vivian Donnell Rodriguez, Executive Director
Pat Marx, Education Coordinator

AWARD

Title: Metro-Dade Art in Public Places Trust
Purpose: To Commission and purchase artwork by contemporary artists in all media to enrich public spaces and contribute to the cultural heritage of Dade County.
Categories of Support: Drawing, Painting, Photography, Printmaking, Public Art, Sculpture, New Genres
Type of Support: Public Art Commission
Year Established: 1973
Duration of Funding: Varies with project
Customary Month or Season of Deadline: Varies with project
Total Number of Applicants: Information not provided
Total Number of Recipients: Information not provided
Funding Amount: Varies with project

APPLICATION PROCEDURE

Requirements: Application form, resume, slides
Restrictions: None
Time Between Application Deadline and Award Notification: Varies with project
Reapplication by Former Recipients: Allowed immediately

SELECTION PROCESS

Method: Board Members
Criteria: Quality of work is the primary criterion. Resume and appropriateness to guidelines are also considered.

OTHER INFORMATION

Publications: Program Guidelines
Activities: Exhibition of recipient's work, slide registry

METROPOLITAN ARTS COMMISSION (MAC)

1120 SW 5th Avenue, Room 518
Portland, OR 97204
503-796-5111
Bill Bulick, Executive Director
Kristin Calhoun, Public Art Assistant

AWARD

Title: Project Grant
Purpose: To provide funding support for individual artists and small to mid-size arts organziations.
Categories of Support: Crafts, Drawing, New Genres, Painting, Photography, Sculpture
Type of Support: Project Grant
Year Established: Information not provided
Duration of Funding: One year
Customary Month or Season of Deadline: Continuing
Total Number of Applicants: 12
Total Number of Recipients: 7
Funding Amount: $500-2,000

APPLICATION PROCEDURE

Requirements: Application form, resume, slides, sample of original work, project description/statement
Restrictions: Applicant may not be currently enrolled in a degree-granting program. Work completed during grant *must be accessible to the Portland metro area.*
Time Between Application Deadline and Award Notification: Two months
Reapplication by Former Recipients: Allowed immediately

SELECTION PROCESS

Method: Peer Panel, Staff Members
Criteria: Quality of work is the primary criterion. Other factors include: resume, appropriateness to guidelines, and project description.

OTHER INFORMATION

Publications: Program Guidelines
Activities: See additional entries for this organization.

METROPOLITAN ARTS COMMISSION (MAC)

1120 SW 5th Avenue, Room 518
Portland, OR 97204
503-796-5111
Bill Bulick, Executive Director
Eloise MacMurray, Public Art Manager

AWARD

Title: Percent for Art Program
Purpose: To commission public art for new or renovated public structures.
Categories of Support: Painting, Photography, Printmaking, Public Art, Sculpture
Type of Support: Public Art Commission
Year Established: 1981
Duration of Funding: Varies with project
Customary Month or Season of Deadline: Continuing
Total Number of Applicants: Information not provided
Total Number of Recipients: Information not provided
Funding Amount: $500-100,000

APPLICATION PROCEDURE

Requirements: Application form, resume, slides, sample of original work, artists' statement/project description, financial statement/project budget
Restrictions: None
Time Between Application Deadline and Award Notification: Varies with project
Reapplication by Former Recipients: Allowed immediately

SELECTION PROCESS

Method: Staff Members, Board Members
Criteria: Quality of work is the primary criterion. Appropriateness to guidelines is also considered.

OTHER INFORMATION

Publications: Program Guidelines
Activities: See additional entries for this organization.

MILLAY COLONY FOR THE ARTS

Steepletop
PO Box 3
Austerlitz, NY 12017-0003
518-392-3103
Ann-Ellen Lesser, Executive Director
Gail Giles, Assistant Director

AWARD

Title: Artists' Residency
Purpose: Gives one month residencies to visual artists, writers, and composers.
Categories of Support: Artists' Books, Drawing, Painting, Photography, Sculpture
Type of Support: Residency
Year Established: 1973
Duration of Funding: One month
Customary Month or Season of Deadline: February, May, and September
Total Number of Applicants: 325
Total Number of Recipients: 60
Funding Amount: Studio, room and board for duration of residency

APPLICATION PROCEDURE

Requirements: Application form, slides
Restrictions: None
Time Between Application Deadline and Award Notification: Three months
Reapplication by Former Recipients: Allowed after one year

SELECTION PROCESS

Method: Peer Panel
Criteria: Quality of work is the primary criterion.

OTHER INFORMATION

Publications: Program Guidelines
Activities: Information not provided

MINNESOTA STATE ARTS BOARD

432 Summit Avenue
St. Paul, MN 55102
612-297-2603
Sam W. Grabarski, Executive Director
Karen Mueller, Program Associate

AWARD

Title: Percent for Art in Public Places Program
Purpose: To select or commission artwork for placement in new or renovated state building sites.
Categories of Support: Crafts, Drawing, New Genres, Painting, Photography, Printmaking, Public Art, Sculpture
Type of Support: Public Art Commission
Year Established: 1984
Duration of Funding: Varies with project
Customary Month or Season of Deadline: February and June
Total Number of Applicants: Information not provided
Total Number of Recipients: Information not provided
Funding Amount: Varies with project

APPLICATION PROCEDURE

Requirements: Application form, resume, slides
Restrictions: None
Time Between Application Deadline and Award Notification: Varies with project
Reapplication by Former Recipients: Allowed immediately

SELECTION PROCESS

Method: Peer Panel Review, Staff Members, Board Members
Criteria: Quality of work is the primary criterion. Resume and appropriateness to guidelines are also considered.

OTHER INFORMATION:

Publications: Program Guidelines, Annual Report
Activities: See additional entries for this organization. Exhibition of recipient's work, subsidized museum purchase of recipient's work.

MONEY FOR WOMEN/BARBARA DEMING MEMORIAL FUND

PO Box 401043
Brooklyn, NY 11240-1043
Pam McAllister, Administrator

AWARD

Title: Individual Grants
Purpose: The Money for Women/Barbara Deming Memorial Fund, Inc. gives small grants to individual feminists in the arts (musicians, artists, dancers, writers, poets, photographers, playwrights, filmmakers) whose work speaks for peace and justice.
Categories of Support: Artists' Books, Crafts, Drawing, New Genres, Painting, Photography, Printmaking, Public Art, Sculpture
Type of Support: Project Grant
Year Established: Information not provided
Duration of Funding: Six months
Customary Month or Season of Deadline: February and July
Total Number of Applicants: 180
Total Number of Recipients: 10
Funding Amount: Up to $1,000

APPLICATION PROCEDURE

Requirements: Application form, resume, slides, project description/statement
Restrictions: US or Canadian citizenship. No funding for educational assistance, research, group projects, or business ventures.
Time Between Application Deadline and Award Notification: Three to four months
Reapplication by Former Recipients: Information not provided

SELECTION PROCESS

Method: Peer Panel
Criteria: Quality of work is the primary criterion. Project description and appropriateness to guidelines are also considered.

OTHER INFORMATION

Publications: Program Guidelines
Activities: Information not provided

MONTGOMERY COUNTY ART IN PUBLIC ARCHITECTURE
110 North Washington Street
Rockville, MD 20850
301-217-6040
Sheila Haggerty, Coordinator

AWARD

Title: Art In Public Architecture
Purpose: Commission artwork for new and renovated county government buildings.
Categories of Support: Public Art
Type of Support: Public Art Commission
Year Established: 1985
Duration of Funding: Varies with project
Customary Month or Season of Deadline: Continuing
Total Number of Applicants: 3,000
Total Number of Recipients: 10
Funding Amount: $5,000-40,000

APPLICATION PROCEDURE

Requirements: Slides
Restrictions: US citizenship
Time Between Application Deadline and Award Notification: Six to nine months
Reapplication by Former Recipients: Allowed immediately

SELECTION PROCESS

Method: Peer Panel
Criteria: Quality of work is the primary criterion. Project description and appropriateness to guidelines are also considered.

OTHER INFORMATION

Publications: Program Guidelines
Activities: Exhibition of recipient's work

MOTHER JONES FUND FOR DOCUMENTARY PHOTOGRAPHY

1663 Mission Street
San Francisco, CA 94103
415-558-8881
Bethany Schoenfeld, Visual Art Program Director

AWARD

Title: Mother Jones Photography Awards
Purpose: To support outstanding in-progress social documentary still photography projects.
Categories of Support: Photography
Type of Support: Project Grant
Year Established: 1990
Duration of Funding: One year
Customary Month or Season of Deadline: May
Total Number of Applicants: 250
Total Number of Recipients: 3
Funding Amount: $5,000-10,000

APPLICATION PROCEDURE

Requirements: Application form, resume, samples of original work, project description/statement
Restrictions: None
Time Between Application Deadline and Award Notification: Five months
Reapplication by Former Recipients: Not allowed

SELECTION PROCESS

Method: Peer Panel
Criteria: Quality of work is the primary criterion. Other factors include: financial need, resume, project description, geographic representation, and appropriateness to guidelines.

OTHER INFORMATION

Publications: Program Guidelines, exhibition catalogues of former recipients
Activities: *Mother Jones* magazine

MTA ARTS FOR TRANSIT PROGRAM

Metropolitan Transit Authority
347 Madison Avenue, 5th Floor
New York, NY 10017
212-878-7452
Wendy Feuer, Executive Director
Cheryl C. Stewart, Manager, Art Programs

AWARD

Title: Permanent Art Program
Purpose: 1% of construction budget in rehabilitated stations devoted to purchase/commission of artwork.
Categories of Support: Crafts, Drawing, New Genres, Painting, Photography, Printmaking, Public Art, Sculpture
Type of Support: Public Art Commission
Year Established: 1985
Duration of Funding: Varies with project
Customary Month or Season of Deadline: Varies with project
Total Number of Applicants: Information not provided
Total Number of Recipients: Information not provided
Funding Amount: Up to $60,000

APPLICATION PROCEDURE

Requirements: Resume, slides, project description/statement
Restrictions: No unsolicited proposals
Time Between Application Deadline and Award Notification: Varies with project
Reapplication by Former Recipients: Information not provided

SELECTION PROCESS

Method: Peer Panel
Criteria: Quality of work is the primary criterion. Other factors include: appropriateness to guidelines, project description, resume, geographic representation, and ethnic background.

OTHER INFORMATION

Publications: Program Guidelines, exhibition catalogues of former recipients
Activities: See additional entries for this organization. Exhibition of recipient's work.

MTA ARTS FOR TRANSIT PROGRAM

Metropolitan Transit Authority
347 Madison Ave., 5th Floor
New York, NY 10017
212-878-7452
Wendy Feuer, Executive Director
Cheryl C. Stewart, Manager, Art Programs

AWARD

Title: Creative Stations Program
Purpose: Up to $5,000 for community based, temporary art projects in stations.
Categories of Support: Crafts, Drawing, New Genres, Painting, Photography, Printmaking, Public Art, Sculpture
Type of Support: Public Art Commission
Year Established: 1985
Duration of Funding: Varies with project
Customary Month or Season of Deadline: Fall
Total Number of Applicants: 40
Total Number of Recipients: 10
Funding Amount: $5,000

APPLICATION PROCEDURE

Requirements: Resume, slides, project description/statement
Restrictions: None
Time Between Application Deadline and Award Notification: Varies with project
Reapplication by Former Recipients: Information not provided

SELECTION PROCESS

Method: Peer Panel Review
Criteria: Quality of work is the primary criterion. Other factors include: appropriateness to guidelines, resume, geographic representation, project description, and ethnic background.

OTHER INFORMATION

Publications: Program Guidelines, exhibition catalogues of former recipients
Activities: See additional entries for this organization. Exhibition of recipient's work.

MUNICIPALITY OF ANCHORAGE PUBLIC ART PROGRAM

Anchorage Museum of History and Art
121 West 7th Avenue
Anchorage , AK 99501
907-343-6473
Patricia B. Wolf, Executive Director
Molly Jones, Curator of Public Art

AWARD

Title: 1% For Art Program
Purpose: Purchase and commission of artworks for public buildings.
Categories of Support: Public Art
Type of Support: Public Art Commission
Year Established: 1978
Duration of Funding: Varies with project
Customary Month or Season of Deadline: Continuing
Total Number of Applicants: Information not provided
Total Number of Recipients: Information not provided
Funding Amount: Varies with project

APPLICATION PROCEDURE

Requirements: Write to Municipality of Anchorage Public Art Program to recieve announcements of competitions for public art projects.
Restrictions: Applicant may not be currently enrolled in a degree-granting program.
Time Between Application Deadline and Award Notification: Varies with project
Reapplication by Former Recipients: Allowed immediately

SELECTION PROCESS

Method: Mayor-appointed jury
Criteria: Quality of work is the primary criterion. Other factors include: resume, project description, and appropriateness to guidelines.

OTHER INFORMATION:

Publications: Program Guidelines
Activities: Exhibition of recipient's work

MUNICIPALITY OF METROPOLITAN SEATTLE (METRO)

MetroArts Program
821 2nd Avenue
Seattle, WA 98199
206-684-1406
Dick Sandaas, Executive Director
Carol Valenta, Art Program Coordinator

AWARD

Title: MetroArts Program
Purpose: To mitigate the adverse affects of transit system construction and increase public enthusiasm for Metro projects.
Categories of Support: New Genres, Public Art
Type of Support: Public Art Commission
Year Established: 1990
Duration of Funding: Through 1992
Customary Month or Season of Deadline: Continuing
Total Number of Applicants: 500
Total Number of Recipients: 21
Funding Amount: $700,000 total for all projects in 1992.

APPLICATION PROCEDURE

Requirements: Resume, slides, project description/statement
Restrictions: Varies with project
Time Between Application Deadline and Award Notification: Varies with project
Reapplication by Former Recipients: Allowed immediately

SELECTION PROCESS

Method: Peer Panel
Criteria: Varies by project

OTHER INFORMATION

Publications: Information not provided
Activities: Exhibition of recipient's work

NATIONAL ENDOWMENT FOR THE ARTS/ AMERICAN CENTER IN PARIS

Visual Arts Program
1100 Pennsylvania Ave., NW
Washington, DC 20506
202-682-5448
Susan Lubowsky, Director
Silvio Lim, Program Specialist

AWARD

Title: American Center/NEA Artist Residencies
Purpose: Living and working studios at the Cité Internationale des Arts in Paris for NEA Fellowship artists.
Categories of Support: Crafts, Drawing, New Genres, Painting, Photography, Printmaking, Sculpture
Type of Support: Residency
Year Established: 1991
Duration of Funding: One year
Customary Month or Season of Deadline: Varies with applicant's medium
Total Number of Applicants: n/a
Total Number of Recipients: n/a
Funding Amount: Housing and studio space for duration of residency

APPLICATION PROCEDURE

Requirements: Artists apply directly to the NEA Visual Arts Program.
Restrictions: Only current NEA Visual Artist Fellowship recipients may apply
Time Between Application Deadline and Award Notification: Six to eight months
Reapplication by Former Recipients: Allowed immediately

SELECTION PROCESS

Method: Peer Panel
Criteria: Quality of work is the primary criterion. Resume and project description are also considered.

OTHER INFORMATION

Publications: Program Guidelines, Annual Report
Activities: See additional entries for this organization.

NATIONAL ENDOWMENT FOR THE ARTS (NEA)
DESIGN ARTS PROGRAM

1100 Pennsylvania Avenue, NW, Room 625
Washington, DC 20506
202-682-5437
Wendy Clark, Senior Program Specialist

AWARD

Title: Design Innovations Grants
Purpose: Recognize and encourage new directions in design.
Categories of Support: Graphic Design, Product Design, Architecture, Landscape Architecture, Industrial Design
Type of Support: Project Grant
Year Established: 1967
Duration of Funding: One year
Customary Month or Season of Deadline: Spring and Fall
Total Number of Applicants: 50
Total Number of Recipients: 6
Funding Amount: $10,000

APPLICATION PROCEDURE

Requirements: Application form, resume, photographs of work, sample of original work, project description/statement, letters of support
Restrictions: US citizenship
Time Between Application Deadline and Award Notification: Six months
Reapplication by Former Recipients: Allowed immediately

SELECTION PROCESS

Method: Peer Panel
Criteria: Quality of work is the primary criterion.

OTHER INFORMATION

Publications: Program Guidelines, write to the NEA for list of other publications.
Activities: See additional entries for this organization. Publishing Program, Design Access (Design Artists' Registry)

NATIONAL ENDOWMENT FOR THE ARTS (NEA)
DESIGN ARTS PROGRAM

1100 Pennsylvania Avenue, NW, Room 625
Washington, DC 20506
202-682-5437
Wendy Clark, Senior Program Specialist

AWARD

Title: Project Grants
Purpose: Funds individual design artists' projects.
Categories of Support: Graphic Design, Product Design, Architecture, Landscape Architecture, Industrial Design
Type of Support: Project Grant
Year Established: 1967
Duration of Funding: One year
Customary Month or Season of Deadline: Spring and Fall
Total Number of Applicants: 178
Total Number of Recipients: 29
Funding Amount: $15,000

APPLICATION PROCEDURE

Requirements: Application form, resume, photographs of work, sample of original work, project/description/statement, letters of support
Restrictions: US citizenship
Time Between Application Deadline and Award Notification: Six months
Reapplication by Former Recipients: Allowed immediately

SELECTION PROCESS

Method: Peer Panel
Criteria: Quality of work is the primary criterion.

OTHER INFORMATION

Publications: Program Guidelines, write to the NEA for list of other publications
Activities: See additional entries for this organization. Publishing Program, Design Access (Design Artists' Registry), Design Innovations Grants.

NATIONAL ENDOWMENT FOR THE ARTS (NEA)
VISUAL ARTS PROGRAM

1100 Pennsylania Avenue, NW
Washington, DC 20506
202-682-5448
Susan Lubowsky, Assistant Director
Silvio Lim, Program Specialist/Fellowships

AWARD

Title: Visual Arts Fellowship Program
Purpose: Grants in this category encourage the creative development of professional artists, enabling them to pursue their work.
Categories of Support: Artists' Books, Drawing, New Genres, Painting, and Printmaking, alternating yearly with Sculpture, Crafts, and Photography
Type of Support: Fellowship
Year Established: 1967
Duration of Funding: One year
Customary Month or Season of Deadline: January and March
Total Number of Applicants: 5,353
Total Number of Recipients: 177
Funding Amount: $5,000 and $20,000

APPLICATION PROCEDURE

Requirements: Application form, resume, slides
Restrictions: Applicant may not be currently enrolled in a degree-granting program. U.S. citizenship.
Time Between Application Deadline and Award Notification: Six - eight months
Reapplication by Former Recipients: Recipients of $5000 fellowships may reapply each cycle. Recipients of $20,000 fellowships may reapply after two 2-year cycles.

SELECTION PROCESS

Method: Peer Panel
Criteria: Quality of work is the primary criterion. Resume is also considered.

OTHER INFORMATION

Publications: Program Guidelines, Annual Report, *Guide to the National Endowment for the Arts*
Activities: Japan Fellowships. See additional entries for this organization

NATIONAL SCULPTURE SOCIETY (NSS)

15 East 26th Street
New York, NY 10010
212-889-6960
Gwen Pier, Executive Director

AWARD

Title: Alex J. Ettl Grant
Purpose: To encourage excellence in figurative sculpture.
Categories of Support: Sculpture
Type of Support: Unrestricted
Year Established: 1989
Duration of Funding: One year
Customary Month or Season of Deadline: October
Total Number of Applicants: 100
Total Number of Recipients: 1
Funding Amount: $5,000

APPLICATION PROCEDURE

Requirements: Resume, photographs of work
Restrictions: US citizenship
Time Between Application Deadline and Award Notification: Two weeks
Reapplication by Former Recipients: Allowed immediately

SELECTION PROCESS

Method: Peer Panel
Criteria: Quality of work is the primary criterion. Appropriateness to guidelines is also considered.

OTHER INFORMATION

Publications: Program Guidelines
Activities: Information not provided

NEBRASKA ARTS COUNCIL (NAC)

1313 Farnam-on-the-Mall
Omaha, NE 68102-1873
402-595-2122
Jennifer S. Clark, Executive Director
Suzanne T. Wise, Visual Arts Coordinator

AWARD

Title: 1% For Art Program
Purpose: State-mandated public art law. All capital construction over $250,000 (renovation) or $500,000 (new) is eligible, with some exceptions.
Categories of Support: Public Art
Type of Support: Public Art Commission
Year Established: 1979
Duration of Funding: Varies with project
Customary Month or Season of Deadline: Varies with project
Total Number of Applicants: Information not provided
Total Number of Recipients: Information not provided
Funding Amount: Varies with project

APPLICATION PROCEDURE

Requirements: Application form, resume, slides. May vary with project.
Restrictions: Varies with project
Time Between Application Deadline and Award Notification: Varies with project
Reapplication by Former Recipients: Allowed immediately

SELECTION PROCESS

Method: Art selection committee
Criteria: Quality of work is the primary criterion. Other factors include: resume, project description, and appropriateness to guidelines.

OTHER INFORMATION:

Publications: Program Guidelines
Activities: See additional entries for this organization. Exhibition of recipient's work.

NEW MEXICO ARTS DIVISION/ART IN PUBLIC PLACES PROGRAM

224 East Palace Avenue
Santa Fe, NM 87501
505-827-6490
Lara Morrow, Executive Director
Anne Green, Public Art Coordinator

AWARD

Title: Art in Public Places Program
Purpose: To acquire a variety of art for public buildings under the state's 1% for art legislation. This program consists of a *slide registry only.* Artists must be included in this registry to be considered for public commissions.
Categories of Support: Public Art
Type of Support: Public Art Commission
Year Established: 1987
Duration of Funding: Varies with project
Customary Month or Season of Deadline: Continuing
Total Number of Applicants: Information not provided
Total Number of Recipients: Information not provided
Funding Amount: n/a

APPLICATION PROCEDURE

Requirements: Resume, slides
Restrictions: None
Time Between Application Deadline and Award Notification: One month
Reapplication by Former Recipients: Allowed immediately

SELECTION PROCESS

Method: Local selection committee
Criteria: Approriateness to guidelines is the primary criterion. Resume and quality of work are also considered.

OTHER INFORMATION

Publications: Program Guidelines, bi-monthly bulletin
Activities: Slide registry

NEW YORK CITY DEPARTMENT OF CULTURAL AFFAIRS

Percent for Art Program
2 Columbus Circle
New York, NY 10019
212-841-4177
Tom Finkelpearl, Executive Director
Karen Hwa, Project Manager

AWARD

Title: Percent For Art Program
Purpose: Commission or purchase artwork for city-owned property.
Categories of Support: Public Art
Type of Support: Public Art Commission
Year Established: 1983
Duration of Funding: Two to five years
Customary Month or Season of Deadline: Varies with project
Total Number of Applicants: Infomation not provided
Total Number of Recipients: Information not provided
Funding Amount: $20,000-200,000

APPLICATION PROCEDURE

Requirements: Application form, resume, slides
Restrictions: None
Time Between Application Deadline and Award Notification: Varies with project
Reapplication by Former Recipients: Allowed immediately

SELECTION PROCESS

Method: Peer Panel
Criteria: Quality of work is the primary criterion. Other factors include: resume, geographic representation, appropriatness to guidelines, and ethnic background.

OTHER INFORMATION

Publications: Program Guidelines
Activities: Exhibition of recipient's work

NEW YORK MILLS ARTS RETREAT (NYMAR)

RR 1, Box 217
New York Mills, MN 56567
218-385-3339
John Davis, Executive Director

AWARD

Title: New York Mills Arts Retreat Residency
Purpose: To provide a place in the country for artists to concentrate on creative projects and ideas while sharing their talents with the community.
Categories of Support: Artists' Books, Crafts, Drawing, New Genres, Painting, Public Art, Sculpture
Type of Support: Residency
Year Established: 1989
Duration of Funding: Up to 2 months
Customary Month or Season of Deadline: Continuing
Total Number of Applicants: 25
Total Number of Recipients: 5
Funding Amount: $700

APPLICATION PROCEDURE

Requirements: Application form, resume, slides, project description/statement
Restrictions: Applicant may not be currently enrolled in a degree-granting program.
Time Between Application Deadline and Award Notification: One month
Reapplication by Former Recipients: Allowed after two years

SELECTION PROCESS

Method: Peer Panel
Criteria: Quality of work is the primary criterion. Resume and project description are also considered.

OTHER INFORMATION

Publications: Program Guidelines
Activities: Information not provided

NEXUS PRESS

535 Means Street
Atlanta, GA 30318
404-577-3579
Louise E. Shaw, Executive Director
Michael Goodman, Director, Nexus Press

AWARD

Title: Nexus Press Residency Program
Purpose: Education and the production of new artists' books.
Categories of Support: Artists' Books
Type of Support: Residency
Year Established: 1984
Duration of Funding: One month
Customary Month or Season of Deadline: May
Total Number of Applicants: 175
Total Number of Recipients: 2
Funding Amount: $2,000-3,000 plus housing

APPLICATION PROCEDURE

Requirements: Resume, slides, project description/statement, book prospectus
Restrictions: Applicant may not be currently enrolled in a degree-granting program.
Time Between Application Deadline and Award Notification: One month
Reapplication by Former Recipients: Allowed immediately

SELECTION PROCESS

Method: Staff Members
Criteria: Quality of work is the primary criterion. Project description is also considered.

OTHER INFORMATION

Publications: Program Guidelines
Activities: Extensive Artists' Book publishing program

OREGON ARTS COMMISSION (OAC)
835 Summer Street, NE
Salem, OR 97301
503-378-3625
Leslie Tuomi, Executive Director
Nancy Lindburg, Artist Services Coordinator

AWARD

Title: Percent for Art Program
Purpose: Purchase of Artwork for state buildings.
Categories of Support: Crafts, Drawing, New Genres, Painting, Photography, Printmaking, Public Art, Sculpture
Type of Support: Purchase
Year Established: 1975
Duration of Funding: One year
Customary Month or Season of Deadline: As needed
Total Number of Applicants: 300
Total Number of Recipients: 30
Funding Amount: $100-100,000

APPLICATION PROCEDURE

Requirements: Application form, resume, slides, project description/statement
Restrictions: None
Time Between Application Deadline and Award Notification: Four months
Reapplication by Former Recipients: Allowed immediately

SELECTION PROCESS

Method: Peer Panel Review, Staff Members
Criteria: Quality of work is the primary criterion. Other factors include: resume, geographic representation, and project description.

OTHER INFORMATION

Publications: Information not provided
Activities: Exhibition of recipient's work

PALENVILLE INTERARTS COLONY

PO Box 59
Palenville, NY 12463
518-678-3332
Joanna M. Sherman, Artistic Director

AWARD

Title: Artist Residency Program
Purpose: Provides an ideal setting for professional artists to reap the benefits of isolation and serenity during physical and spiritual rejuvenation.
Categories of Support: Crafts, Drawing, Printmaking, Sculpture
Type of Support: Residency
Year Established: 1982
Duration of Funding: Up to eight weeks
Customary Month or Season of Deadline: April
Total Number of Applicants: 126
Total Number of Recipients: 22
Funding Amount: Fee waivers dependent on financial need

APPLICATION PROCEDURE

Requirements: Application form, resume, slides, sample of original work, project description/statement, three references
Restrictions: None
Time Between Application Deadline and Award Notification: One month
Reapplication by Former Recipients: Allowed immediately (once)

SELECTION PROCESS

Method: Peer Panel
Criteria: Quality of work is the primary criterion. Appropriateness to guidelines and ethnic background are also considered.

OTHER INFORMATION

Publications: Program Guidelines
Activities: Exhibition of recipient's work

PALM BEACH COUNTY COUNCIL OF THE ARTS

Art in Public Places Committee
PO Box 3366
West Palm Beach, FL 33401-2371
305-471-2905
William E. Ray, Executive Director
Paul R. Aho, Director, Art in Public Places

AWARD

Title: Art in Public Places-Palm Beach County
Purpose: To Enhance visual environments of major county facilites and spaces.
Categories of Support: Public Art
Type of Support: Public Art Commission
Year Established: 1982
Duration of Funding: Varies with project
Customary Month or Season of Deadline: Varies with project
Total Number of Applicants: 200
Total Number of Recipients: 20
Funding Amount: $500-50,000

APPLICATION PROCEDURE

Requirements: Resume, slides
Restrictions: None
Time Between Application Deadline and Award Notification: Three - six months
Reapplication by Former Recipients: Allowed immediately

SELECTION PROCESS

Method: Peer Panel, Board Members
Criteria: Quality of work is the primary criterion. Other factors include: resume, geographic representation, and appropriateness to guidelines.

OTHER INFORMATION

Publications: n/a
Activities: Exhibition of recipient's work, slide registry

PHILADELPHIA OFFICE OF ARTS AND CULTURE
Percent for Art Program
1680 Municipal Services Building
Philadelphia, PA 19102-1684
215-686-8684
Rita Roosevelt, Executive Director
Joan MacKeith, Percent for Art Program Coordinator

AWARD
Title: Percent for Art Program
Purpose: Development and implementation of public art for visual artists. Open competitions for visual artists.
Categories of Support: Public Art
Type of Support: Public Art
Year Established: 1959
Duration of Funding: Varies with project
Customary Month or Season of Deadline: Varies with project
Total Number of Applicants: 300+
Total Number of Recipients: 7
Funding Amount: $30,000-70,000

APPLICATION PROCEDURE
Requirements: Application form, resume, slides, project description/statement, project budget
Restrictions: None
Time Between Application Deadline and Award Notification: Varies with project
Reapplication by Former Recipients: Allowed immediately

SELECTION PROCESS
Method: Peer Panel
Criteria: Quality of work is the primary criterion. Other factors include: resume, project description, and ethnic background.

OTHER INFORMATION
Publications: Program Guidelines
Activities: Exhibition of recipient's work, slide registry

PHOTOGRAPHIC RESOURCE CENTER (PRC)

602 Commonwealth Avenue
Boston, MA 02215
617-353-0700
Stan Trecker, Executive Director
Emily Terry, Program Director

AWARD

Title: Leopold Godowsky, Jr. Color Photography Award
Purpose: To support outstanding work in color photography worldwide. Eligibility for the award rotates to a different global region every two years.
Categories of Support: Photography
Type of Support: Unrestricted
Year Established: 1987
Duration of Funding: Two years
Customary Month or Season of Deadline: Continuing
Total Number of Applicants: 75
Total Number of Recipients: 3 awards, 3 honorable mentions
Funding Amount: $10,000 total awarded

APPLICATION PROCEDURE

Requirements: Resume, slides, clippings, reviews
Restrictions: Applicant must be 18 years of age or older and not currently enrolled in a degree-granting program. Write to Photographic Resource Center for current geographic eligibility restrictions.
Time Between Application Deadline and Award Notification: 1 1/2 years
Reapplication by Former Recipients: Not allowed

SELECTION PROCESS

Method: Peer Panel
Criteria: Quality of work is the primary criterion. Geographic representation is also considered.

OTHER INFORMATION

Publications: Information not provided
Activities: Information not provided

PILCHUCK GLASS SCHOOL

Emerging Artists-in Residence Program
107 South Main Street #324
Seattle, WA 98104
206-621-8422
Marjorie Levy, Executive Director

AWARD

Title: (Winter) Emerging Artist-in-Residence Program
Purpose: To provide emerging visual artists an opportunity to work in glass with technical assistants and excellent facilities and supplies.
Categories of Support: Crafts, New Genres, Sculpture, Printmaking.
Type of Support: Residency
Year Established: 1990
Duration of Funding: Four months
Customary Month or Season of Deadline: April
Total Number of Applicants: 40
Total Number of Recipients: 5
Funding Amount: $1,000 plus housing for duration of residency

APPLICATION PROCEDURE

Requirements: Application form, resume, slides, statement/project description, application fee, two lettters of recommendation
Restrictions: Applicant must be 18 years of age or older and not currently enrolled in a degree-granting program.
Time Between Application Deadline and Award Notification: One month
Reapplication by Former Recipients: Not allowed

SELECTION PROCESS

Method: Peer Panel Review, Staff Members
Criteria: Quality of work is the primary criterion. Resume and project description are also considered.

OTHER INFORMATION

Publications: School Catalog
Activities: See additional entries for this organization. Exhibition of recipient's work.

POLLOCK-KRASNER FOUNDATION

PO Box 4957
New York, NY 10185
212-517-5400
Charles C. Bergman, Executive Director
Linda Selvin, Grants Manager

AWARD

Title: Pollock-Krasner Foundation Grant
Purpose: Grants are awarded to professional visual artists for their personal, professional, or medical needs. Equal weight is given to merit and financial need.
Categories of Support: Drawing, Painting, Printmaking, Sculpture
Type of Support: Unrestricted
Year Established: 1985
Duration of Funding: One year
Customary Month or Season of Deadline: Continuing
Total Number of Applicants: Information not provided
Total Number of Recipients: 193
Funding Amount: $1,000-30,000

APPLICATION PROCEDURE

Requirements: Application form, resume, slides, cover letter
Restrictions: Funds may not be used for legal fees, purchase of real estate, or costs related to production of commissioned works.
Time Between Application Deadline and Award Notification: Three - nine months
Reapplication by Former Recipients: Allowed after one year

SELECTION PROCESS

Method: Peer Panel, Board Members
Criteria: Quality of work is the primary criterion. Financial need is also considered.

OTHER INFORMATION

Publications: Program Guidelines, Annual Report
Activities: Information not provided

PRINCE GEORGE'S COUNTY ART IN PUBLIC PLACES

CAB Room 5032
Upper Marlboro, MD 20772
301-985-5132
Anne C. Palumbo, Program Coordinator

AWARD

Title: Art in Public Places
Purpose: Site-specific commissions or purchase of artworks through 1% for art program.
Categories of Support: Artists' Books, Crafts, Drawing, New Genres, Painting, Photography, Printmaking, Public Art, Sculpture
Type of Support: Public Art Commission
Year Established: 1990
Duration of Funding: Varies with project
Customary Month or Season of Deadline: Varies with project
Total Number of Applicants: 240
Total Number of Recipients: 2 finalists, 10 semi-finalists
Funding Amount: Finalists: $60,000-200,000 Semi-Finalists: $1,500-1,000

APPLICATION PROCEDURE

Requirements: Resume, slides
Restrictions: May vary with project
Time Between Application Deadline and Award Notification: Two months
Reapplication by Former Recipients: Allowed immediately

SELECTION PROCESS

Method: Peer Panel, Staff Members, Board Members
Criteria: Quality of work is the primary criterion. Other factors include: resume, project description, geographic representation (when specified), and ethnic background (when specified).

OTHER INFORMATION

Publications: Program Guidelines, calls for entries
Activities: Exhibition of recipient's work, slide registry

PUBLIC ART FUND INC.

1285 Avenue of the Americas, 3rd Floor
New York, NY 10019-6071
212-541-8423
James Clark, Executive Director

AWARD

Title: Public Art Fund/New York City Department of Transportation Artist in Residence Program
Purpose: This residency program gives artists access to the NYC DOT sign shop for the creation of original signage, with the final products displayed on New York's streets as functional signs. The program represents an exceptional opportunity for artists to explore issues related to symbology, signage, and information.
Categories of Support: Public Art/New Genres
Type of Support: Residency
Year Established: 1989
Duration of Funding: Six months
Customary Month or Season of Deadline: May
Total Number of Applicants: Information not provided
Total Number of Recipients: 1
Funding Amount: $2,500 artist's fee and equipment access

APPLICATION PROCEDURE

Requirements: Resume, project description/statement, slides
Restrictions: None
Time Between Application Deadline and Award Notification: Three months
Reapplication by Former Recipients: Information not provided

SELECTION PROCESS

Method: Selection panel
Criteria: Quality of work is the primary criterion. Project description and appropriateness to guidelines are also considered.

OTHER INFORMATION

Publications: Program Guidelines, exhibition catalogue of recipients
Activities: Exhibition of recipients' work, slide registry

PYRAMID ATLANTIC

6001 66th Avenue, Suite 103
Riverdale, MD 20737
301-459-7154
Helen Frederick, Executive Director

AWARD

Title: MID-BOOK Pyramid Atlantic Artist Book Publishing Residency
Purpose: Publishing program established to produce two Artists' Books per residency: one in offset and one in letterpress. Our goal is to produce books that are rich in color and language, innovative in structure, and authentic to contemporary human concerns. Artists from all media are encouraged to apply.
Categories of Support: Artists' Books, Printmaking, Papermaking
Type of Support: Residency
Year Established: Information not provided
Duration of Funding: One to three months
Customary Month or Season of Deadline: Continuing
Total Number of Applicants: 25
Total Number of Recipients: 12
Funding Amount: Access to equipment and technical assistance (valued at $2,500)

APPLICATION PROCEDURE

Requirements: Application form, resume, project description/statement, slides
Restrictions: Applicant may not be currently enrolled in a degree-granting program. U.S. citizenship.
Time Between Application Deadlineand Award Notification: Three months
Reapplication by Former Recipients: Allowed after three years

SELECTION PROCESS

Method: Peer panel, staff members
Criteria: Quality of work is the primary criterion. Other factors include: project description, appropriateness to guidelines, and ethnic background.

OTHER INFORMATION

Publications: Program guidelines
Activities: See additional entries for this organization. Exhibition of recipient's work, slide registry.

RAGDALE FOUNDATION

1260 North Green Bay Road
Lake Forest, IL 60045
708-234-1063
Michael Wilkerson, Executive Director

AWARD

Title: Ragdale Foundation Residencies
Purpose: To provide time, studio space, and interaction with other artists, writers and composers for qualified visual artists.
Categories of Support: Artists' Books, Drawing, New Genres, Painting, Public Art, Sculpture
Type of Support: Residency
Year Established: 1976
Duration of Funding: Two weeks to two months
Customary Month or Season of Deadline: Three deadlines each year. Write to Ragdale Foundation for current deadlines.
Total Number of Applicants: 500
Total Number of Recipients: 150
Funding Amount: Housing and studio space at a nominal fee. Full and partial fee waivers available according to need.

APPLICATION PROCEDURE

Requirements: Application form, resume, slides, project description/statement, financial statement (if fee waiver requested)
Restrictions: None
Time Between Application Deadline and Award Notification: One to two months
Reapplication by Former Recipients: Allowed after one year

SELECTION PROCESS

Method: Peer Panel
Criteria: Quality of work is the primary criterion. Other factors include: Resume, geographic representation, project description, and ethnic background.

OTHER INFORMATION

Publications: Program Guidelines, Annual newsletter
Activities: Information not provided

ROCKEFELLER FOUNDATION

Bellagio Center Office
1133 Avenue of the Americas
New York, NY 10036
212-869-8500
Susan E. Garfield, Manager, Bellagio Center Office

AWARD

Title: Residential Program for Scholars and Artists
Purpose: Provides a setting for artists to complete a specific project at the foundation's Bellagio Center at Lake Como, Italy. Candidates working toward an expected exhibition are given preference.
Categories of Support: Drawing, New Genres, Painting, Photography, Printmaking, Public Art, Sculpture
Type of Support: Residency
Year Established: Information not provided
Duration of Funding: Five weeks
Customary Month or Season of Deadline: Four deadlines per year. Write to the Rockefeller Foundation for current deadlines.
Total Number of Applicants: 600
Total Number of Recipients: 7
Funding Amount: Room and board, studio for duration of residency

APPLICATION PROCEDURE

Requirements: Application form, resume, slides, project description/statement
Restrictions: Applicant may not be currently enrolled in degree-granting program and should have a solid history of achievement. Not for emerging artists.
Time Between Application Deadline and Award Notification: Three - four months
Reapplication by Former Recipients: Allowed after ten years

SELECTION PROCESS

Method: Staff Members
Criteria: Quality of work is the primary criterion. Resume is also considered.

OTHER INFORMATION

Publications: Program Guidelines
Activities: Information not provided

ROCKY MOUNTAIN WOMEN'S INSTITUTE

7150 Montview Boulevard
Denver, CO 80220
303-871-6923
Cheryl Bezio-Gorham, Executive Director

AWARD

Title: Annual Associateship
Purpose: Provides stipends and a working environment to artists and scholars to allow them to concentrate on their professional disciplines.
Categories of Support: Artists' Books, Crafts, Drawing, New Genres, Painting, Photography, Printmaking, Sculpture
Type of Support: Unrestricted
Year Established: Information not provided
Duration of Funding: One academic year
Customary Month or Season of Deadline: March
Total Number of Applicants: 176
Total Number of Recipients: 7
Funding Amount: $1,000

APPLICATION PROCEDURE

Requirements: Application form, resume, slides, project description/statement
Restrictions: Applicant may not be currently enrolled in a degree-granting program.
Time Between Application Deadline and Award Notification: 2 1/2 months
Reapplication by Former Recipients: Not allowed

SELECTION PROCESS

Method: Peer Panel, Staff Members, Board Members
Criteria: Quality of work is the primary criterion. Financial need is also considered.

OTHER INFORMATION

Publications: Program Guidelines
Activities: Exhibition of recipient's work

ROSWELL MUSEUM RESIDENCIES

Roswell Musuem and Art Center
100 West 11th Street
Roswell, NM 88201
505-624-6744
Stuart Arends, Program Director

AWARD

Title: Artists in Residence Program
Purpose: Provides professional artists in varying disciplines with three to twelve month residencies for unhindered productive time.
Categories of Support: Drawing, New Genres, Painting, Photography, Printmaking, Sculpture
Type of Support: Residency
Year Established: 1967
Duration of Funding: Three to twelve months
Customary Month or Season of Deadline: Varies
Total Number of Applicants: 300
Total Number of Recipients: 1
Funding Amount: $500/month stipend, room and board, studio

APPLICATION PROCEDURE

Requirements: Application form, resume, slides, project description/statement
Restrictions: None
Time Between Application Deadline and Award Notification: Four months
Reapplication by Former Recipients: Not allowed. Former recipients may be invited back.

SELECTION PROCESS

Method: Peer Panel, Staff Members, Board Members
Criteria: Quality of work is the primary criterion. Project description is also considered.

OTHER INFORMATION

Publications: Program Guidelines, exhibition catalogues of former recipients
Activities: Possible exhibition of recipient's work

SANTA FE ARTS COMMISSION (SFAC)

Percent for Art Program
P.O. Box 909
Santa Fe, NM 87504-8909
505-984-6707
Sabrina V. Platt, Executive Director

AWARD

Title: 1% For Art Program
Purpose: Placement of public art throughout the city of Santa Fe.
Categories of Support: Public Art
Type of Support: Public Art Commission
Year Established: 1987
Duration of Funding: Varies with project
Customary Month or Season of Deadline: Continuing
Total Number of Applicants: 58
Total Number of Recipients: 2
Funding Amount: $10,000-125,000

APPLICATION PROCEDURE

Requirements: Resume, slides, project description/statement
Restrictions: None
Time Between Application Deadline and Award Notification: Varies with project
Reapplication by Former Recipients: Allowed immediately

SELECTION PROCESS

Method: Peer Panel
Criteria: Quality of work is the primary criterion. Resume and project description are also considered.

OTHER INFORMATION

Publications: Information not provided
Activities: Exhibition of recipient's work.

SCULPTURE SPACE INC.

12 Gates Street
Utica, NY 13502
315-724-8381
Sylvia De Swaan, Executive Director

AWARD

Title: Funded Residency
Purpose: To support artists by providing free use of studio space, access to equipment, and industrial resources.
Categories of Support: Sculpture
Type of Support: Residency
Year Established: 1981
Duration of Funding: Two months
Customary Month or Season of Deadline: Information not provided
Total Number of Applicants: 50
Total Number of Recipients: 4
Funding Amount: $200-2,000

APPLICATION PROCEDURE

Requirements: Resume, project description/statement, slides
Restrictions: Applicant may not be currently enrolled in a degree-granting program.
Time Between Application Deadline and Award Notification: Three months
Reapplication by Former Recipients: Information not provided

SELECTION PROCESS

Method: Peer panel
Criteria: Quality of work is the primary criterion.

OTHER INFORMATION

Publications: Program Guidelines, newsletter
Activities: Information not provided

SEATTLE ARTS COMMISSION

305 Harrison Street
Seattle, WA 98109
206-684-7171
T. Ellen Sollod, Executive Director
Victoria Cruz, Public Art Program

AWARD

Title: Public Art Program (1% For Art)
Purpose: This program administers a wide range of artwork projects, from major outdoor installations, wall pieces for display in city buildings, and architect/design team projects.
Categories of Support: Artists' Books, Crafts, Drawing, New Genres, Painting, Photography, Printmaking, Public Art, Sculpture
Type of Support: Commission/Purchase
Year Established: 1973
Duration of Funding: Varies with project
Customary Month or Season of Deadline: Continuing
Total Number of Applicants: Information not provided
Total Number of Recipients: Approx. 30 projects per year
Funding Amount: $500,000 total yearly expenditure for program

APPLICATION PROCEDURE

Requirements: Varies with project
Restrictions: Varies with project
Time Between Application Deadline and Award Notification: Varies with project
Reapplication by Former Recipients: Allowed once every three-year cycle

SELECTION PROCESS

Method: Selection committee
Criteria: Quality of work is the primary criterion. Project description and appropriateness to guidelines are also considered.

OTHER INFORMATION::

Publications: Program Guidelines
Activities: n/a

MARIE WALSH SHARPE ART FOUNDATION

711 North Tejon, Suite B
Colorado Springs, CO 80903
719-635-3220
Joyce E. Robinson, Executive Director
Kim Taylor, Administrative Assistant

AWARD

Title: The Space Program
Purpose: Offers 14 free studio spaces in New York City to visual artists 21 and over. The studios are non live-in and are available for periods up to one year with an opportunity to reapply for a second year. Studios are available beginning June 1, 1992.
Categories of Support: Drawing, New Genres, Painting, Photography (no facilities), Printmaking (no facilites), Sculpture
Type of Support: Workspace
Year Established: 1990
Duration of Funding: One year with an opportunity to reapply for a second year
Customary Month or Season of Deadline: January
Total Number of Applicants: 350
Total Number of Recipients: 17
Funding Amount: Studio space in Manhattan for duration of residency

APPLICATION PROCEDURE

Requirements: Resume, slides, narrative statement describing why studio space is needed, statement specifying start date and length of residency
Restrictions: Applicant must be 21 years of age or older and not currently enrolled in a degree-granting program. US citizenship.
Time Between Application Deadline and Award Notification: Two months
Reapplication by Former Recipients: Allowed immediately

SELECTION PROCESS

Method: Peer Panel
Criteria: Quality of work is the primary criterion. Resume and narrative statement are also considered.

OTHER INFORMATION

Publications: Program Guidelines
Activities: Artists' Hotline

SIERRA ARTS FOUNDATION

200 Flint Street
Reno, NV 89501
702-329-1324
Virginia Keeney, Executive Director
Stephanie Sparks, Program Director

AWARD

Title: Honoraria
Purpose: Disburses artists' fees to visual artists exhibiting in the Sierra Art Center's Gallery.
Categories of Support: Artists' Books, Crafts, Drawing, New Genres, Painting, Photography, Printmaking, Sculpture
Type of Support: Honoraria
Year Established: 1988
Duration of Funding: One month
Customary Month or Season of Deadline: Continuing
Total Number of Applicants: Information not provided
Total Number of Recipients: Information not provided
Funding Amount: Varies with project

APPLICATION PROCEDURE

Requirements: Resume, slides, project description/statement, letters of recommendation
Restrictions: Applicant may not be currently enrolled in a degree-granting program.
Time Between Application Deadline and Award Notification: Varies with project
Reapplication by Former Recipients: Allowed immediately

SELECTION PROCESS

Method: Peer Panel
Criteria: Quality of work is the primary criterion. Other factors vary with project.

OTHER INFORMATION:

Publications: Newsletters, brochure
Activities: Exhibition of recipient's work, Art-in-Education Program.

AARON SISKIND FOUNDATION

73 Warren Street
New York, NY 10017

AWARD

Title: Individual Photographer Fellowships
Purpose: Supports on-going creative work in all photographic media.
Categories of Support: Photography
Type of Support: Unrestricted
Year Established: 1991
Duration of Funding: One year
Customary Month or Season of Deadline: April
Total Number of Applicants: 700
Total Number of Recipients: 11
Funding Amount: Up to $5,000

APPLICATION PROCEDURE

Requirements: Application form, resume, slides, project description/statement (optional)
Restrictions: Applicant may not be currently enrolled in a degree-granting program.
Time Between Application Deadline and Award Notification: Two months
Reapplication by Former Recipients: Allowed after one year

SELECTION PROCESS

Method: Peer Panel
Criteria: Quality of work is the primary criterion.

OTHER INFORMATION

Publications: Program Guidelines
Activities: Information not provided

W. EUGENE SMITH MEMORIAL FUND

International Center for Photography
1130 5th Avenue
New York, NY 10028
212-679-3288
Howard Chapnick, Executive Director

AWARD

Title: W. Eugene Smith Grant in Humanistic Photography
Purpose: The fund and grant was established in 1979 to seek out and encourage independent voices in photography.
Categories of Support: Photography
Type of Support: Unrestricted
Year Established: 1979
Duration of Funding: One year
Customary Month or Season of Deadline: July
Total Number of Applicants: Information not provided
Total Number of Recipients: 1
Funding Amount: $20,000

APPLICATION PROCEDURE

Requirements: Application form, slides, samples of original work, project description/statement, clippings
Restrictions: None
Time Between Application Deadline and Award Notification: Four months
Reapplication by Former Recipients: Information not provided

SELECTION PROCESS

Method: Peer Panel
Criteria: Quality of work is the primary criterion. Project description/statement is also considered.

OTHER INFORMATION::

Publications: Program Guidelines
Activities: Information not provided

SOUTHWEST CRAFT CENTER (SWCC)
Visiting Artists Program
300 Augusta Street
San Antonio, TX 78205
512-224-1848
Ric Collier, Executive Director
Margo Cassis, Director of Programs

AWARD
Title: Visiting Artist/Artist-in-Residence
Purpose: The Center provides an alternative worksite for artists and participants to collaborate and explore mutually beneficial projects.
Categories of Support: Artist's Books, Crafts, Drawing, Painting, New Genres, Photography, Printmaking, Public Art, Sculpture
Type of Support: Project Grant
Year Established: 1984
Duration of Funding: One year
Customary Month or Season of Deadline: Information not provided
Total Number of Applicants: Information not provided
Total Number of Recipients: 50
Funding Amount: $1,000-5,000

APPLICATION PROCEDURE
Requirements: Resume, slides, project description/statement, project budget
Restrictions: Texas state residency may be required in *some cases.*
Time Between Application Deadline and Award Notification: Varies with project
Reapplication by Former Recipients: Allowed immediately

SELECTION PROCESS
Method: Staff members
Criteria: Quality of work is the primary criterion. Project description is also considered.

OTHER INFORMATION
Publications: Exhibition catalogues of former recipients
Activities: Information not provided

SPOKANE ARTS COMMISSION

808 West Spokane Falls Boulevard
Spokane, WA 99201
509-625-6050
Sue Ellen Heflin, Arts Director

AWARD

Title: Percent for Art Program
Purpose: Enhancement of public areas through the acquisition of artwork with 1% of construction costs over $25,000 set aside for the purchase and/or commissioning of artwork.
Categories of Support: Public Art
Type of Support: Public Art Commission
Year Established: 1982
Duration of Funding: Varies with project
Customary Month or Season of Deadline: Varies with project
Total Number of Applicants: Information not provided
Total Number of Recipients: Information not provided
Funding Amount: Varies with project

APPLICATION PROCEDURE

Requirements: Varies with project
Restrictions: Varies with project
Time Between Application Deadline and Award Notification: Varies with project
Reapplication by Former Recipients: Varies with project

SELECTION PROCESS

Method: Peer Panel, Board Members
Criteria: Quality of work is the primary criterion. Project description and appropriateness to guidelines are also considered.

OTHER INFORMATION::

Publications: Commission announcements
Activities: Exhibition of recipient's work

STATE ARTS COUNCIL OF OKLAHOMA

2101N. Lincoln Boulevard, Suite 640
Oklahoma City, OK 73105
405-521-2931
Betty Price, Executive Director
James Huelsman, Arts Education Director

AWARD

Title: Artists-in-Residence Program
Purpose: To encourage a cooperative commitment among artists, educators, and the community for making the arts an integral part of the total learning experience for all Oklahomans.
Categories of Support: Drawing, Painting, Photography, Printmaking, Sculpture
Type of Support: Residency
Year Established: 1969
Duration of Funding: Two years
Customary Month or Season of Deadline: Summer
Total Number of Applicants: Information not provided
Total Number of Recipients: Information not provided
Funding Amount: Information not provided

APPLICATION PROCEDURE

Requirements: Application form, resume
Restrictions: None
Time Between Application Deadline and Award Notification: Varies with project
Reapplication by Former Recipients: Allowed immediately

SELECTION PROCESS

Method: Peer Panel, Staff Members, Board Members.
Criteria: Quality of work is the primary criterion.

OTHER INFORMATION::

Publications: Program Guidelines
Activities: Information not provided

STUDIOS MIDWEST
PO Box 291
Galesburg, IL 61401
309-344-1177 or
309-342-2010
Todd Moore, Director

AWARD
Title: Studios Midwest Residency
Purpose: Eight week residency program for six artists in Galesburg, IL.
Categories of Support: Artists' Books, Crafts, Drawing, New Genres, Painting, Photography, Printmaking, Public Art, Sculpture
Type of Support: Residency
Year Established: 1985
Duration of Funding: Two months (June-August)
Customary Month or Season of Deadline: March
Total Number of Applicants: 40
Total Number of Recipients: 6
Funding Amount: Housing and studio for duration of residency.

APPLICATION PROCEDURE
Requirements: Application form, resume, slides, project description/statement
Restrictions: None
Time Between Application Deadline and Award Notification: One month
Reapplication by Former Recipients: Allowed immediately

SELECTION PROCESS
Method: Peer Panel
Criteria: Quality of work is the primary criterion.

OTHER INFORMATION::
Publications: Program Guidelines, Annual Report
Activities: Exhibition of recipient's work

UCROSS FOUNDATION

2836 US Highway 14-16
Clearmont, WY 82835
307-737-2291
Elizabeth Guheen, Executive Director

AWARD

Title: Ucross Foundation Residency
Purpose: Provides residencies and studio space for visual artists.
Categories of Support: Artists' Books, Crafts, Drawing, New Genres, Painting, Photography, Printmaking, Public Art, Sculpture
Type of Support: Residency
Year Established: 1983
Duration of Funding: Two weeks - four months
Customary Month or Season of Deadline: March and October
Total Number of Applicants: 130
Total Number of Recipients: 16
Funding Amount: Room and board, studio space for duration of residency

APPLICATION PROCEDURE

Requirements: Application form, resume, slides, sample of original work, project description/statement
Restrictions: None
Time Between Application Deadline and Award Notification: Six weeks
Reapplication by Former Recipients: Allowed after two years

SELECTION PROCESS

Method: Peer Panel
Criteria: Quality of work is the primary criterion. Resume and project description are also considered.

OTHER INFORMATION::

Publications: Program Guidelines, newsletter
Activities: Information not provided

URBAN INSTITUTE FOR CONTEMPORARY ARTS (UICA)

1064 Race Street NE
Grand Rapids, MI 49503
616-454-7000
Paul Wittenbraker, Executive Director
Dorothy Bradshaw, Associate Director

AWARD

Title: Artist-in-Residence Program
Purpose: Artists are awarded large studios in an Institute building and given a solo show. Residencies last two years and the artist may reapply for a one-year extension. Artists-in-Residence are free to use any facilites in the building.
Categories of Support: Artists' Books, Crafts, Drawing, Painting, Photography, Printmaking, Sculpture, New Genres
Type of Support: Residency
Year Established: Information not provided
Duration of Funding: Two years
Customary Month or Season of Deadline: April
Total Number of Applicants: 50
Total Number of Recipients: 3
Funding Amount: Studio for duration of residency

APPLICATION PROCEDURE

Requirements: Resume, slides, project description
Restrictions: None
Time Between Application Deadline and Award Notification: Three to four months
Reapplication by Former Recipients: Allowed immediately (once)

SELECTION PROCESS

Method: Out-of-State Peer Panel
Criteria: Quality of work is the primary criterion. Resume and project description are also considered.

OTHER INFORMATION

Publications: Program Guidelines
Activities: Exhibition of recipient's work

VILLA MONTALVO CENTER FOR THE ARTS

PO Box 158
Saratoga, Ca 95070
408-741-3421
Elisabeth Challener, Executive Director
Lori A. Wood, Artist-in-Residence Program Coordinator

AWARD

Title: Villa Montalvo Artist-in-Residence Program
Purpose: Montalvo is a 19 room 1912 villa on 176 acres of parkland. We can accommodate five artists at a time, two in the villa and three in separate cottages. Throughout the summer we have a full calendar of concerts and performances on the grounds for which artists receive free tickets, but for which they must spare some quiet time.
Categories of Support: Artists' Books, Drawing, New Genres, Painting, Public Art, Sculpture, Photography (darkroom facilites under construction)
Type of Support: Residency
Year Established: c.1940
Duration of Funding: One - three months
Customary Month or Season of Deadline: April and October
Total Number of Applicants: 34
Total Number of Recipients: 10
Funding Amount: $500-800 stipends for those who apply for aid

APPLICATION PROCEDURE

Requirements: Application form, resume, slides, project description/statement, three references, financial statement (for those applying for aid)
Restrictions: None
Time Between Application Deadline and Award Notification: Six to eight weeks
Reapplication by Former Recipients: Allowed after one year

SELECTION PROCESS

Method: Peer Panel
Criteria: Quality of work is the primary criterion. Resume and project description are also considered.

OTHER INFORMATION::

Publications: Program Guidelines, Villa Montalvo subscriber's magazine, schedule of summer events
Activities: Exhibition of recipient's work, readings and other events as decided by current group of artists.

VIRGINIA CENTER FOR THE CREATIVE ARTS (VCCA)

Mt. San Angelo
PO Box VCCA
Sweet Briar, VA 24595
804-946-7236
William Smart, Executive Director
Craig Pleasants, Assistant Director

AWARD

Title: VCCA Residency
Purpose: To allow time and studio space for exceptional artists to concentrate on their work.
Categories of Support: Artists' Books, Drawing, New Genres, Painting, Photography, Sculpture
Type of Support: Residency
Year Established: 1971
Duration of Funding: One to three months
Customary Month or Season of Deadline: January, May, and September
Total Number of Applicants: 3,000+
Total Number of Recipients: 300
Funding Amount: Subsidies and fee waivers according to financial need

APPLICATION PROCEDURE

Requirements: Application form, resume, slides
Restrictions: None
Time Between Application Deadline and Award Notification: Two - three months
Reapplication by Former Recipients: Allowed immediately

SELECTION PROCESS

Method: Peer Panel
Criteria: Quality of work is the primary criterion. Financial need and resume are also considered.

OTHER INFORMATION::

Publications: Program Guidelines
Activities: Exhibition of recipient's work

LUDWIG VOGELSTEIN FOUNDATION
PO Box 4924
Brooklyn, NY 11240-4924
Frances Pishny, Executive Director

AWARD

Title: Ludwig Vogelstein Foundation Grant
Purpose: For individuals in the arts and humanities, usually with no other source of funding.
Categories of Support: Drawing, Painting, Sculpture
Type of Support: Unrestricted
Year Established: 1975
Duration of Funding: One year
Customary Month or Season of Deadline: Late fall
Total Number of Applicants: 250
Total Number of Recipients: 25
Funding Amount: $1,500 average

APPLICATION PROCEDURE

Requirements: Guidelines under revision at time of publication. Write to Ludwig Vogelstein Foundation for new guidelines.
Restrictions: Guidelines are being revised.
Time Between Application Deadline and Award Notification: Guidelines are being revised
Reapplication By Former Recipients: Guidelines are being revised

SELECTION PROCESS

Method: Board Members
Criteria: Quality of work is the primary criterion. Financial need is also considered.

OTHER INFORMATION

Publications: Program Guidelines
Activities: n/a

VOLCANO ART CENTER (VAC)

PO Box 104
Hawaii National Park, HI 96718-0104
808-967-8222
John Campbell, Executive Director
Cherie Newton, Program Director

AWARD

Title: Artists In the Park: Residencies and Exhibitions
Purpose: To provide artists with undisturbed time in the Hawaii Volcanoes National Park to draw inspiration from the unique environment and to create original artwork.
Categories of Support: Artists' Books, Crafts, Drawing, New Genres, Painting, Photography
Type of Support: Residency
Year Established: 1985
Duration of Funding: Two weeks to two months
Customary Month or Season of Deadline: Continuing
Total Number of Applicants: Information not provided
Total Number of Recipients: 5
Funding Amount: $500-1,000

APPLICATION PROCEDURE

Requirements: Application form, resume, slides, samples of original work, project description/statement, financial statement
Restrictions: None
Time Between Application Deadline and Award Notification: Up to six months
Reapplication by Former Recipients: Not allowed

SELECTION PROCESS

Method: Staff members
Criteria: Quality of work is the primary criterion. Project description and appropriateness to guidelines are also considered.

OTHER INFORMATION

Publications: Program Guidelines, Annual Report
Activities: Exhibition of recipient's work

WALKER'S POINT CENTER FOR THE ARTS (WPCA)

911 National Avenue
Milwaukee, WI 53204
414-672-2787
Jane Brite, Executive Director/Curator
Frank Lewis, Administrator

AWARD

Title: Artists' Honoraria
Purpose: Exhibition fees to artists exhibiting at WPCA.
Categories of Support: New Genres
Type of Support: Project Grant
Year Established: 1990
Duration of Funding: One year
Customary Month or Season of Deadline: Continuing
Total Number of Applicants: 46
Total Number of Recipients: 6
Funding Amount: $500-1,000

APPLICATION PROCEDURE

Requirements: Resume, project description/statement, slides, project budget
Restrictions: Applicant must be18 years of age or older.
Time Between Application Deadline And award Notification: Varies with project
Reapplication by Former Recipients: Allowed after two years

SELECTION PROCESS

Method: Peer Panel, Staff Members
Criteria: Quality of work is the primary criterion. Project description is also considered.

OTHER INFORMATION

Publications: Program Guidelines, programs and press packets from former recipients' exhibitions
Activities: Exhibition of recipient's work

WATERSHED CENTER FOR THE CERAMIC ARTS

RR 1, Box 845
Cochran Road
Edgecomb, ME 04556
207-882-6075
Holly Walker, Executive Director

AWARD

Title: Artists Invite Artists
Purpose: To bring together a core group of artists who would like the opportunity to work around each other and possibly collaborate.
Categories of Support: Crafts, New Genres, Painting, Public Art, Sculpture
Type of Support: Residency
Year Established: 1991
Duration of Funding: Two - four weeks
Customary Month or Season of Deadline: Summer
Total Number of Applicants: 11
Total Number of Recipients: 9
Funding Amount: Varies by season

APPLICATION PROCEDURE

Requirements: Resume, slides, project description/statement
Restrictions: None
Time Between Application Deadline and Award Notification: Information not provided
Reapplication by Former Recipients: Allowed after one year

SELECTION PROCESS

Method: Peer Panel, Staff Members, Board Members
Criteria: Quality of work is the primary criterion. Other factors include: resume, geographic representation, and ethnic background.

OTHER INFORMATION

Publications: Program Guidelines, Annual Report
Activities: See additional entries for this organization. Exhibition of recipient's work, slide registry.

WETHERHOLT GALLERIES

3050 K Street, NW Suite 125
Washington, DC 20001
202-944-4278
Roger O. Wetherholt, Executive Director
Sonya Berhardt, Vice President

AWARD

Title: The Bernhardt-Wetherholt Emerging Artists' Award
Purpose: To support undiscovered/emerging visual artists and showcase their work through Wetherholt Galleries.
Categories of Support: New Genres, Painting, Photography, Sculpture
Type of Support: Unrestricted
Year Established: 1991
Duration of Funding: One year
Customary Month or Season of Deadline: December
Total Number of Applicants: Information not provided
Total Number of Recipients: Information not provided
Funding Amount: $500

APPLICATION PROCEDURE

Requirements: Resume, slides, project description/statement
Restrictions: None
Time Between Application Deadline and Award Notification: One month
Reapplication by Former Recipients: Not allowed

SELECTION PROCESS

Method: Staff Members, Board Members
Criteria: Quality of work is the primary criterion. Project description and appropriateness to guidelines are also considered.

OTHER INFORMATION::

Publications: Program Guidelines
Activities: Exhibition of recipient's work, slide registry

WOMEN'S STUDIO WORKSHOP (WSW)
PO Box 489
Rosendale, NY 12472
914-658-9133
Ann E. Kalmbach, Executive Director
Lisa Kellogg, Program Director

AWARD
Title: Artists-in-Residence
Purpose: To publish hand-printed, limited edition books.
Categories of Support: Artists' Books
Type of Support: Project Grant
Year Established: 1979
Duration of Funding: Six weeks
Customary Month or Season of Deadline: December
Total Number of Applicants: 50
Total Number of Recipients: 2
Funding Amount: $2,250

APPLICATION PROCEDURE
Requirements: Application form, resume, slides, project description/statement, financial statement
Restrictions: Applicant may not be currently enrolled in a degree-granting program.
Time Between Application Deadline and Award Notification: Information not provided
Reapplication by Former Recipients: Allowed after two years

SELECTION PROCESS
Method: Peer Panel
Criteria: Quality of work is the primary criterion. Appropriateness to guidelines is also considered.

OTHER INFORMATION::
Publications: Program Guidelines
Activities: Exhibition of recipient's work

HELENE WURLITZER FOUNDATION

PO Box 545
Taos, NM 87571
505-758-2413
Henry R. Sauerwein Jr., Executive Director

AWARD

Title: Residency
Purpose: Provide time and space for artists to pursue their own work.
Categories of Support: Artists' Books, Crafts, Drawing, New Genres, Painting, Photography, Printmaking, Public Art, Sculpture
Type of Support: Residency
Year Established: 1953
Duration of Funding: Three months
Customary Month or Season of Deadline: Continuing
Total Number of Applicants: Information not provided
Total Number of Recipients: 12
Funding Amount: Room, board, and studio for duration of residency.

APPLICATION PROCEDURE

Requirements: Application form, resume, slides
Restrictions: None
Time Between Application Deadline and Award Notification: Information not provided
Reapplication by Former Recipients: Allowed after three years

SELECTION PROCESS

Method: Board Members
Criteria: Quality of work is the primary criterion.

OTHER INFORMATION

Publications: Information not provided
Activities: Information not provided

YADDO
Box 395
Saratoga Springs, NY 12866
518-584-0746
Admissions Committee

AWARD
Title: Yaddo Residency
Purpose: To provide visual artists with time, space, and isolation for the creation of artwork.
Categories of Support: Drawing, Painting, Printmaking, Photography, Sculpture
Type of Support: Residency
Year Established: 1926
Duration of Funding: Two to eight weeks
Customary Month or Season of Deadline: January and August
Total Number of Applicants: Information not provided
Total Number of Recipients: Up to 35
Funding Amount: Residency fee waivers according to financial need; artists are invited to Yaddo irrespective of their ability to pay.

APPLICATION PROCEDURE
Requirements: Application form, slides
Restrictions: None
Time Between Application Deadline and Award Notification: Four months
Reapplication by Former Recipients: Information not provided

SELECTION PROCESS
Method: Selection Committee
Criteria: Quality of work is the primary criterion. Level of professional acheivement is also considered.

OTHER INFORMATION::
Publications: Program Guidelines
Activities: Information not provided

YELLOW SPRINGS INSTITUTE

1645 Art School Road
Malvern, PA 19425
215-827-9111
John Clauser, Director
Vesna Todorovic Miksic, Director of Programs and Development

AWARD

Title: Yellow Springs Institute Residency Fellowship Program
Purpose: Residency Fellowships are for the development of new and experimental work in dance, sound research, performance art, experimental theater, and interdisciplinary forms.
Categories of Support: New Genres
Type of Support: Residency
Year Established: 1979
Duration of Funding: Varies with project
Customary Month or Season of Deadline: November
Total Number of Applicants: 200+
Total Number of Recipients: 14
Funding Amount: $500 stipend, housing and studio for duration of residency

APPLICATION PROCEDURE

Requirements: Application form, resume, project description/statement, video/audio tapes, other documentation depending on media
Restrictions: Applicant may not be currently enrolled in a degree-granting program.
Time Between Application Deadline and Award Notification: Two months
Reapplication by Former Recipients: Allowed after one year

SELECTION PROCESS

Method: Peer Panel
Criteria: Quality of work is the primary criterion.

OTHER INFORMATION

Publications: Program Guidelines, brochure
Activities: n/a

ZONE ART CENTER

395 Dwight Street
Springfield, MA 01103
413-732-1995
Brendan Stecchini, Executive Director

AWARD

Title: Massachusetts Cultural Council Projects Awards
Purpose: ZONE Art Center applies with selected artists for state-funded new projects awards. ZONE also supports selected artists for specific exhibitions and projects through its own resources including funds received from the National Endowment for the Arts and the Massachusetts Cultural Council.
Categories of Support: Drawing, New Genres, Painting, Photography, Printmaking, Public Art, Sculpture
Type of Support: Project Grant
Year Established: 1982
Duration of Funding: Varies with project
Customary Month or Season of Deadline: Varies with project
Total Number of Applicants: 30
Total Number of Recipients: 15
Funding Amount: Up to $5,000

APPLICATION PROCEDURE

Requirements: Resume, slides, project description/statement
Restrictions: Applicant may not be currently enrolled in a degree-granting program.
Time Between Application Deadline and Award Notification: Up to six months
Reapplication by Former Recipients: Allowed immediately

SELECTION PROCESS

Method: Peer Panel, Board Members
Criteria: Quality of work is the primary criterion. Project description and geographic representation are also considered.

OTHER INFORMATION

Publications: Brochure
Activities: Exhibition of recipient's work

REGIONAL SOURCES

Since funding organizations may change their policies, procedures, and award amounts, artists should always obtain current information and application guidelines directly from the funding sources before submitting material for award consideration. Exact deadlines are not included for this reason. For current information on new sources of support, contact appropriate state arts councils, regional arts organizations, and sources of information listed in the Bibliography and Resource Organizations section.

ARTS MIDWEST

528 Hennepin Avenue, Suite 310
Minneapolis, MN 55403
612-341-0755
David Fraher, Executive Director
Jeanne Lakso, Senior Program Director

<u>AWARD</u>

Title: Arts Midwest/NEA Visual Artist Fellowships
Purpose: Direct support and wider recognition for exceptional professional visual artists.
Categories of Support: Crafts, Photography, and Sculpture in odd-numbered years, Painting and works on paper in even-numbered years
Type of Support: Unrestricted
Year Established: 1985
Duration of Funding: One year
Customary Month or Season of Deadline: March
Total Number of Applicants: 1,364
Total Number of Recipients: 25
Funding Amount: $5,000

<u>APPLICATION PROCEDURE</u>

Requirements: Application form, resume, slides
Restrictions: Applicant must be a resident of IA, IL, IN, MI, MN, ND, OH, SD, or WI, not currently enrolled in a degree-granting program.
Time Between Application Deadline and Award Notification: Three months
Reapplication by Former Recipients: Allowed after five years

<u>SELECTION PROCESS</u>

Method: Peer Panel
Criteria: Quality of work is the primary criterion. Resume is also considered.

<u>OTHER INFORMATION</u>

Publications: Program Guidelines, Annual Report, exhibition catalogues of former recipients, Directory of Visual Arts Exhibition Spaces
Activities: Exhibition of recipient's work, subsidized museum purchase of recipient's work, exhibition subsidy for recipient's work

BUSH FOUNDATION

East 900 1st National Bank Building
332 Minnesota Street
St. Paul, MN 55101
612-227-0891
Humphrey Doermann, Executive Director
Sally Fox Dixon, Program Director

AWARD

Title: Bush Artist Fellowships
Purpose: To buy time for artists to do their own work.
Categories of Support: Artists' Books, Drawing, New Genres, Painting, Photography, Printmaking, Public Art, Sculpture
Type of Support: Unrestricted
Year Established: 1976
Duration of Funding: Six - eighteen months
Customary Month or Season of Deadline: Fall
Total Number of Applicants: 560
Total Number of Recipients: 15
Funding Amount: $26,000 plus $7,000. production and travel stipend

APPLICATION PROCEDURE

Requirements: Application form, resume, slides, sample of original work
Restrictions: Applicant must be a resident of MN, SD, ND, or western WI, not currently enrolled in a degree-granting program.
Time Between Application Deadline and Award Notification: Four months
Reapplication by Former Recipients: Allowed after five years

SELECTION PROCESS

Method: Peer Panel
Criteria: Quality of work is the primary criterion. Resume and project description/statement are also considered.

OTHER INFORMATION

Publications: Program Guidelines, Annual Report,exhibition catalogues of former recipients
Activities: Information not provided

CHESTER SPRINGS STUDIOS

1668 Art School Road
PO Box 329
Chester Springs, PA 19425
215-827-7277
Lindsay Brinton, Executive Director

AWARD

Title: Artist's Residency
Purpose: To provide time and studio space for visual artists to focus on their own work. Small, temporary site-specific installations may be commissioned by the studio for some artists-in-residence.
Categories of Support: Artists' Books, Crafts, Drawing, New Genres, Painting, Photography, Printmaking, Public Art, Sculpture
Type of Support: Residency
Year Established: 1989
Duration of Funding: One Month
Customary Month or Season of Deadline: March
Total Number of Applicants: 30
Total Number of Recipients: 4
Funding Amount: $1,000-1,500

APPLICATION PROCEDURE

Requirements: Application form, resume, slides, project description/statement
Restrictions: Applicant must be a resident of PA, DE, MD, or NJ, not currently enrolled in a degree-granting program.
Time Between Application Deadline and Award Notification: Two to three weeks
Reapplication by Former Recipients: Allowed after three years

SELECTION PROCESS

Method: Juror
Criteria: Quality of work is the primary criterion. Project description and appropriateness to guidelines are also considered.

OTHER INFORMATION

Publications: Program Guidelines
Activities: Exhibition of recipient's work (planned), Slide Registry (planned)

CONTEMPORARY ARTS CENTER (CAC)

PO Box 30498
New Orleans, LA 70190
504-523-1216
Annette Carlozzi, Executive Director
Lew Thomas, Curator

AWARD

Title: Regional Artists Project
Purpose: Supports experimental projects and encourages regional artists to explore new definitions of or boundaries between cultures, ethnic traditions, and arts disciplines. This program is part of the Presenting and Commissioning Program (formerly Inter-Arts) of the National Endowment for the Arts.
Categories of Support: Artists' Books, Crafts, Drawing, New Genres, Painting, Photography, Printmaking, Public Art, Sculpture
Type of Support: Project Grant
Year Established: 1986
Duration of Funding: One year
Customary Month or Season of Deadline: Spring
Total Number of Applicants: 75
Total Number of Recipients: 8
Funding Amount: $1,500-7,000

APPLICATION PROCEDURE

Requirements: Application form, resume, slides, project description/statement, financial statement
Restrictions: Applicant must be a resident of LA, AR, AL, or MS.
Time Between Application Deadline and Award Notification: Four - five months
Reapplication by Former Recipients: Allowed immediately

SELECTION PROCESS

Method: Peer panel
Criteria: Quality of work is the primary criterion. Other factors include: project description, appropriateness to guidelines, ethnic background, geographic representation and financial need.

OTHER INFORMATION

Publications: Program Guidelines
Activities: n/a

DALLAS MUSEUM OF ART

Clare Hart DeGoyler Memorial Fund
1717 North Harwood
Dallas, TX 75201
214-922-1234
Debra Wittrup, Director, Awards to Artists

AWARD

Title: Clare Hart DeGoyler Memorial Fund
Purpose: Recognize exceptional talent and promise in young visual artists.
Categories of Support: Artists' Books, Crafts, Drawing, New Genres, Painting, Photography, Printmaking, Sculpture, Film/Video
Type of Support: Unrestricted
Year Established: 1980
Duration of Funding: One year
Customary Month or Season of Deadline: March
Total Number of Applicants: 75
Total Number of Recipients: 5
Funding Amount: Up to $1,500

APPLICATION PROCEDURE

Requirements: Resume, slides, project description/statement, project budget, two letters of recommendation
Restrictions: Applicant must be a resident of TX, OK, NM, CO, or AZ, 15-25 years of age.
Time Between Application Deadline and Award Notification: Three months
Reapplication by Former Recipients: Not allowed

SELECTION PROCESS

Method: Board Members
Criteria: Quality of work is the primary criterion.

OTHER INFORMATION

Publications: Program Guidelines
Activities: See additional entries for this organization.

DIVERSE WORKS INC./MEXIC-ARTE
1117 East Freeway
Houston, TX 77002
713-223-8346
Michael Peranteau, Co-Director
Caroline Huber, Co-Director

AWARD

Title: New Forms Regional Initiative Grants Program
Purpose: Provides funds for works that challenge traditional art disciplines and explore new forms of art and culture. Projects that are innovative, adventurous, and which explore new definitions of art forms and/or cultural traditions are considered for funding. The program is a part of the Pesenting and Commissioning Program (formerly Inter-arts) of the National Endowment for the Arts.
Categories of Support: Artists' Books, Crafts, Drawing, New Genres, Painting, Photography, Printmaking, Public Art, Sculpture
Type of Support: Project Grant
Year Established: 1986
Duration of Funding: One year
Customary Month or Season of Deadline: Late spring
Total Number of Applicants: 200
Total Number of Recipients: 12
Funding Amount: $3,000-5,000

APPLICATION PROCEDURE

Requirements: Application form, resume, slides, project description/statement, samples of original work, project budget
Restrictions: Applicant must be a resident of TX, OK, NM, or AZ, not currently enrolled in a degree-granting program.
Time Between Application Deadline and Award Notification: Three months
Reapplication by Former Recipients: Allowed after one year

SELECTION PROCESS

Method: Peer panel
Criteria: Quality of work project description are the primary criteria. Appropriateness to guidelines and resume are also considered.

OTHER INFORMATION

Publications: Program Guidelines
Activites: Information not provided

HEADLANDS CENTER FOR THE ARTS

944 Fort Barry
Sausalito, CA 94965
415-331-2787
Jennifer Dowley, Executive Director
Ann Chamberlain, Program Director

AWARD

Title: Artist-in-Residence Program
Purpose: To provide artists in all media from different cultural and geographic backgrounds an opportunity to develop new work and exchange ideas in the context of the Marin Headlands, a 13,000 acre National Park on the Pacific coast, 15 minutes from San Francisco.
Categories of Support: Artists' Books, Crafts, Drawing, New Genres, Painting, Photography, Printmaking, Public Art, Sculpture
Type of Support: Residency
Year Established: 1987
Duration of Funding: Nine months
Customary Month or Season of Deadline: Late summer
Total Number of Applicants: 250
Total Number of Recipients: 25
Funding Amount: $800/month stipend, housing and studio

APPLICATION PROCEDURE

Requirements: Resume, letter of intent, slides
Restrictions: Applicant must be a resident of MN, OH, NC, or the San Francisco Bay area.
Time Between Application Deadline and Award Notification: Four months
Reapplication by Former Recipients: Allowed after five years

SELECTION PROCESS

Method: Peer panel, Staff members
Criteria: Quality of work is the primary criterion. Appropriateness to guidelines is also considered.

OTHER INFORMATION

Publications: Program Guidelines
Activities: Lectures and performances during residency

HELENA PRESENTS

9 Placer Street
Helena, MT 59601
406-443-0287
Arnie Malina, Executive Director

AWARD

Title: New Forms Regional Grants
Purpose: Provides funds for works that challenge traditional art disciplines and explore new art and cultural forms. The program is a part of the Presenting and Commissioning Program (formerly Inter-Arts) of the National Endowment for the Arts.
Categories of Support: Artists' Books, Crafts, Drawing, New Genres, Painting, Photography, Printmaking, Public Art, Sculpture
Type of Support: Project Grant
Year Established: 1988
Duration of Funding: One year
Customary Month or Season of Deadline: February
Total Number of Applicants: 166
Total Number of Recipients: 10
Funding Amount: $1,000-5,000

APPLICATION PROCEDURE

Requirements: Application form, resume, slides, project description/statement
Restrictions: Applicant must be a resident of MT, CO, WY, UT, NV, or ID not currently enrolled in a degree-granting program.
Time Between Application Deadline and Award Notification: Three months
Reapplication by Former Recipients: Allowed after one year

SELECTION PROCESS

Method: Peer Panel
Criteria: Quality and innovative nature of work are the primary criteria.

OTHER INFORMATION

Publications: Program Guidelines
Activities: Program co-administered with Colorado Dance/New Performance Festival, Boulder, CO. See additional entries for this organization.

INTERMEDIA ARTS MINNESOTA (IAM)

425 Ontario Street, SE
Minneapolis, MN 55414
612-627-4444
Thomas Borrup, Executive Director
Al Kostars, Director of Artist Programs

AWARD

Title: Intermedia Arts/McKnight Interdisciplinary Fellowships
Purpose: To support outstanding work by regional artists who exhibit an established committment to exploring the changing relationship between artistic disciplines, diverse cultural forms, and traditional expressions.
Categories of Support: New Genres
Type of Support: Unrestricted
Year Established: 1992
Duration of Funding: One year
Customary Month or Season of Deadline: Fall
Total Number of Applicants: Information not provided
Total Number of Recipients: Information not provided
Funding Amount: $8,000-12,000

APPLICATION PROCEDURE

Requirements: Application form, resume, slides, video/audio tapes, scripts
Restrictions: Applicant must be resident of IA, KS, NE, MN, ND, SD, or WI.
Time Between Application Deadline and Award Notification: Three to five months
Reapplication by Former Recipients: Allowed after three years

SELECTION PROCESS

Method: Peer Panel
Criteria: Quality of work is the primary criterion. Resume and ethnic background are also considered.

OTHER INFORMATION

Publications: Program Guidelines, Exhibition Catalogues of recipients (planned)
Activities: See additional entries for this organization.

INTERMEDIA ARTS MINNESOTA (IAM)

425 Ontario Street, SE
Minneapolis, MN 55414
612-627-4444
Thomas Borrup, Executive Director
Al Kostars, Director of Artist Programs

AWARD

Title: *Diverse Visions* Regional Grants Program
Purpose: To encourage artists to investigate diverse issues and concerns in their work while challenging traditional, conventional, and widely accepted contemporary aproaches when creating, producing, and presenting that work. The program is a part of the Presenting and Commissioning Program (formerly Inter-Arts) of the National Endowment for the Arts.
Categories of Support: New Genres
Type of Support: Project Grant
Year Established: 1984
Duration of Funding: One year
Customary Month or Season of Deadline: April
Total Number of Applicants: 99
Total Number of Recipients: 7
Funding Amount: Up to $5,000

APPLICATION PROCEDURE

Requirements: Application form, resume, slides, artists' statement/project description, proposed budget, audio/video tapes, scripts
Restrictions: Applicant must be a resident of IA, MN, SD, ND, WI, NE, or KS, not currently enrolled in a degree-granting program.
Time Between Application Deadline and Award Notification: Three months
Reapplication by Former Recipients: Allowed after three years

SELECTION PROCESS

Method: Peer Panel Review
Criteria: Quality of work is the primary criterion. Appropriateness to guidelines is also considered.

OTHER INFORMATION

Publications: Program Guidelines
Activities: See additional entries for this organization.

LOS ANGELES CONTEMPORARY EXHIBITIONS (LACE)

Artists' Project Grants
1804 Industrial Street
Los Angeles, CA 90021
213-624-5650
Gwen Darien, Executive Director

AWARD

Title: LACE Artist's Project Grants
Purpose: To fund new forms of art: this program is made possible by the New Forms Regional Initiative, co-funded by the Presenting and Commissioning Program (formerly Inter-Arts) of the National Endowment for the Arts, the Rockefeller Foundation, and the Andy Warhol Foundation for the Visual Arts.
Categories of Support: New Genres
Type of Support: Project Grant
Year Established: 1984
Duration of Funding: One year
Customary Month or Season of Deadline: Spring
Total Number of Applicants: 171
Total Number of Recipients: 8
Funding Amount: $2,000-5,000

APPLICATION PROCEDURE

Requirements: Resume, slides, project description/statement
Restrictions: Applicant must be a resident of southern CA or HI, not currently enrolled in a degree-granting program.
Time Between Application Deadline and Award Notification: Six weeks
Reapplication by Former Recipients: Allowed immediately

SELECTION PROCESS

Method: Peer Panel
Criteria: Quality of work is the primary criterion. Project description is also considered.

OTHER INFORMATION

Publications: Information not provided
Activities: See additional entries for this organization. Exhibition of recipient's work, performance and video programs.

MID-AMERICA ARTS ALLIANCE (M-AAA)
912 Baltimore Avenue, Suite 700
Kansas City, MO 64105
816-412-1388
Henry Moran, Executive Director
Linda Bailey, Fellowship Coordinator

AWARD

Title: M-AAA/NEA Visual Artists' Fellowships
Purpose: Direct support and wider recognition for exceptional professional visual artists.
Categories of Support: Artists' Books, Crafts, Drawing, Painting, Photography, Printmaking, Sculpture. Categories offered are designed to complement those offered by the NEA in a given year.
Type of Support: Unrestricted
Year Established: 1983
Duration of Funding: One year
Customary Month or Season of Deadline: January
Total Number of Applicants: 762
Total Number of Recipients: 20
Funding Amount: $5,000

APPLICATION PROCEDURE

Requirements: Application form, resume, slides
Restrictions: Applicant must be a resident of AR, KS, MO, NE, OK, or TX, not currently enrolled in a degree-granting program.
Time Between Application Deadline and Award Notification: Three months
Reapplication by Former Recipients: Not allowed

SELECTION PROCESS

Method: Peer Panel
Criteria: Quality of work is the primary criterion. Resume is also considered.

OTHER INFORMATION

Publications: Exhibition Catalogues of former recipients
Activities: Matching subsidies to institutions exhibiting work by fellowship recipients

MID-ATLANTIC ARTS FOUNDATION (MAAF)

11 East Chase Street, Suite 2A
Baltimore, MD 21202
301-539-6659
Michael Braun, Executive Director
Heather Tunis, Director of Visual Arts

AWARD

Title: MAAF/NEA Regional Visual Arts Fellowships
Purpose: Direct support and wider recognition for exceptional professional visual artists.
Categories of Support: Artists' Books, Crafts, Drawing, New Genres, Painting, Photography, Printmaking, Sculpture. Categories are offered to complement those offered by the NEA in a given year.
Type of Support: Unrestricted
Year Established: 1988
Duration of Funding: One year
Customary Month or Season of Deadline: January
Total Number of Applicants: 1,559
Total Number of Recipients: 20
Funding Amount: $5,000

APPLICATION PROCEDURE

Requirements: Application form, resume, slides, self-addressed stamped envelope.
Restrictions: Applicant must be a resident of DE, DC, MD, NJ, NY, PA, USVI, VA, or WV, not currently enrolled in a degree-granting program.
Time Between Application Deadline and Award Notification: Six months
Reapplication by Former Recipients: Not allowed

SELECTION PROCESS

Method: Peer Panel
Criteria: Quality of work is the primary criterion. Resume is also considered.

OTHER INFORMATION

Publications: Program Guidelines
Activities: See additional entries for this organization.

MID-ATLANTIC ARTS FOUNDATION (MAAF)

11 East Chase Street, Suite 2A
Baltimore, MD 21202
301-539-6659
Michael Braun, Executive Director
Heather Tunis, Director of Visual Arts

AWARD

Title: Visual Arts Residency Program
Purpose: The main thrust of the program is to provide artists with time and opportunities to develop their work. Funded projects further the exchange, accessibility and professional development of contemporary and traditional visual artists in the Mid-Atlantic region. Application must be through a sponsoring non-profit host organization.
Categories of Support: Artists' Books, Crafts, Drawing, New Genres, Painting, Photography, Printmaking, Public Art, Sculpture
Type of Support: Residency
Year Established: 1985
Duration of Funding: Varies with project
Customary Month or Season of Deadline: July
Total Number of Applicants: 65
Total Number of Recipients: 29
Funding Amount: $1,350-4,550

APPLICATION PROCEDURE

Requirements: Application form, resume, slides, project description/statement, financial statement provided by host organization.
Restrictions: Applicant must be a resident of DE, DC, MD, NJ, NY, PA, USVI, VA, or WV. Applicant must reside outside of the host organization's state but within the Mid-Atlantic region.
Time Between Application Deadline and Award Notification: Four months
Reapplication by Former Recipients: Allowed immediately. Residents may be funded for two consecutive years through different host organizations but must then wait one year before reapplying.

SELECTION PROCESS

Method: Peer Panel Review
Criteria: Quality of work is the primary criterion. Other factors include: project description, resume, and economic need.

OTHER INFORMATION

Publications: Program Guidelines
Activities: See additional entries for this organization.

MOUNTLAKE TERRACE ARTS COMMISSION

5303 228th Street, SW
Mountlake Terrace, WA 98043
206-776-8956
Selection Committee

AWARD

Title: 1% For Art Program
Purpose: Commission public art for city buildings
Categories of Support: Public Art
Type of Support: Public Art Commission
Year Established: 1976
Duration of Funding: Varies with project
Customary Month or Season of Deadline: Varies with project
Total Number of Applicants: 27
Total Number of Recipients: 1
Funding Amount: Up to $8,000

APPLICATION PROCEDURE

Requirements: Resume, slides, project budget
Restrictions: Applicant must be a resident of the Northwestern US.
Time Between Application Deadline and Award Notification: Varies with project
Reapplication by Former Recipients: Allowed immediately

SELECTION PROCESS

Method: Board Members
Criteria: Project description is the primary criterion. Appropriateness to guidelines and quality of work are also considered.

OTHER INFORMATION

Publications: Projects are advertised as they become available.
Activities: Exhibition of recipient's work

NEW ENGLAND FOUNDATION FOR THE ARTS (NEFA)

678 Massachusetts Avenue
Cambridge, MA 02144
617-492-2914
Fax: 617-876-0702
Holly Sidford, Executive Director
Michael Moore, Deputy Director

AWARD

Title: Regional Fellowships for Visual Artists
Purpose: Provides direct support for artists to pursue their own work. The program is a cooperative venture of the New England Foundation for the Arts and the Presenting and Commissioning Program (formerly Inter-Arts) of the National Endowment for the Arts. Awards are not project-specific and are based solely on the quality of the artists' work.
Categories of Support: Artists' Books, Crafts, Drawing, Painting, Photography, Printmaking, Sculpture
Type of Support: Unrestricted
Year Established: 1989
Duration of Funding: One year
Customary Month or Season of Deadline: January
Total Number of Applicants: 459
Total Number of Recipients: 14
Funding Amount: $5,000

APPLICATION PROCEDURE

Requirements: Application form, resume, slides
Restrictions: Applicant must be a resident of the New England region not currently enrolled in a degree-granting program. US citizenship.
Time Between Application Deadline and Award Notification: Three months
Reapplication by Former Recipients: Allowed after two years

SELECTION PROCESS

Method: Peer Panel
Criteria: Quality of work is the primary criterion. Resume and appropriateness to guidelines are also considered.

OTHER INFORMATION

Publications: Program Guidelines, Annual Report
Activities: See additional entries for this organization. Exhibition of recipient's work

NEW ENGLAND FOUNDATION FOR THE ARTS (NEFA)

678 Massachusetts Avenue
Cambridge, MA 02144
617-492-2914
Holly Sidford, Executive Director
Michael Moore, Deputy Director

AWARD

Title: New Forms Regional Initiative
Purpose: Designed to support projects by lesser-known artists whose work explores new definitions of cultures, disciplines, and/or traditions. This includes experimental work that is innovative in form or content, collaborations and traditional work which explores new forms and/or contexts.
Categories of Support: Public Art
Type of Support: Project Grant
Year Established: 1989
Duration of Funding: One year
Customary Month or Season of Deadline: January
Total Number of Applicants: 232
Total Number of Recipients: 18
Funding Amount: $2,000-5,000

APPLICATION PROCEDURE

Requirements: Application form, resume, slides, project description/statement, financial statement.
Restrictions: Applicant must be a resident of the New England region, US citizenship.
Time Between Application Deadline and Award Notification: Three months
Reapplication by Former Recipients: Allowed immediately

SELECTION PROCESS

Method: Peer Panel Review
Criteria: Quality of work is the primary criterion. Project description is also considered.

OTHER INFORMATION

Publications: Program Guidelines, Annual Report
Activities: See additional entries for this organization.

NEW LANGTON ARTS CENTER (NLA)

1246 Folsom
San Francisco, CA 94103
415-626-5416
Renny Pritikin, Executive Director
Shauna O'Donnell, Program Coordinator

AWARD

Title: New Forms Regional Initiative
Purpose: To support new artists projects which extend traditional forms and culture. The program is part of the Presenting and Commissioning Program (formerly Inter-Arts) of the National Endowment for the Arts.
Categories of Support: New Genres
Type of Support: Project Grant
Year Established: 1986
Duration of Funding: One year
Customary Month or Season of Deadline: February
Total Number of Applicants: 233
Total Number of Recipients: 15
Funding Amount: $3,000-5,000

APPLICATION PROCEDURE

Requirements: Application form, resume, slides, project description/statement, video/audio tapes, scripts
Restrictions: Applicant must be a resident of AK, WA, OR, or northern CA, not currently enrolled in a degree-granting program.
Time Between Application Deadline and Award Notification: Two months
Reapplication by Former Recipients: Allowed after two years

SELECTION PROCESS

Method: Peer Panel
Criteria: Quality of work is the primary criterion. Project description and appropriateness to guidelines are also considered.

OTHER INFORMATION

Publications: Program Guidelines
Activities: Information not provided

PAINTED BRIDE ART CENTER

230 Vine Street
Philadelphia, PA 19106
215-925-9914
Gerry Givnish, Executive Director
Steve Gerba, New Forms Program Director

AWARD

Title: New Forms Regional Grants Program
Purpose: For independent artists' projects which explore new definitions of, or the boundaries between cultures, disciplines, and/or traditions. This grant is part of the Preting and Commissioning Program (formerly Inter-Arts) of the National Endowment for the Arts.
Categories of Support: New Genres
Type of Support: Project Grant
Year Established: 1984
Duration of Funding: One year
Customary Month or Season of Deadline: April
Total Number of Applicants: Information not provided
Total Number of Recipients: 21
Funding Amount: $2,000-5,000

APPLICATION PROCEDURE

Requirements: Application form, resume, slides, other documentation depending on media, project budget
Restrictions: Applicant must be a resident of PA, NJ, DE, MD, VA, WV, or DC, not currently enrolled in a degree-granting program.
Time Between Application Deadline and Award Notification: Six months
Reapplication by Former Recipients: Allowed after one year

SELECTION PROCESS

Method: Peer Panel
Criteria: Quality of work is the primary criterion.

OTHER INFORMATION

Publications: Program Guidelines
Activities: Exhibition of recipient's work

PYRAMID ATLANTIC

6001 66th Avenue, Suite 103
Riverdale, MD 20737
301-459-7154
Helen Frederick, Executive Director

AWARD

Title: Artists' Residency Program
Purpose: To allow artists from all disciplines to experiment at the Pyramid Atlantic facilities, a center for Handpapermaking, Printmaking, and the Art of the Book.
Categories of Support: Artists' Books, Printmaking, Papermaking
Type of Support: Residency
Year Established: Information not provided
Duration of Funding: One to three months
Customary Month or Season of Deadline: Continuing
Total Number of Applicants: 40
Total Number of Recipients: 12
Funding Amount: Varies with project

APPLICATION PROCEDURE

Requirements: Applicants apply through the Mid-Atlantic Arts Foundation. Contact Pyramid Atlantic for current requirements.
Restrictions: Applicant must be a resident of the Mid-Atlantic region (excluding MD).
Time Between Application Deadline and Award Notification: Three months
Reapplication by Former Recipients: Allowed after three years

SELECTION PROCESS

Method: Peer Panel Review
Criteria: Quality of work is the primary criterion. Other factors include: resume, geographic representation, ethnic background, and project description.

OTHER INFORMATION

Publications: Program Guidelines
Activities: See additional entries for this organization. Exhibition of recipient's work, slide registry.

RANDOLPH STREET GALLERY

756 N. Milwaukee
Chicago, IL 60622
312-666-773
Peter Taub, Executive Director
Nilaja Niyonu, NFRG Coordinator

AWARD

Title: New Forms Regional Grant Program
Purpose: Project funding for individual artists or small collaborative groups making artwork extending beyond historical tradition, whether that tradition be one of artistic form or cultural content. This grant is part of the Presenting and Commissioning Program (formerly Inter-Arts) of the National Endowment for the Arts.
Categories of Support: New Genres
Type of Support: Project Grant
Year Established: 1989
Duration of Funding: One year
Customary Month or Season of Deadline: Spring
Total Number of Applicants: 257
Total Number of Recipients: 14
Funding Amount: Up to $4,000

APPLICATION PROCEDURE

Requirements: Application form, resume, slides, project description/statement, project budget
Restrictions: Applicant must be a resident of IL, IN, MI, MO, or OH, not currently enrolled in a degree-granting program. US citizenship.
Time Between Application Deadline and Award Notification: Two - five months
Reapplication by Former Recipients: Allowed after two years

SELECTION PROCESS

Method: Peer Panel
Criteria: Appropriateness to guidelines is the primary criterion. Other factors include: quality of work, project description, and geographic representation.

OTHER INFORMATION

Publications: Program Guidelines
Activities: Information not provided

ROSENBERG GALLERY, GOUCHER COLLEGE

Dulaney Valley Road
Baltimore, MD 21204
301-337-6073
Helen Glazer, Exhibitions Director

AWARD

Title: Site-Specific Installation Exhibit
Purpose: To give artists the opportunity to create a site-specific installation. The artist is asked to give a public lecture in conjunction with the exhibit.
Categories of Support: New Genres
Type of Support: Project Grant
Year Established: 1989
Duration of Funding: Four to six weeks
Customary Month or Season of Deadline: Continuing
Total Number of Applicants: Information not provided
Total Number of Recipients: 1
Funding Amount: $500-1,000

APPLICATION PROCEDURE

Requirements: Resume, project description/statement, slides
Restrictions: Applicant must be a resident of the Mid-Atlantic region.
Time Between Application Deadline and Award Notification: Information not provided
Reapplication by Former Recipients: Allowed after four years

SELECTION PROCESS

Method: Staff members
Criteria: Quality of work is the primary criterion. Other factors include: resume, project description, appropriateness to guidelines, and ethnic background.

OTHER INFORMATION

Publications: Exhibition catalogues of former recipients
Activities: Exhibition of recipient's work

SOUTHERN ARTS FEDERATION (SAF)

1293 Peachtree Street, NE, Suite 500
Atlanta, GA 30309
404-874-7244
Jeffrey A. Kesper, Executive Director
Rick Fisher, Director of Visual and Media Arts

AWARD

Title: SAF/NEA Visual Artists Fellowships
Purpose: Direct support and wider recognition for exceptional professional visual artists within the region.
Categories of Support: Artists' Books, Crafts, Drawing, Painting, Photography, Printmaking, Sculpture. Categories offered are designed to complement those offered by the NEA in a given year.
Type of Support: Unrestricted
Year Established: 1984
Duration of Funding: One year
Customary Month or Season of Deadline: March
Total Number of Applicants: 500
Total Number of Recipients: 20
Funding Amount: $5,000

APPLICATION PROCEDURE

Requirements: Application form, resume, slides, self-addressed stamped envelope
Restrictions: Applicant must be a resident of AL, FL, GA, KY, LA, MS, NC, SC, or TN, not currently enrolled in a degree-granting program. May not be a prior recipient of an NEA fellowship.
Time Between Application Deadline and Award Notification: Four months
Reapplication by Former Recipients: Not allowed

SELECTION PROCESS

Method: Peer Panel
Criteria: Quality of work is the primary criterion. Resume and project description are also considered.

OTHER INFORMATION

Publications: Program Guidelines, exhibition catalogues of former recipients, Artists' Books
Activities: Exhibition of recipient's work, slide registry

WESTERN STATES ARTS FEDERATION (WESTAF)
236 Montezuma Ave.
Santa Fe, NM 87501
505-988-1166
Donald A. Meyer, Executive Director
Violetta Romero, Fellowship Program Administrator

AWARD

Title: WESTAF/NEA Regional Fellowships for Visual Artists
Purpose: Direct support and wider recognition for exceptional professional visual artists within the region.
Categories of Support: Artists' Books, Crafts, Drawing, Painting, Photography, Printmaking, Sculpture. Categories of support are designed to complement those offered by the NEA in a given year.
Type of Support: Unrestricted
Year Established: 1988
Duration of Funding: One year
Customary Month or Season of Deadline: April
Total Number of Applicants: 1,563
Total Number of Recipients: 20
Funding Amount: $5,000

APPLICATION PROCEDURE

Requirements: Application form, resume, slides
Restrictions: Applicant must be a resident of AK, AZ, CA, CO, ID, MT, NV, NM, OR, UT, or WY, not currently enrolled in a degree-granting program.
Time Between Application Deadline and Award Notification: Two months
Reapplication by Former Recipients: Allowed after four years

SELECTION PROCESS

Method: Peer Panel
Criteria: Quality of work is the primary criterion. Resume is also considered.

OTHER INFORMATION

Publications: Program Guidelines, Annual Report, exhibition catalogues of former recipients
Activities: Matching stipends to qualified non-profit exhibiting institutions for exhibition of recipient's work.

STATE AND LOCAL SOURCES

Since funding organizations may change their policies, procedures, and award amounts, artists should always obtain current information and application guidelines directly from the funding sources before submitting material for award consideration. Exact deadlines are not included for this reason. For current information on new sources of support, contact appropriate state arts councils, regional arts organizations, and sources of information listed in the Bibliography and Resource Organizations section.

ALABAMA STATE COUNCIL ON THE ARTS AND HUMANITIES (ASCAH)

One Dexter Avenue
Montgomery, AL 36104
205-242-4076
Al Head, Executive Director
Randy Shoults, Community Development Program Manager

AWARD

Title: Visual Artist Fellowship
Purpose: To support, encourage, and promote individual artists.
Categories of Support: Crafts, Drawing, Painting, Photography, Printmaking, Sculpture, New Genres
Type of Support: Unrestricted
Year Established: 1978
Duration of Funding: One year
Customary Month or Season of Deadline: May
Total Number of Applicants: 36
Total Number of Recipients: 3
Funding Amount: $7,500

APPLICATION PROCEDURE

Requirements: Application form, slides, resume (optional), project description (optional)
Restrictions: Applicant must be an Alabama state resident (3 years)
Time Between Application Deadline and Award Notification: Information not provided
Reapplication by Former Recipients: Allowed after three years

SELECTION PROCESS

Method: Peer Panel, Staff Members, Board Members
Criteria: Quality of work is the primary criterion. Appropriateness to guidelines is also considered.

OTHER INFORMATION

Publications: Program Guidelines
Activities: Exhibition of recipient's work, slide registry, publicity, Media Fellowship, Folklife Apprenticeship Grant, Project Assistance

ALASKA STATE COUNCIL ON THE ARTS (ASCA)

411 West 4th Avenue, Suite 1E
Anchorage, AK 99501-2343
907-279-1558
Christine D'Arcy, Executive Director
Jean Palmer, Grants Officer

AWARD

Title: Individual Artist Fellowship
Purpose: Assists experienced, professional artists in the creation of original works of art and in the development of their professional artistic careers.
Categories of Support: Crafts, Drawing, Painting, Photography, Printmaking, Sculpture
Type of Support: Unrestricted
Year Established: 1980
Duration of Funding: One year
Customary Month or Season of Deadline: October
Total Number of Applicants: 69
Total Number of Recipients: 6
Funding Amount: $5,000

APPLICATION PROCEDURE

Requirements: Application form, resume, slides, project description/statement
Restrictions: Applicant must be an Alaska state resident, not currently enrolled in a degree-granting program. Visual artists apply in odd-numbered years only.
Time Between Application Deadline and Award Notification: Eight weeks
Reapplication by Former Recipients: Allowed after three years

SELECTION PROCESS

Method: Peer Panel
Criteria: Quality of work is the primary criterion. Resume and project description are also considered.

OTHER INFORMATION

Publications: Program Guidelines, Annual Report, bulletin issued eight times per year
Activities: See additional entries for this organization.

ALASKA STATE COUNCIL ON THE ARTS (ASCA)

Artist Travel Grant Program
411 West 4thAvenue, Suite 1E
Anchorage, AK 99501-2343
907-279-1558
Christine D'Arcy, Executive Director
Jean Palmer, Grants Officer

AWARD

Title: Travel Grant
Purpose: Cash awards to individual artists to enable them to attend events which will enhance their artistic skills or professional standing.
Categories of Support: Artists' Books, Crafts, Drawing, Painting, Photography, Printmaking, Sculpture
Type of Support: Travel Grant
Year Established: 1980
Duration of Funding: One year
Customary Month or Season of Deadline: 30 days prior to travel
Total Number of Applicants: 35
Total Number of Recipients: 24
Funding Amount: 2/3 cost of travel - $600 maximum

APPLICATION PROCEDURE

Requirements: Application form, resume, slides, artists' statement/project description
Restrictions: Applicant must be an Alaska state resident not currently enrolled in a degree-granting program.
Time Between Application Deadline and Award Notification: Varies with project
Reapplication by Former Recipients: Allowed after one year

SELECTION PROCESS

Method: Staff Members
Criteria: Quality of work is the primary criterion. Project description and appropriateness to guidelines are also considered.

OTHER INFORMATION

Publications: Program Guidelines, Annual Report, bulltin issued eight times per year
Activities: See additional entries for this organization.

JUNEAU ARTS AND HUMANITIES COUNCIL (JAHC)

PO Box 20562
Juneau, AK 99802-0562
907-586-2787
Natalee Rothaus, Executive Director

AWARD

Title: Individual Artists' Assistance Program
Purpose: This program awards funds to experienced artists of exceptional talent to produce original works of art or advance their careers. Artists in any creative discipline may apply. This program enables artists to set aside time to create, present, research, purchase materials, attend workshops, or cover loss of artistic materials resulting from theft, fire, and other emergencies.
Categories of Support: Artists' Books, Crafts, Drawing, New Genres, Painting, Photography, Printmaking, Public Art, Sculpture
Type of Support: Unrestricted
Year Established: 1976
Duration of Funding: One year
Customary Month or Season of Deadline: October and February
Total Number of Applicants: 5
Total Number of Recipients: 3
Funding Amount: Up to $1,000

APPLICATION PROCEDURE

Requirements: Application form, resume, slides, sample of original work, project description/statement, financial statement
Restrictions: Applicant must be a city of Juneau (AK) resident.
Time Between Application Deadline and Award Notification: Two weeks
Reapplication by Former Recipients: Allowed after one year

SELECTION PROCESS

Method: Peer Panel, Staff Members, Board Members
Criteria: Quality of work is the primary criterion. Financial need and resume are aslo considered.

OTHER INFORMATION:

Publications: Program Guidelines
Activities: Information not provided

ARIZONA COMMISSION ON THE ARTS (ACA)

417 West Roosevelt Street
Phoenix, AZ 85003
602-255-5882
Shelley Cohn, Executive Director
Krista Elrick, Visual Arts Director

AWARD

Title: Visual Arts Fellowships
Purpose: Fellowships recognize the excellence of professional Arizona artists. The funds are unrestricted and are intended to allow individual artists to set aside time to work, to purchase supplies and materials and for other purposes that will contribute to their artistic growth and development. Supported media rotate on a three-year cycle.
Categories of Support: Artists' Books, Crafts, Drawing, Painting, Photography, Printmaking, Sculpture. Media rotate every three years. Write Arizona Commission on the Arts for current listing.
Type of Support: Unrestricted
Year Established: Information not provided
Duration of Funding: One year
Customary Month or Season of Deadline: September
Total Number of Applicants: 89
Total Number of Recipients: 4
Funding Amount: $5,000-7,500

APPLICATION PROCEDURE

Requirements: Application form, resume, slides, project description/statement
Restrictions: Applicant must be an Arizona state resident not currently enrolled in a degree-granting program.
Time Between Application Deadline and Award Notification: Four months
Reapplication by Former Recipients: Allowed after three years

SELECTION PROCESS

Method: Peer Panel
Criteria: Quality of work is the primary criterion.

OTHER INFORMATION

Publications: Program Guidelines
Activities: See additional entries for this organization.

ARIZONA COMMISSION ON THE ARTS (ACA)

417 West Roosevelt Street
Phoenix, AZ 85003
602-255-5882
Shelley Cohn, Executive Director
Krista Elrick, Visual Arts Director

AWARD

Title: Artists' Projects
Purpose: To support individual artists in all disciplines for project-related costs. Support for projects that allow the artist increased time to research and develop ideas or new works that stretch the artist's work or seek to advance the art form, and projects involving interdisciplinary collaborations with other artists or non-artists are encouraged.
Categories of Support: Artists' Books, Crafts, Drawing, New Genres, Painting, Photography, Printmaking, Public Art, Sculpture
Type of Support: Project Grant
Year Established: 1990
Duration of Funding: One year
Customary Month or Season of Deadline: September
Total Number of Applicants: 79
Total Number of Recipients: 5
Funding Amount: Up to $5,000

APPLICATION PROCEDURE

Requirements: Application form, resume, slides, project description/statement, financial statement
Restrictions: Applicant must be an Arizona state resident and not currently enrolled in a degree-granting program.
Time Between Application Deadline and Award Notification: Six months
Reapplication by Former Recipients: Not allowed

SELECTION PROCESS

Method: Peer Panel
Criteria: Quality of work is the primary criterion. Resume and project description are also considered.

OTHER INFORMATION

Publications: Program Guidelines
Activities: See additional entries for this organization.

CASA GRANDE ARTS & HUMANITIES COMMISSION

300 E. 4th Street
Casa Grande, AZ 85222
602-421-8600
Nelda M. Donohue, City Clerk

AWARD

Title: Project Commissions
Purpose: Commissions public art for city buildings
Categories of Support: Public Art
Type of Support: Public Art Commission
Year Established: 1986
Duration of Funding: One year
Customary Month or Season of Deadline: Varies with project
Total Number of Applicants: 15
Total Number of Recipients: 1 (artist/architect team)
Funding Amount: Up to $20,000

APPLICATION PROCEDURE

Requirements: Proposal for specific project
Restrictions: Applicant must be an Arizona state resident.
Time Between Application Deadline and Award Notification: Varies with project
Reapplication by Former Recipients: Allowed immediately

SELECTION PROCESS

Method: Board Members
Criteria: Appropriateness to guidelines is the primary criterion. Project description and quality of work are also considered.

OTHER INFORMATION

Publications: Announcement of commission opportunities
Activities: Exhibition of recipient's work

CONTEMPORARY FORUM OF THE PHOENIX ART MUSEUM

Contempoary Forum
Phoenix Art Museum
1625 N. Central Avenue
Phoenix, AZ 85004
602-257-1880
Bruce Kurtz, Executive Director

AWARD

Title: Arizona Artists' Materials Fund Grants
Purpose: To provide funds for materials for artists working in Arizona
Categories of Support: Artists' Books, Crafts, Drawing, New Genres, Painting, Photography, Printmaking, Sculpture
Type of Support: Unrestricted
Year Established: 1986
Duration of Funding: One year
Customary Month or Season of Deadline: January
Total Number of Applicants: 220
Total Number of Recipients: 4
Funding Amount: $1,000

APPLICATION PROCEDURE

Requirements: Resume, slides, project description/statement
Restrictions: Applicant must be an Arizona state resident not currently enrolled in a degree-granting program.
Time Between Application Deadline and Award Notification: Four months
Reapplication by Former Recipients: Not allowed

SELECTION PROCESS

Method: Peer Panel
Criteria: Quality of work is the primary criterion.

OTHER INFORMATION

Publications: Program Guidelines
Activities: See additional entries for this organization.

TUCSON/PIMA ARTS COUNCIL (T/PAC)

PO Box 27210
Tucson, AZ 85726
602-624-0595
Dian Magie, Executive Director
Patty White, Visual Arts Program Coordinator

AWARD

Title: Individual Artist Fellowships
Purpose: To recognize Pima county artists for their artistic acheivement. Visual artists apply every other year.
Categories of Support: Crafts, Drawing, New Genres, Painting, Photography, Printmaking, Sculpture
Type of Support: Unrestricted
Year Established: 1986
Duration of Funding: One year
Customary Month or Season of Deadline: Fall
Total Number of Applicants: 213
Total Number of Recipients: 9
Funding Amount: $2,500

APPLICATION PROCEDURE

Requirements: Application form, resume, slides, project description/statement
Restrictions: Applicant must be a Pima county (AZ) resident not currently enrolled in a degree-granting program.
Time Between Application Deadline and Award Notification: Three months
Reapplication by Former Recipients: Allowed after three years

SELECTION PROCESS

Method: Peer Panel
Criteria: Quality of work is the primary criterion.

OTHER INFORMATION

Publications: Program Guidelines, Bi-Monthly Newsletter
Activities: Exhibition of recipient's work

ARKANSAS ARTS COUNCIL (AAC)
225 East Markham, Suite 200
Little Rock, AR 72201
501-324-9337
Bill Puppione, Executive Director
Sally Williams, Program Coordinator

AWARD

Title: Individual Artists' Programs-Fellowship Grants
Purpose: Makes awards to individual artists in recognition of their artistic accomplishments. These awards enable artists to set aside time for creating their art, to improve their skills, or to enhance their artistic careers.
Categories of Support: Crafts, Drawing, New Genres, Painting, Photography, Printmaking, Sculpture. Supported media rotate on a yearly basis.
Type of Support: Unrestricted
Year Established: 1986
Duration of Funding: One year
Customary Month or Season of Deadline: February
Total Number of Applicants: 45
Total Number of Recipients: 10
Funding Amount: Up to $10,000

APPLICATION PROCEDURE

Requirements: Application form, slides.
Restrictions: Applicant must be a state resident, 18 years of age or older, not currently enrolled in a degree-granting program.
Time Between Application Deadline and Award Notification: Three months
Reapplication by Former Recipients: Allowed after three years

SELECTION PROCESS

Method: Peer Panel, Board Members
Criteria: Quality of work is the primary criterion.

OTHER INFORMATION

Publications: Program Guidelines
Activities: Occasional exhibition of recipient's work

ARTS COUNCIL OF SANTA CLARA COUNTY

4 North Second Street, Suite 505
San Jose, CA 95113
408-998-2787
Patricia Hollihan, Executive Director
Lawrence Thoo, Associate Director

AWARD

Title: Artist Fellowships
Purpose: To encourage the development of a strong community of artists that celebrates the rich variety of cultural and ethnic traditions represented among the people of Santa Clara County.
Categories of Support: Media rotate on a yearly basis. Interested applicants should contact the council well before the deadline.
Type of Support: Unrestricted
Year Established: 1989
Duration of Funding: One year
Customary Month or Season of Deadline: Spring
Total Number of Applicants: 20
Total Number of Recipients: 6
Funding Amount: $1,500+

APPLICATION PROCEDURE

Requirements: Application form, resume, slides
Restrictions: Applicant must be a Santa Clara county (CA) resident,18 years of age or older, not currently enrolled in a degree-granting program.
Time Between Application Deadline and Award Notification: Three months
Reapplication by Former Recipients: Allowed after one year

SELECTION PROCESS

Method: Peer Panel, Board Members
Criteria: Quality of work is the primary criterion. Resume is also considered.

OTHER INFORMATION

Publications: Program Guidelines, Annual Report
Activities: Artist Registry, Arts Connect. See additional entries for this organization.

ARTS COUNCIL OF SANTA CLARA COUNTY

4 North Second Street, Suite 505
San Jose, CA 95113
408-998-2787
Patricia Hollihan, Executive Director
Lawrence Thoo, Associate Director

AWARD

Title: Fund for New Works
Purpose: To support local presentation of new and innovative art in all fields. The council is especially interested in projects that provide opportunities for children.
Categories of Support: Artists' Books, Crafts, Drawing, New Genres, Painting, Photography, Printmaking, Public Art, Sculpture.
Type of Support: Project Grant
Year Established: 1991
Duration of Funding: Two years
Customary Month or Season of Deadline: January
Total Number of Applicants: Information not provided
Total Number of Recipients: Information not provided
Funding Amount: Up to $15,000

APPLICATION PROCEDURE

Requirements: Application form, slides, project description/statement, initial letter of intent with brief description of project
Restrictions: Applicant must be a Santa Clara county (CA) resident.
Time Between Application Deadline and Award Notification: Information not provided
Reapplication by Former Recipients: Information not provided

SELECTION PROCESS

Method: Peer Panel, Board Members.
Criteria: Quality of work is the primary criterion. Other factors include: project description, appropriateness to guidelines, potential degree of public interaction with project.

OTHER INFORMATION

Publications: Program Guidelines, Annual Report
Activities: Artist Registry, Arts Connect. See additional entries for this organization.

CALIFORNIA ARTS COUNCIL (CAC)
2411 Alhambra Boulevard
Sacramento, CA 95817
916-739-3186
Kathi Stockdale, Acting Executive Director
Carol Shiffman, Manager, Artists-in-Residence Program

AWARD

Title: Artists-in-Residence Award
Purpose: Long term projects completed while working with public workshops, enabling participants to better understand the art form and develop creativity through it.
Categories of Support: Artists' Books, Crafts, Drawing, New Genres, Painting, Photography, Printmaking, Sculpture
Type of Support: Residency
Year Established: 1976
Duration of Funding: Three to eleven months
Customary Month or Season of Deadline: February
Total Number of Applicants: 350
Total Number of Recipients: 190
Funding Amount: $1,200-9,000

APPLICATION PROCEDURE

Requirements: Application form, resume, slides, project description/statement, financial statement, support statement by project sponsor
Restrictions: Applicant must be a California state resident
Time Between Application Deadline and Award Notification: Varies with project
Reapplication by Former Recipients: Allowed after one year

SELECTION PROCESS

Method: Peer Panel Review
Criteria: The project description is the primary criterion. Quality of work and appropriateness to guidelines are also considered.

OTHER INFORMATION

Publications: Program Guidelines
Activities: See additional entries for this organization.

CALIFORNIA ARTS COUNCIL

2411 Alhambra Boulevard
Sacramento, CA 95817
916-739-3186
Kathi Stockdale, Acting Executive Director
Carol Shiffman, Artists' Fellowship Program Manager

AWARD

Title: Artists' Fellowship Program
Purpose: To recognize California artists in many disciplines who are the primary creators of their art. Applicants must show five years professional experience. Visual artists apply every fourth year.
Categories of Support: Artists' Books, Crafts, Drawing, New Genres, Painting, Photography, Printmaking, Sculpture
Type of Support: Unrestricted
Year Established: 1988
Duration of Funding: Information not provided
Customary Month or Season of Deadline: Fall
Total Number of Applicants: 1,200
Total Number of Recipients: 67
Funding Amount: $5,000

APPLICATION PROCEDURE

Requirements: Application form, resume, slides, artists' statement/project description
Restrictions: Applicant must be a California state resident not currently enrolled in a degree-granting program. Visual artists may apply every fourth year. Write to California Arts Council for current guidelines.
Time Between Application Deadline and Award Notification: Six months
Reapplication by Former Recipients: Allowed after eight years

SELECTION PROCESS

Method: Peer Panel Review
Criteria: Quality of work is the primary criterion. Resume and appropriateness to guidelines are also considered.

OTHER INFORMATION

Publications: Program Guidelines
Activities: See additional entries for this organization.

CALIFORNIA COMMUNITY FOUNDATION

Brody Arts Fund
606 South Olive Street, Suite 2400
Los Angeles, CA 90014-1526
213-413-4042
Jack Shakely, President
Susan Fong, Program Officer

AWARD

Title: Fellowship/Grant
Purpose: Aid to emerging multi-cultural artists whose work is rooted in the community. This program has a three year cycle in which visual artists will be funded in 1992. Arts organizations with budgets up to $100,000 are invited to apply in any cycle.
Categories of Support: Artists' Books, Crafts, Drawing, New Genres, Painting, Photography, Printmaking, Public Art, Sculpture
Type of Support: Unrestricted
Year Established: Information not provided
Duration of Funding: One year
Customary Month or Season of Deadline: Information not provided
Total Number of Applicants: 201
Total Number of Recipients: 12
Funding Amount: $2,500

APPLICATION PROCEDURE

Requirements: Application form, resume, slides
Restrictions: Applicant must be a Los Angeles county resident not currently enrolled in a degree-granting program. Visual artists may apply every three years.
Time Between Application Deadline and Award Notification: Four months
Reapplication by Former Recipients: Allowed after three years

SELECTION PROCESS

Method: Peer Panel
Criteria: Quality of work is the primary criterion. Other factors include: financial need, gender, geographic representation within L.A. county, and ethnic background.

OTHER INFORMATION

Publications: Program Guidelines
Activities: Informational meetings scheduled prior to deadline. See additional entries for this organization.

CALIFORNIA COMMUNITY FOUNDATION

J. Paul Getty Trust for the Visual Arts
606 South Olive Street, Suite 2400
Los Angeles, CA 90014-1526
213-413-4042
Jack Shakely, Executive Director
Susan Fong, Program Officer

AWARD

Title: J. Paul Getty Trust Fund for the Visual Arts
Purpose: Assistance to and recognition of mid-career artists and organizations with budgets between $100,000 - 1,500,000
Categories of Support: Artists' Books, Crafts, Drawing, New Genres, Painting, Photography, Printmaking, Sculpture
Type of Support: Unrestricted
Year Established: 1987
Duration of Funding: One year
Customary Month or Season of Deadline: August
Total Number of Applicants: 322
Total Number of Recipients: 5
Funding Amount: $15,000

APPLICATION PROCEDURE

Requirements: Application form, resume, slides, project description/statement, financial statement
Restrictions: Applicant must be a Los Angeles county resident 35 years of age or older.
Time Between Application Deadline and Award Notification: Information not provided
Reapplication by Former Recipients: Allowed immediately

SELECTION PROCESS

Method: Peer Panel
Criteria: Quality of work is the primary criterion. Other factors include: resume, project description, and geographic representation.

OTHER INFORMATION

Publications: Program Guidelines
Activities: See additional entries for this organization.

CITY OF LOS ANGELES CULTURAL AFFAIRS DEPARTMENT (LACAD)

433 South Spring Street
10th Floor
Los Angeles, CA 90013
213-620-8635
Adolfo Nodal, General Manager
Roella Hsieh Louie, Grants Director

AWARD

Title: Artist in the Community Program
Purpose: To bring professional artists into direct contact with the public and to offer art experiences within community settings to non-artists.
Categories of Support: Artists' Books, Crafts, Drawing, New Genres, Painting, Photography, Printmaking, Public Art, Sculpture
Type of Support: Project Grant
Year Established: 1989
Duration of Funding: One year
Customary Month or Season of Deadline: September
Total Number of Applicants: 241
Total Number of Recipients: 72
Funding Amount: $1,500-15,000

APPLICATION PROCEDURE

Requirements: Application form, resume, slides, project description/statement, financial statement, host venue for project
Restrictions: Applicant must be a Los Angeles county resident. Projects may be done in the city of Los Angeles only.
Time Between Application Deadline and Award Notification: Nine months
Reapplication by Former Recipients: Allowed immediately

SELECTION PROCESS

Method: Peer Panel, City Allocations Committee, Cultural Affairs Commission, City Council, Mayor's Office approval
Criteria: Quality of work is the primary criterion. Other factors include: resume, project description, geographic representation, appropriateness to guidelines, and ethnic background.

OTHER INFORMATION

Publications: Program Guidelines
Activities: Information not provided

MARIN ARTS COUNCIL

251 North San Pedro, Road
San Rafael, CA 94903
415-499-8350
Jeanne Bogardus, Executive Director
Beky Carter, Grants Coordinator

<u>AWARD</u>

Title: Individual Artist Grants
Purpose: General support with no restrictions for Marin county resident artists.
Categories of Support: Crafts, Drawing, New Genres, Painting, Photography, Printmaking, Sculpture
Type of Support: Unrestricted
Year Established: 1985
Duration of Funding: One year
Customary Month or Season of Deadline: January and May
Total Number of Applicants: 318
Total Number of Recipients: 28
Funding Amount: $1,000-10,000

<u>APPLICATION PROCEDURE</u>

Requirements: Application form, slides, sample of original work, self-addressed stamped envelope
Restrictions: Applicant must be a Marin County (CA) resident. US citizenship.
Time Between Application Deadline and Award Notification: Three months
Reapplication by Former Recipients: Allowed after three years

<u>SELECTION PROCESS</u>

Method: Peer Panel
Criteria: Quality of work is the primary criterion.

<u>OTHER INFORMATION</u>:

Publications: Program Guidelines, *Artists' Dialogue*, *Arts Resources in Marin County*
Activities: Information not provided

PASADENA ARTS DIVISION

150 South Los Robles, Suite 420
Pasadena, CA 91101
818-568-1220
Denise Nelson Nash, Executive Director

AWARD

Title: Grants-in-Aid/Public Art
Purpose: To support Pasadena resident artists and arts organizations.
Categories of Support: Artists' Books, Drawing, New Genres, Painting, Photography, Printmaking, Public Art, Sculpture
Type of Support: Unrestricted
Year Established: 1989
Duration of Funding: One year
Customary Month or Season of Deadline: Varies with project
Total Number of Applicants: 104
Total Number of Recipients: 36
Funding Amount: $181,000 total program funding for 1992

APPLICATION PROCEDURE

Requirements: Application form, resume, slides, project description
Restrictions: Applicant must be city of Pasadena resident, not currently enrolled in a degree-granting program.
Time Between Application Deadline and Award Notification: Varies with project
Reapplication by Former Recipients: Allowed after one year

SELECTION PROCESS

Method: Peer Panel, Staff Members, Board Members
Criteria: Quality of work is the primary criterion. Resume and project description are also considered.

OTHER INFORMATION

Publications: Program Guidelines
Activities: Exhibition of recipient's work, Citywide Arts Education Program

COLORADO COUNCIL ON THE ARTS AND HUMANITIES (CCAH)
750 Pennsylvania Street
Denver, CO 80203-3699
303-894-2617
Barbara Neal, Executive Director
Daniel Salazar, Director, Individual Artist Programs

AWARD
Title: Folk Arts Master/Apprenticeships
Purpose: Encourage the continuing vitality of traditional folk arts in Colorado
Categories of Support: Crafts
Type of Support: Apprenticeship
Year Established: 1985
Duration of Funding: Two months
Customary Month or Season of Deadline: September
Total Number of Applicants: 30
Total Number of Recipients: 16
Funding Amount: Up to $2,000

APPLICATION PROCEDURE
Requirements: Application form, slides, project description/statement, financial statement, lesson plan
Restrictions: Applicant must be a Colorado state resident
Time Between Application Deadline and Award Notification: Three months
Reapplication by Former Recipients: Allowed immediately

SELECTION PROCESS
Method: Peer Panel
Criteria: Quality of work is the primary criterion. Other factors include: geographic representation, project description, and ethnic background.

OTHER INFORMATION
Publications: Program Guidelines, Annual Report, exhibition catalogues of former recipients
Activities: See additional entries for this organization. Exhibition of recipient's work. Slide registry, artists' registry

COLORADO COUNCIL ON THE ARTS AND HUMANITIES (CCAH)
750 Pennsylvania Street
Denver, CO 80203-3699
303-866-2617
Barbara Neal, Executive Director
Daniel Salazar, Director, Individual Artist Programs

AWARD
Title: COVisions: Project Grants for Individual Artists
Purpose: Encourage and showcase new work within the originating community.
Categories of Support: Artists' Books, Crafts, Drawing, New Genres, Painting, Photography, Printmaking, Public Art, Sculpture
Type of Support: Project Grant
Year Established: 1990
Duration of Funding: One year
Customary Month or Season of Deadline: December
Total Number of Applicants: 118
Total Number of Recipients: 10
Funding Amount: Up to $2,500

APPLICATION PROCEDURE
Requirements: Application form, slides, project description/statement, exhibition/presentation plan, financial statement
Restrictions: Applicant must be a Colorado state resident.
Time Between Application Deadline and Award Notification: Three months
Reapplication by Former Recipients: Allowed after one year

SELECTION PROCESS
Method: Peer Panel Review
Criteria: Quality of work is the primary criterion. Other factors include: geographic representation, appropriateness to guidelines, and project description.

OTHER INFORMATION
Publications: Program Guidelines
Activities: See additional entries for this organization. Slide registry, artists' registry

COLORADO COUNCIL ON THE ARTS AND HUMANITIES (CCAH)

750 Pennsylvania Street
Denver, CO 80203-3699
303-894-2617
Barbara Neal, Executive Director
Daniel Salazar, Director, Individual Artist Programs

AWARD

Title: Creative Fellowship
Purpose: Acknowledge outstanding accomplishment among Colorado artists and provide direct financial support for artists to set aside time for professional development.
Categories of Support: Artists' Books, Crafts, Drawing, New Genres, Painting, Photography, Printmaking, Sculpture
Type of Support: Unrestricted
Year Established: 1984
Duration of Funding: One year
Customary Month or Season of Deadline: November
Total Number of Applicants: 436
Total Number of Recipients: 16
Funding Amount: $4,000

APPLICATION PROCEDURE

Requirements: Application form, slides
Restrictions: Applicant must be a Colorado state resident
Time Between Application Deadline and Award Notification: Six months
Reapplication by Former Recipients: Allowed after three years

SELECTION PROCESS

Method: Peer Panel (Out-of-State Juror)
Criteria: Quality of work is the primary criterion.

OTHER INFORMATION

Publications: Program Guidelines, Annual Report, exhibition catalogues of Former Recipients
Activities: See additional entries for this organization. Exhibition of recipient's work, slide registry, promotional catalog of recipients.

CONNECTICUT COMMISSION ON THE ARTS

227 Lawrence Street
Hartford, CT 06106
203-566-7076 or 4770
John Ostrout, Executive Director
Linda Dente, Visual Arts Coordinator

<u>AWARD</u>

Title: Artist Grants
Purpose: To encourage the development of Connecticut's finest creative artists. Visual artists apply every other year.
Categories of Support: Crafts, Drawing, New Genres, Painting, Photography, Printmaking, Sculpture
Type of Support: Project Grant
Year Established: 1965
Duration of Funding: One year
Customary Month or Season of Deadline: January
Total Number of Applicants: 350
Total Number of Recipients: 20
Funding Amount: $5,000

<u>APPLICATION PROCEDURE</u>

Requirements: Application form, resume, slides, project description/statement
Restrictions: Applicant must be a Connecticut state resident (four years), not currently enrolled in a degree-granting program. Visual artists apply every other year. Write to Connecticut Commission on the Arts for current guidelines.
Time Between Application Deadline and Award Notification: Six months
Reapplication by Former Recipients: Allowed after four years

<u>SELECTION PROCESS</u>

Method: Peer Panel, Board Members
Criteria: Quality of work is the primary criterion. Resume and project description are also considered.

<u>OTHER INFORMATION</u>

Publications: Program Guidelines
Activities: n/a

D.C. COMMISSION ON THE ARTS AND HUMANITIES (DCCAH)

410 8th Street, NW #500
Washington, DC 20004
202-724-5613
Pamela G. Holt, Executive Director
Jann Darsie, Program Coordinator

AWARD

Title: Individual Artist Fellowship
Purpose: To reward and encourage artistic excellence among DC's artists
Categories of Support: Artists' Books, Crafts, Drawing, New Genres, Painting, Photography, Printmaking, Sculpture
Type of Support: Unrestricted
Year Established: 1975
Duration of Funding: One year
Customary Month or Season of Deadline: Spring
Total Number of Applicants: 130
Total Number of Recipients: 20
Funding Amount: $5,000

APPLICATION PROCEDURE

Requirements: Application form, resume, slides, letters of recommendation
Restrictions: Applicant must be a District of Columbia resident 18 years of age or older.
Time Between Application Deadline and Award Notification: Eight months
Reapplication by Former Recipients: Allowed after two years

SELECTION PROCESS

Method: Peer Panel, Board Members
Criteria: Quality of work is the primary criterion. Resume is also considered.

OTHER INFORMATION

Publications: Program Guidelines
Activities: See additional entries for this organization. Possible exhibition of recipient's work, professional referrals.

D.C. COMMISSION ON THE ARTS AND HUMANITIES (DCCAH)

410 8th Street, NW #500
Washington, DC 20004
202-724-5613
Pamela G. Holt, Executive Director
Jann Darsie, Program Coordinator

AWARD

Title: City Arts Projects Program
Purpose: To support projects that encourage growth of arts activities, especially east of the Anacostia River.
Categories of Support: Artists' Books, Crafts, Drawing, New Genres, Painting, Photography, Printmaking, Sculpture
Type of Support: Project Grant
Year Established: 1991
Duration of Funding: 11 months
Customary Month or Season of Deadline: Spring
Total Number of Applicants: n/a
Total Number of Recipients: n/a
Funding Amount: $1,000-5,000

APPLICATION PROCEDURE

Requirements: Application form, resume, slides, project description/statement, project budget
Restrictions: Applicant must be a District of Columbia resident.
Time Between Application Deadline and Award Notification: Eight months
Reapplication by Former Recipients: Allowed immediately

SELECTION PROCESS

Method: Peer Panel Review, Board Members
Criteria: Quality of work is the primary criterion. Resume and project description are also considered.

OTHER INFORMATION

Publications: Program Guidelines
Activities: See additional entries for this organization.

DELAWARE STATE ARTS COUNCIL

Carvel State Building,
820 North French Street
Wilmington, DE 19801
302-577-3540
Cecelia Fitzgibbon, Executive Director
Barbara King, Visual Arts Coordinator

AWARD

Title: Individual Artist Fellowship
Purpose: To enable recipients to set aside time to produce art, purchase materials, and advance their careers. Funds may be used to offset costs incurred in producing his or her creative work, including the costs of materials and supplies.
Categories of Support: Artists' Books, Crafts, Drawing, New Genres, Painting, Photography, Printmaking, Sculpture
Type of Support: Unrestricted
Year Established: 1980
Duration of Funding: One year
Customary Month or Season of Deadline: Early March
Total Number of Applicants: 75
Total Number of Recipients: 12
Funding Amount: $2,000-5,000

APPLICATION PROCEDURE

Requirements: Application form, resume, slides, sample of original work
Restrictions: Applicant must be a Delaware state resident, 18 years of age or older, not currently enrolled in a degree-granting program. No travel outside US, no captital expenditures.
Time Between Application Deadline and Award Notification: Seven months
Reapplication by Former Recipients: Allowed after three years

SELECTION PROCESS

Method: Juror
Criteria: Quality of work is the primary criterion. Other factors include: financial need, resume, project description, geographic representation, and ethnic background.

OTHER INFORMATION

Publications: Program Guidelines, 15 year report, institution listing
Activities: Artist/Slide Registry,management training, exhibitions

ARTS ASSEMBLY OF JACKSONVILLE, INC./ JACKSONVILLECOMMUNITY FOUNDATION

128 East Forsyth Street, 3rd Floor
Jacksonville, FL 32202
904-358-3600
Barbara Benisch, Executive Director
Page D. Mankin, Grants and Services Manager

AWARD

Title: Career Opportunity Grants for Artists
Purpose: To assist artists in attaining the next level of development in the pursuit of a professional artistic career. Money may be used for projects, equipment, training, or for travel required in the research of new ideas.
Categories of Support: Artists' Books, Crafts, Drawing, New Genres, Painting, Photography, Printmaking, Public Art, Sculpture
Type of Support: Project Grant
Year Established: 1990
Duration of Funding: One year
Customary Month or Season of Deadline: June
Total Number of Applicants: 44
Total Number of Recipients: 11
Funding Amount: $800-5,000

APPLICATION PROCEDURE

Requirements: Application form, slides, project description/statement
Restrictions: Applicant must be a resident of Duval, Clay, Nassau, St. Johns, or Baker counties (FL), not currently enrolled in a degree-granting program.
Time Between Application Deadline and Award Notification: Four months
Reapplication by Former Recipients: Allowed immediately

SELECTION PROCESS

Method: Peer Panel
Criteria: Quality of work is the primary criterion. Project description and ethnic background are also considered.

OTHER INFORMATION

Publications: Program Guidelines
Activities: Exhibition of recipient's work

ARTS COUNCIL OF HILLSBOROUGH COUNTY

1000 North Ashley, Suite 316
Tampa, FL 33602
813-229-6547
Susan Edwards, Director, Program Services

AWARD

Title: Emerging Artist Grants
Purpose: Emerging artist grants are designed to help young or emerging artists take a decisive career step.
Categories of Support: Artists' Books, Crafts, Drawing, New Genres, Painting, Photography, Printmaking, Sculpture
Type of Support: Project Grant
Year Established: 1988
Duration of Funding: One year
Customary Month or Season of Deadline: Fall and Spring
Total Number of Applicants: 70
Total Number of Recipients: 15
Funding Amount: Up to $1,500

APPLICATION PROCEDURE

Requirements: Application form, resume, slides
Restrictions: Applicant must be a Hillsborough County (FL) resident .
Time Between Application Deadline and Award Notification: One month
Reapplication by Former Recipients: Allowed immediately (twice)

SELECTION PROCESS

Method: Peer Panel, Board Members
Criteria: Quality of work is the primary criterion. Resume is also considered.

OTHER INFORMATION

Publications: Program Guidelines
Activities: Graphic Services Bureau

FLORIDA STATE ARTS COUNCIL

The Capital, Division of Cultural Affairs
Tallahassee, FL 32399
904-487-2980
Ms. Peyton C. Fearington, Executive Director
Blair Sands, Arts Administrator

AWARD

Title: Florida Individual Artist Fellowship Program
Purpose: Designed to address the need for a direct, in-state support system for practicing, professional creative artists of exceptional talent and demonstrated ability who work and reside in Florida.
Categories of Support: Artists' Books, Crafts, Drawing, New Genres, Painting, Photography, Printmaking, Sculpture
Type of Support: Unrestricted
Year Established: 1975
Duration of Funding: One year
Customary Month or Season of Deadline: January
Total Number of Applicants: 535
Total Number of Recipients: 34
Funding Amount: $5,000

APPLICATION PROCEDURE

Requirements: Application form, resume, slides, project description/statement
Restrictions: Applicant must be a Florida state resident 18 years of age or older, not currently enrolled in a degree-granting program.
Time Between Application Deadline and Award Notification: Eight months
Reapplication by Former Recipients: Allowed after five years

SELECTION PROCESS

Method: Peer Panel
Criteria: Quality of work is the primary criterion. Appropriateness to guidelines and resume are also considered.

OTHER INFORMATION

Publications: Program Guidelines, exhibition catalogues of former recipients, Monthly Newsletter
Activities: See additional entries for this organization. Exhibition of recipient's work.

FLORIDA DANCE ASSOCIATION

Miami-Dade Community College
300 NE 2nd Avenue, Suite 1410
Miami, FL 33132-2204
305-237-3413
Rebecca Terrell, Executive Director
Tom Thielen, Director of Services

AWARD

Title: New Forms Florida: Grants for Artists' Projects
Purpose: The program is designed to support artists whose projects explore intersections or boundaries between artistic disciplines and/or cultures, explore or expand the role of the artist in society and the ways in which artists interact with their communities. The program is part of the Presenting and Commissioning Program (formerly Inter-Arts) of the National Endowment for the Arts.
Categories of Support: New Genres
Type of Support: Project Grant
Year Established: 1990
Duration of Funding: One year
Customary Month or Season of Deadline: March-April
Total Number of Applicants: 66
Total Number of Recipients: 11
Funding Amount: $1,000-5,000

APPLICATION PROCEDURE

Requirements: Application form, resume, slides, sample of original work, project description/statement, financial statement
Restrictions: Applicant must be a Florida state resident. Project collaborators may be from out of state.
Time Between Application Deadline and Award Notification: Four months
Reapplication by Former Recipients: Allowed immediately

SELECTION PROCESS

Method: Peer Panel
Criteria: Quality of work is the primary criterion. Other factors include: financial need, resume, geographic representation, appropriateness to guidelines, and ethnic background.

OTHER INFORMATION

Publications: Program Guidelines, Annual Report
Activities: Exhibition of recipient's work

PINELLAS COUNTY ARTS COUNCIL (PCAC)

400 Pierce Boulevard
Clearwater, FL 34616
813-462-3327
Judith Powers-Jones

AWARD

Title: Artists Resource Fund (ARF) Grant
Purpose: Designed to provide Pinellas County (FL) artists with a source of non-governmental financial assistance for professional development.
Categories of Support: Artists' Books, Crafts, Painting, Drawing, Photography, Printmaking, Public Art, Sculpture, New Genres
Type of Support: Project Grant
Year Established: 1990
Duration of Funding: One year
Customary Month or Season of Deadline: January
Number of Applicants: Information not provided
Total Number of Recipients: Information not provided
Funding Amount: Up to $1,000

APPLICATION PROCEDURE

Requirements: Application form, resume, slides, additional support material dependent on media
Restrictions: Applicant must be a Pinellas County (FL) resident 18 years of age or older, not currently enrolled in a degree-granting program.
Time Between Application Deadline and Award Notification: Information not provided
Reapplication by Former Recipients: Allowed after three years

SELECTION PROCESS

Method: Peer Panel
Criteria: Quality of work is the primary criterion. Resume and project description are also considered.

OTHER INFORMATION

Publications: Program Guidelines
Activities: Information not provided

SOUTH FLORIDA CULTURAL CONSORTIUM (SFCC)

c/o Metro-Dade County Cultural Affairs Council
111 NW First Street, Suite 625
Miami, FL 33301
305-375-4634
Betty Stoetzer, Executive Director

AWARD

Title: Visual and Media Arts Fellowships
Purpose: To assist eligible visual and media artists through direct grants awarded solely on the basis of creative excellence, to improve artistic skills and encourage career development.
Categories of Support: Drawing, Painting, Photography, Printmaking, New Genres, Sculpture, Film/Video
Type of Support: Unrestricted
Year Established: 1987
Duration of Funding: One year
Customary Month or Season of Deadline: October
Total Number of Applicants: 350
Total Number of Recipients: 6
Funding Amount: $15,000

APPLICATION PROCEDURE

Requirements: Application form, slides, resume
Restrictions: Applicant must be a resident of Martin, Palm Beach, Broward, Dade or Monroe Counties (FL), 18 years of age or older.
Restrictions: Two months
Reapplication by Former Recipients: Not allowed

SELECTION PROCESS

Method: Peer Panel
Criteria: Quality of work is the primary criterion.

OTHER INFORMATION

Publications: Program Guidelines, exhibition catalogues of former recipients
Activities: Exhibition of recipient's work

CITY OF ATLANTA BUREAU OF CULTURAL AFFAIRS
236 Forsyth Street SW, Suite 402
Atlanta, GA 30303
404-653-7160
Emily L. Allen, Program Administrator

AWARD
Title: Mayor's Fellowship in the Arts
Purpose: To recognize and reward the on-going achievements of practicing, professional artists of exceptional talent who live and create in the city of Atlanta.
Categories of Support: Artists' Books, Crafts, Drawing, New Genres, Painting, Photography, Printmaking, Sculpture
Type of Support: Unrestricted
Year Established: Information not provided
Duration of Funding: Nine months
Customary Month or Season of Deadline: November
Total Number of Applicants: Information not provided
Total Number of Recipients: 2
Funding Amount: $8,000

APPLICATION PROCEDURE
Requirements: Application form
Restrictions: Applicant must be a city of Atlanta resident.
Time Between Application Deadline and Award Notification: Five months
Reapplication by Former Recipients: Allowed immediately

SELECTION PROCESS
Method: Peer Panel
Criteria: Quality of work is the primary criterion. Resume and appropriateness to guidelines are also considered.

OTHER INFORMATION
Publications: Program Guidelines
Activities: See additional entries for this organization.

CITY OF ATLANTA BUREAU OF CULTURAL AFFAIRS
236 Forsyth Street SW, Suite 402
Atlanta, GA 30303
404-653-7160
Emily L. Allen, Executive Director

AWARD

Title: Artist Project Grants
Purpose: To provide funding for practicing, professional artists residing in the city of Atlanta. Matching funds must be produced by the applicant.
Categories of Support: Artists' Books, Crafts, Drawing, New Genres, Painting, Photography, Printmaking, Sculpture
Type of Support: Project Grant
Year Established: Information not provided
Duration of Funding: One year
Customary Month or Season of Deadline: October
Total Number of Applicants: Information not provided
Total Number of Recipients: Information not provided
Funding Amount: Up to $2,750

APPLICATION PROCEDURE

Requirements: Application form, resume, slides, project description/statement
Restrictions: Applicant must be a city of Atlanta resident.
Time Between Application Deadline and Award Notification: Information not provided
Reapplication by Former Recipients: Allowed after one year

SELECTION PROCESS

Method: Peer Panel Review
Criteria: Quality of work is the primary criterion. Resume and project description are also considered.

OTHER INFORMATION

Publications: Program Guidelines
Activities: See additional entries for this organization.

DEKALB COUNCIL FOR THE ARTS, INC. (DCA)

PO Box 875
Decatur, GA 30031
404-371-8826
Judy B. Turner, Acting Executive Director
Thea Beasley, Assistant to the Acting Director

AWARD

Title: Mini-Grants Program
Purpose: To promote the growth and development of the arts in DeKalb County and to help individual artists and cultural organizations improve the quality of their work.
Categories of Support: Artists' Books, Crafts, Drawing, New Genres, Painting, Photography, Printmaking, Public Art, Sculpture
Type of Support: Project Grant
Year Established: 1983
Duration of Funding: One year
Customary Month or Season of Deadline: December
Total Number of Applicants: 37
Total Number of Recipients: 32
Funding Amount: Up to $1,500 for individuals, up to $3,000 for organizations

APPLICATION PROCEDURE

Requirements: Application form, resume, slides, project description/statement
Restrictions: Applicant must be a DeKalb County (GA) resident.
Time Between Application Deadline and Award Notification: Information not provided
Reapplication by Former Recipients: Allowed immediately

SELECTION PROCESS

Method: Peer Panel
Criteria: Quality of work is the primary criterion. Project description and appropriateness to guidelines are also considered.

OTHER INFORMATION

Publications: Program Guidelines
Activities: Slide registry

FULTON COUNTY ARTS COUNCIL

42 Spring Street
Atlanta, GA 30311
404-586-4941, 730-5780
Veronica Njoku, Assistant Director

AWARD

Title: Independent Artists' Grant Program
Purpose: The program is designed to provide funds to individual visual artists producing or presenting works in Fulton county. Practicing professional artists are eligible.
Categories of Support: Artists' Books, Crafts, Drawing, New Genres, Painting, Photography, Printmaking, Sculpture
Type of Support: Project Grant
Year Established: 1981
Duration of Funding: One year
Customary Month or Season of Deadline: January
Total Number of Applicants: 50
Total Number of Recipients: 13
Funding Amount: Up to $7,500

APPLICATION PROCEDURE

Requirements: Application form, resume, slides, project budget
Restrictions: Applicant must be a Fulton county (GA) resident.
Time Between Application Deadline and Award Notification: Six months
Reapplication by Former Recipients: Allowed after one year

SELECTION PROCESS

Method: Peer Panel, Board Members
Criteria: Quality of work is the primary criterion. Resume and project description are also considered.

OTHER INFORMATION

Publications: Program Guidelines, Bi-Annual Report
Activities: Slide registry

GEORGIA COUNCIL FOR THE ARTS (GCA)

2082 E. Exchange Place, Suite 100
Tucker, GA 30084
404-651-7920
Betsey Weltner, Executive Director
Richard Waterhouse, Visual Arts Coordinator

AWARD

Title: Individual Artists Grant Program
Purpose: To provide income for artists whose work demonstrates artistic merit and whose careers potentially benefit from completion of a particular project.
Categories of Support: Artists' Books, Crafts, Drawing, New Genres, Painting, Photography, Printmaking, Public Art, Sculpture
Type of Support: Project Grant
Year Established: 1981
Duration of Funding: One year
Customary Month or Season of Deadline: April
Total Number of Applicants: 138
Total Number of Recipients: 39
Funding Amount: Up to $5,000

APPLICATION PROCEDURE

Requirements: Application form, resume, slides, project description/statement, financial statement
Restrictions: Applicant must be a Georgia state resident not currently enrolled in a degree-granting program.
Time Between Application Deadline and Award Notification: Information not provided
Reapplication by Former Recipients: Allowed after two years

SELECTION PROCESS

Method: Peer Panel
Criteria: Quality of work is the primary criterion. Other factors include: financial need, resume, geographic representation, appropriateness to guidelines, project description, and ethnic background.

OTHER INFORMATION

Publications: Program Guidelines
Activities: Slide registry

IDAHO COMMISSION ON THE ARTS
304 West State Street
Boise, ID 83720
208-334-2119
Margot H. Knight, Executive Director
Jaqueline Crist, Artists' Services Program Director

AWARD

Title: Fellowships
Purpose: Fellowships are awarded to individual artists of exceptional talent in recognition of outstanding work. Visual artists may apply for funding in even-numbered years only.
Categories of Support: Artists' Books, Crafts, Drawing, New Genres, Painting, Photography, Printmaking, Sculpture
Type of Support: Unrestricted
Year Established: 1985
Duration of Funding: One year
Customary Month or Season of Deadline: April
Total Number of Applicants: 35
Total Number of Recipients: 3
Funding Amount: $5,000

APPLICATION PROCEDURE

Requirements: Write to Idaho Commission on the Arts for specific application procedures.
Restrictions: Applicant must be an Idaho state resident 18 years of age or older, not currently enrolled in a degree-granting program. Visual artists apply for funding in even-numbered years only.
Time Between Application Deadline and Award Notification: Four months
Reapplication by Former Recipients: Allowed after five years

SELECTION PROCESS

Method: Peer Panel
Criteria: Quality of work is the primary criterion.

OTHER INFORMATION

Publications: Program Guidelines
Activities: See additional entries for this organization. Folk and Traditional Arts Programs, Arts in Education Program, Artists- in-Residence Program

IDAHO COMMISSION ON THE ARTS

304 West State Street
Boise, ID 83720
208-334-2119
Margot H. Knight, Executive Director
Jaqueline Crist, Artists' Services Program Director

AWARD

Title: WORKSITES Awards
Purpose: WORKSITES are awarded to artists for the purpose of working or training with a master, for attendance at a colony, release time from employment for the creation of new work, or travel required to investigate new ideas. Visual artists may apply for funding in even-numbered years only
Categories of Support: Artists' Books, Crafts, Drawing, New Genres, Painting, Photography, Printmaking, Public Art, Sculpture
Type of Support: Project Grant
Year Established: 1985
Duration of Funding: One year
Customary Month or Season of Deadline: April
Total Number of Applicants: Information not provided
Total Number of Recipients: Information not provided
Funding Amount: Up to $5,000

APPLICATION PROCEDURE

Requirements: Write to Idaho Commission on the Arts for specific application procedures.
Restrictions: Applicant must be an Idaho state resident 18 years of age or older, not currently enrolled in a degree-granting program. Visual artists may apply for funding in even-numbered years only
Time Between Application Deadline and Award Notification: Four months
Reapplication by Former Recipients: Allowed after five years

SELECTION PROCESS

Method: Peer Panel Review
Criteria: Quality of work is the primary criterion. Resume is also considered.

OTHER INFORMATION

Publications: Program Guidelines
Activities: See additional entries for this organization. Folk and Traditional Arts Programs, Arts in Education Program, Artists- in-Residence Program

ILLINOIS ARTS COUNCIL (IAC)
100 West Randolph, Suite 10-500
Chicago, IL 60601
312-814-6750
toll free 800-237-6994
Rhoda Pierce, Acting Executive Director
Rose Parisi, Artists' Services Coordinator

AWARD

Title: Artist Fellowship Program
Purpose: Non-matching fellowships are awarded to Illinois artists to enable them to pursue their artistic goals.
Categories of Support: Artists' Books, Crafts, Drawing, New Genres, Painting, Photography, Printmaking, Sculpture
Type of Support: Unrestricted
Year Established: 1977
Duration of Funding: Nine months
Customary Month or Season of Deadline: September
Total Number of Applicants: 795
Total Number of Recipients: 54
Funding Amount: $500-15,000

APPLICATION PROCEDURE

Requirements: Application form, resume, slides, statement, audio/video tapes, scripts
Restrictions: Applicant must be an Illinois state resident not currently enrolled in a degree-granting program.
Time Between Application Deadline and Award Notification: Three months
Reapplication by Former Recipients: Varies with amount of funding

SELECTION PROCESS

Method: Peer Panel, Board Members
Criteria: Quality of work is the primary criterion. Resume is also considered.

OTHER INFORMATION

Publications: Program Guidelines, Annual Report
Activities: See additional entries for this organization.

ILLINOIS ARTS COUNCIL (IAC)

100 West Randolph, Suite 10-500
Chicago, IL 60601
312-814-6750
toll free 800-237-6994
Rhoda Pierce, Acting Executive Director
Rose Parisi, Artist Services Coordinator

AWARD

Title: Special Assistance Grant
Purpose: Project-specific matching grant program. Artists may apply for assistance with exhibition/documentation expenses, technical assistance, conference/seminar/workshop attendance.
Categories of Support: Artists' Books, Crafts, Drawing, New Genres, Painting, Photography, Printmaking, Public Art, Sculpture
Type of Support: Project Grant
Year Established: 1977
Duration of Funding: Varies with project
Customary Month or Season of Deadline: Continuing
Total Number of Applicants: 37
Total Number of Recipients: 24
Funding Amount: Up to $1,500

APPLICATION PROCEDURE

Requirements: Application form, resume, slides, sample of original work, project description/statement, financial statement
Restrictions: Applicant must be an Illinois state resident not currently enrolled in a degree-granting program.
Time Between Application Deadline and Award Notification: Two months
Reapplication by Former Recipients: Allowed after one year

SELECTION PROCESS

Method: Staff Members
Criteria: Quality of work is the primary criterion. Resume and project description are also considered.

OTHER INFORMATION

Publications: Program Guidelines, Annual Report
Activities: See additional entries for this organization.

ARTS COUNCIL OF INDIANAPOLIS
47 South Pennsylvania, Suite 703
Indianapolis, IN 46204
317-631-3301
Norman Brandenstein, Director of Services

AWARD
Title: Fellowships
Purpose: To recognize and support the accomplishments of Indianapolis-based artists. Visual Arts fellowships are offered on a three-year alternating cycle. Write for current information.
Categories of Support: Artists' Books, Crafts, Drawing, New Genres, Painting, Photography, Printmaking, Sculpture
Type of Support: Unrestricted
Year Established: 1986
Duration of Funding: One year
Customary Month or Season of Deadline: Continuing
Total Number of Applicants: Information not provided
Total Number of Recipients: Information not provided
Funding Amount: $1,000-5,000

APPLICATION PROCEDURE
Requirements: Applcation form, resume, slides, project description/statement
Restrictions: Applicant must be an Indianapolis metro area resident.
Time Between Application Deadline and Award Notification: Varies
Reapplication by Former Recipients: Allowed immediately.

SELECTION PROCESS
Method: Peer Panel
Criteria: Quality of work is the primary criterion.

OTHER INFORMATION
Publications: Program Guidelines, *Start With Art* exhibition catalogues
Activities: Technical Assistance Grant Program, Professional Development Program, *Start With Art* juried exhibition, Artists' Registry

INDIANA ARTS COMMISSION
402 W. Washington, Room 072
Indianapolis, IN 46201-2741
317-232-1268
Thomas B. Schorgl, Executive Director
Robert Burnett, Visual Arts Specialist

AWARD

Title: Individual Artist Fellowship
Purpose: Direct support grants designed to foster the development of Indiana artists. For activities significant to the artists' professional growth and recognition.
Categories of Support: Artists' Books, Crafts, Drawing, New Genres, Painting, Photography, Printmaking, Sculpture
Type of Support: Unrestricted
Year Established: 1984
Duration of Funding: One year
Customary Month or Season of Deadline: April
Total Number of Applicants: 239
Total Number of Recipients: 29
Funding Amount: $2,000 and $5,000

APPLICATION PROCEDURE

Requirements: Application form, resume, slides, project description/statement
Restrictions: Applicant must be an Indiana state resident. US citizenship.
Time Between Application Deadline and Award Notification: Two months
Reapplication by Former Recipients: Allowed immediately

SELECTION PROCESS

Method: Peer Panel
Criteria: Quality of work is the primary criterion. Project description and resume are also considered.

OTHER INFORMATION

Publications: Program Guidelines, Annual Report, Artists' Directory, Artist Fellowship Catalogue
Activities: Arts Projects and Series Program, Technical Assistance Program, project support

IOWA ARTS COUNCIL (IAC)
Department of Cultural Affairs
Capitol Complex
1223 East Court
Des Moines, IA 50319
515-281-4006
Natalie A. Hala, Executive Director
Bruce Williams, Director of Creative Artists and Visual Arts

AWARD

Title: Artist Mini-Grants
Purpose: Artist Mini-Grants provide direct assistance to Iowa artists to support opportunities in four areas: projects, professional development, training, and arts education.
Categories of Support: Artists' Books, Crafts, Drawing, New Genres, Painting, Photography, Printmaking, Public Art, Sculpture
Type of Support: Project Grant
Year Established: 1990
Duration of Funding: One year
Customary Month or Season of Deadline: Varies with project
Total Number of Applicants: four to six per month
Total Number of Recipients: Information not provided
Funding Amount: $500 maximum

APPLICATION PROCEDURE

Requirements: Application form, resume, slides, artists' statement/project description, letters of support from other participants
Restrictions: Applicant must be an Iowa state resident 18 years of age or older, not currently enrolled in a degree-granting program.
Time Between Application Deadline and Award Notification: Two months
Reapplication by Former Recipients: Allowed immediately

SELECTION PROCESS

Method: Staff Members
Criteria: Quality of work is the primary criterion. Project description and appropriatenesss to guidelines are also considered.

OTHER INFORMATION

Publications: Program Guidelines, summary of funded applicants
Activities: See additional entries for this organization. Slide registry.

IOWA ARTS COUNCIL (IAC)

Department of Cultural Affairs
Capitol Complex
1223 East Court
Des Moines, IA 50319
515-281-4006
Natalie A. Hala, Executive Director
Bruce Williams, Director of Creative Artists and Visual Arts

AWARD

Title: Artist Project Grants Program
Purpose: Artist Project Grants provide direct support to Iowa artists to support projects that are designed and managed by artists to meet their specific needs.
Categories of Support: Artists' Books, Crafts, Drawing, New Genres, Painting, Photography, Printmaking, Public Art, Sculpture
Type of Support: Project Grant
Year Established: 1991
Duration of Funding: One year
Customary Month or Season of Deadline: January
Total Number of Applicants: Information not provided
Total Number of Recipients: Information not provided
Funding Amount: $2,000 average

APPLICATION PROCEDURE

Requirements: Application form, resume, slides, artists' statement/project description, letters of support from other participants
Restrictions: Applicant must be an Iowa state resident 18 years of age or older, not currently enrolled in a degree-granting program.
Time Between Application Deadline and Award Notification: Three months
Reapplication by Former Recipients: Allowed immediately

SELECTION PROCESS

Method: Peer Panel Review, Board Members
Criteria: Quality of work is the primary criterion. Project description and appropriateness to guidelines are also considered.

OTHER INFORMATION

Publications: Program Guidelines
Activities: See additional entries for this organization.

KANSAS ARTS COMMISSION

Jayhawk Tower
700 Jackson, Suite 1004
Topeka, KS 66603-3714
913-296-3335
Conchita Reyes, Arts Program Coordinator

<u>AWARD</u>

Title: Kansas Artists Fellowships
Purpose: Recognizes excellence and promotes the further development of Kansas artists. Applicants may apply to both the Fellowship Program and the Professional Development Grant Program simultaneously.
Categories of Support: Artists' Books, Crafts, Drawing, New Genres, Painting, Photography, Printmaking, Public Art, Sculpture
Type of Support: Unrestricted
Year Established: 1989
Duration of Funding: One year
Customary Month or Season of Deadline: October
Total Number of Applicants: Information not provided
Total Number of Recipients: Information not provided
Funding Amount: $5,000

<u>APPLICATION PROCEDURE</u>

Requirements: Application form, resume, slides, project description/statement
Restrictions: Applicant must be a Kansas state resident.
Time Between Application Deadline and Award Notification: Six months
Reapplication by Former Recipients: Not allowed

<u>SELECTION PROCESS</u>

Method: Peer Panel
Criteria: Quality of work is the primary criterion.

<u>OTHER INFORMATION</u>:

Publications: Program Guidelines, Annual Report
Activities: See additional entries for this organization.

KANSAS ARTS COMMISSION

Jayhawk Tower
700 Jackson, Suite 1004
Topeka, KS 66603-3714
913-296-3335
Conchita Reyes, Executive Director

AWARD

Title: Professional Development Grant
Purpose: The program provides financial assistance for costs related to exhibition preparation, technical assistance and training, or other activities which will further the applicant's artistic career.
Categories of Support: Artists' Books, Crafts, Drawing, New Genres, Painting, Photography, Printmaking, Public Art, Sculpture
Type of Support: Project Grant
Year Established: 1989
Duration of Funding: Varies with project
Customary Month or Season of Deadline: October
Total Number of Applicants: Information not provided
Total Number of Recipients: Information not provided
Funding Amount: $100-500

APPLICATION PROCEDURE

Requirements: Application form, resume, slides, project description/statement, project budget
Restrictions: Applicant must be a Kansas state resident.
Time Between Application Deadline and Award Notification: Varies with project
Reapplication by Former Recipients: Not allowed

SELECTION PROCESS

Method: Staff Members
Criteria: Quality of work is the primary criterion. Project description is also considered.

OTHER INFORMATION

Publications: Program Guidelines, Annual Report
Activities: See additional entries for this organization.

KENTUCKY ARTS COUNCIL (KAC)

31 Fountain Place
Frankfort, KY 40601
502-564-3757
C. Martin Newell, Executive Director
Irwin Peickett, Director of Visual Arts and Fellowships

AWARD

Title: Kentucky Artists Fellowship and Artists Grants
Purpose: To aid and promote Kentucky's individual artists.
Categories of Support: Artists' Books, Crafts, Drawing, New Genres, Painting, Photography, Printmaking, Public Art, Sculpture
Type of Support: Unrestricted
Year Established: 1972
Duration of Funding: One year
Customary Month or Season of Deadline: March
Total Number of Applicants: 265
Total Number of Recipients: 20
Funding Amount: $7,500

APPLICATION PROCEDURE

Requirements: Application form, resume(optional), slides, project description
Restrictions: Applicant must be a Kentucky state resident not currently enrolled in a degree-granting program.
Time Between Application Deadline and Award Notification: Three to four months
Reapplication by Former Recipients: Allowed after four years

SELECTION PROCESS

Method: Peer Panel, Board Members
Criteria: Quality of work is the primary criterion. Other factors include: financial need, resume, and geographic representation, and ethnic background.

OTHER INFORMATION:

Publications: Program Guidelines, exhibition catalogues of former recipients
Activities: Exhibition of recipient's work, slide registry

KENTUCKY FOUNDATION FOR WOMEN

Heyburn Building, Suite 1215
Louisville, KY 40202
502-562-0045
Ann Stewart Anderson, Executive Director
Pat Buster, Assistant to the Director

AWARD

Title: Kentucky Foundation for Women Grants Program
Purpose: To support Kentucky women who use the arts for social change—specifically for the equality of all women regardless of class, age, sexual preference, or color.
Categories of Support: Artists' Books, Crafts, Drawing, New Genres, Painting, Photography, Printmaking, Public Art, Sculpture
Type of Support: Unrestricted
Year Established: 1985
Duration of Funding: One year
Customary Month or Season of Deadline: October
Total Number of Applicants: 250
Total Number of Recipients: 50
Funding Amount: $100-10,000

APPLICATION PROCEDURE

Requirements: Application form, resume, slides, financial statement, letters of recommendation
Restrictions: Applicant must be a Kentucky state resident . Visual arts applications considered for odd-numbered years only.
Time Between Application Deadline and Award Notification: Four months
Reapplication by Former Recipients: Allowed immediately

SELECTION PROCESS

Method: Peer Panel, Board Members
Criteria: Quality of work is the primary criterion.

OTHER INFORMATION:

Publications: Program Guidelines
Activities: Information not provided

LOUISIANA DIVISION OF THE ARTS

PO Box 44247
Baton Rouge, LA 70804
504-342-8180
Emma Burnette, Executive Director
Ann Russo, Program Coordinator

AWARD

Title: Individual Artist Fellowships
Purpose: Non-matching awards to provide support to Louisiana fine artists
Categories of Support: Artists' Books, Crafts, Drawing, New Genres, Painting, Photography, Printmaking, Sculpture
Type of Support: Unrestricted
Year Established: 1979
Duration of Funding: One year
Customary Month or Season of Deadline: March
Total Number of Applicants: 90
Total Number of Recipients: 3
Funding Amount: $5,000

APPLICATION PROCEDURE

Requirements: Application form, resume, slides, project description/statement
Restrictions: Applicant must be a Louisiana state resident not currently enrolled in a degree-granting program.
Time Between Application Deadline and Award Notification: Three months
Reapplication by Former Recipients: Not allowed

SELECTION PROCESS

Method: Peer Panel
Criteria: Quality of work is the primary criterion. Resume and project description are also considered.

OTHER INFORMATION:

Publications: Program Guidelines, exhibition catalogues of former recipients (through the Masur Museum, Monroe, LA)
Activities: Project Assistance Grants, Artists' Roster, Art-in-Education Program

CARINA HOUSE: MONHEGAN RESIDENCY

Farnsworth Art Museum
PO Box 466
Rockland, ME 04841
207-596-6457
Christopher Crossman, Executive Director
Suzette McAroy, Curator

AWARD

Title: Carina House Residency for Maine Artists
Purpose: Provides two 6-week residencies for Maine artists on Monhegan Island. Accomodations, studio, and stipend provided.
Categories of Support: Drawing, Painting, Photography, Printmaking, Sculpture
Type of Support: Residency
Year Established: 1989
Duration of Funding: Six weeks
Customary Month or Season of Deadline: March
Total Number of Applicants: 34
Total Number of Recipients: 2
Funding Amount: $600 stipend, housing and studio

APPLICATION PROCEDURE

Requirements: Resume, slides, project description/statement
Restrictions: Applicant must be a Maine state resident 21 years of age or older, not currently enrolled in a degree-granting program.
Time Between Application Deadline and Award Notification: One month
Reapplication by Former Recipients: Not allowed

SELECTION PROCESS

Method: Peer Panel
Criteria: Quality of work is the primary criterion. Other factors include: financial need, resume, and appropriateness to guidelines.

OTHER INFORMATION

Publications: Program Guidelines
Activities: Information not provided

MAINE ARTS COMMISSION

55 Capital Street, Station 25
Augusta, ME 04333
207-289-2724
Alden C. Wilson, Executive Director
Kathy Ann Jones, Museum/Visual Arts Associate

AWARD

Title: Individual Artist Fellowships
Purpose: To provide financial support for artists to advance their careers, acknowledge artistic excellence, and promote public awareness of Maine artists.
Categories of Support: Artists' Books, Crafts, Drawing, New Genres, Painting, Photography, Printmaking, Public Art, Sculpture
Type of Support: Unrestricted
Year Established: 1988
Duration of Funding: One year
Customary Month or Season of Deadline: September
Total Number of Applicants: 108
Total Number of Recipients: 6
Funding Amount: $3,000

APPLICATION PROCEDURE

Requirements: Application form, resume
Restrictions: Applicant must be a state resident 18 years of age or older, not currently enrolled in a degree-granting program.
Time Between Application Deadline and Award Notification: Five months
Reapplication by Former Recipients: Allowed after six years

SELECTION PROCESS

Method: Peer Panel, Board approval
Criteria: Quality of work is the primary criterion.

OTHER INFORMATION:

Publications: Program Guidelines, Annual Report, exhibition catalogues of former recipients
Activities: Exhibition of recipient's work.

ARTS COUNCIL OF MONTGOMERY COUNTY

10701 Rockville Pike
Rockville, MD 20852
301-530-6744
Sarah Stout, Acting Director
Maura Doern, Project Coordinator

AWARD

Title: Individual Artist Fellowships
Purpose: These grants are for artists in Montgomery County and the results are intended to benefit the citizens of the county.
Categories of Support: Artists' Books, Crafts, Drawing, New Genres, Painting, Photography, Printmaking, Public Art, Sculpture
Type of Support: Unrestricted
Year Established: 1976
Duration of Funding: One year
Customary Month or Season of Deadline: April
Total Number of Applicants: 36
Total Number of Recipients: 12
Funding Amount: $500

APPLICATION PROCEDURE

Requirements: Application form, resume, slides
Restrictions: Applicant must be a Montgomery County (MD) resident.
Time Between Application Deadline and Award Notification: Two months
Reapplication by Former Recipients: Allowed immediately

SELECTION PROCESS

Method: Peer Panel
Criteria: Quality of work is the primary criterion. Appropriateness to guidelines is also considered.

OTHER INFORMATION

Publications: Program Guidelines
Activities: Slide registry

HOWARD COUNTY ARTS COUNCIL (HCAC)
8510 High Ridge Road
Ellicott City, MD 21043
301-313-2787
Mary E. Toth, Executive Director
Carla Dunlap, Director of Programming and Facilities

AWARD

Title: Arts Grants
Purpose: To foster excellence, diversity, and vitality of arts offerings for Howard County residents, broaden opportunities for Howard County artists and arts organizations, and increase the availability of arts activities in Howard County.
Categories of Support: Artists' Books, Crafts, Drawing, New Genres, Painting, Photography, Printmaking, Public Art, Sculpture
Type of Support: Project Grant
Year Established: 1987
Duration of Funding: One year
Customary Month or Season of Deadline: June
Total Number of Applicants: 36
Total Number of Recipients: 30
Funding Amount: Up to $10,000

APPLICATION PROCEDURE

Requirements: Application through a sponsoring non-profit art organization only.
Restrictions: Applicant must both reside and be employed in Howard County.
Time Between Application Deadline and Award Notification: One month
Reapplication by Former Recipients: Allowed immediately

SELECTION PROCESS

Method: Peer Panel, Staff Members, Board Members
Criteria: Quality of work is the primary criterion. Other factors include: resume, project description, and appropriateness to guidelines.

OTHER INFORMATION

Publications: Program Guidelines
Activities: Information not provided

MASSACHUSETTS CULTURAL COUNCIL
80 Boylston Street, Suite 1000
Boston, MA 02116
617-727-3668
TDD 617-338-9153
Rose Austin, Executive Director
Karen Rose, Sercice Coordinator, Visual Arts

AWARD

Title: Individual Project Support
Purpose: Support to artists' projects with a strong public element. Supported media rotate on a yearly basis.
Categories of Support: Artists'Books, Crafts, Drawing, New Genres, Painting, Photography, Printmaking, Public Art, Sculpture. Media rotate on a yearly basis.
Type of Support: Project Grant
Year Established: 1992
Duration of Funding: One year
Customary Month or Season of Deadline: Spring
Total Number of Applicants: 92
Total Number of Recipients: 29
Funding Amount: $2,000-5,000

APPLICATION PROCEDURE

Requirements: Application form, resume, slides, project description/statement, financial statement
Restrictions: Applicant must be a Massachusetts state resident, 18 years of age or older, not currently enrolled in a degree-granting program.
Time Between Application Deadline and Award Notification: Four months
Reapplication by Former Recipients: Allowed after one year

SELECTION PROCESS

Method: Peer Panel
Criteria: Quality of work is the primary criterion. Other factors include: appropriateness to guidelines, community accesibility, and project description are also considered.

OTHER INFORMATION

Publications: Program Guidelines
Activities: State Arts Lottery-decentralized local project-based funding program

ARTS FOUNDATION OF MICHIGAN

Creative Artists' Grants
1553 Woodward Avenue,Suite 1553
Detroit, MI 48228
313-964-2244
Kimberly Adams, Executive Director

AWARD

Title: Creative Artists' Grants
Purpose: For individuals to create new and significant projects with a strong public interaction element. This program is funded by the Michigan Council for Arts and Cultural Affairs. Artists apply through a sponsoring non-profit arts organization.
Categories of Support: Artists' Books, Crafts, Drawing, New Genres, Painting, Photography, Printmaking, Public Art, Sculpture
Type of Support: Project Grant
Year Established: 1992
Duration of Funding: One year
Customary Month or Season of Deadline: May
Total Number of Applicants: n/a (new program)
Total Number of Recipients: n/a (new program)
Funding Amount: up to $10,000

APPLICATION PROCEDURE

Requirements: Application form, resume, slides, project description/statement
Restrictions: Applicant must be a Michigan state resident. Applications are through a sponsoring non-profit arts organization only.
Time Between Application Deadline and Award Notification: Three months
Reapplication by Former Recipients: Allowed immediately

SELECTION PROCESS

Method: Board Members
Criteria: Quality of work is the primary criterion. Other factors include: resume, appropriateness to guidelines, and community accesibility are also considered.

OTHER INFORMATION

Publications: Program Guidelines
Activities: See other entries for this organization

ARTS FOUNDATION OF MICHIGAN

General Grants Program
1553 Woodward Avenue,Suite 1553
Detroit, MI 48228
313-964-2244
Kimberly Adams, Executive Director

AWARD

Title: General Grants Program
Purpose: For individuals to create new and significant projects with a strong public interaction element.
Categories of Support: Artists' Books, Crafts, Drawing, New Genres, Painting, Photography, Printmaking, Public Art, Sculpture
Type of Support: Project Grant
Year Established: 1976
Duration of Funding: One year
Customary Month or Season of Deadline: May
Total Number of Applicants: 200
Total Number of Recipients: 36
Funding Amount: $500-3,500

APPLICATION PROCEDURE

Requirements: Application form, resume, slides, project description/statement
Restrictions: Applicant must be a Michigan state resident. Applications are through a sponsoring non-profit arts organization only.
Time Between Application Deadline and Award Notification: Three months
Reapplication by Former Recipients: Allowed immediately

SELECTION PROCESS

Method: Board Members
Criteria: Quality of work is the primary criterion. Other factors include: resume, appropriateness to guidelines, and community accesibility are also considered.

OTHER INFORMATION

Publications: Program Guidelines
Activities: See other entries for this organization. Subsidized awards program for juried competitions.

FORECAST PUBLIC ARTWORKS

2955 Bloomington Avenue South
Minneapolis, MN 55407
612-721-4394
John M. Walley, Executive Director
Julie Marckel, Projects Manager

AWARD

Title: Public Art Affairs
Purpose: To offer research/development and project grants for emerging public artists for the creation of temporary works of public art in Minnesota communities.
Categories of Support: Painting, Public Art, Sculpture, New Genres
Type of Support: Project Grant
Year Established: 1989
Duration of Funding: One year
Customary Month or Season of Deadline: May
Total Number of Applicants: 25
Total Number of Recipients: 9
Funding Amount: $800-4,000

APPLICATION PROCEDURE

Requirements: Application form, resume, slides, project description/statement, samples of original work
Restrictions: Applicant must be a Minnesota state resident.
Time Between Application Deadline and Award Notification: Three weeks
Reapplication by Former Recipients: Information not provided

SELECTION PROCESS

Method: Peer panel
Criteria: Quality of work is the primary criterion. Other factors include: resume, project description, and appropriateness to guidelines.

OTHER INFORMATION

Publications: Program Guidelines, exhibition catalogues of former recipients
Activities: Information not provided

INTERMEDIA ARTS MINNESOTA (IAM)

425 Ontario Street, SE
Minneapolis,MN 55414
612-627-4444
Thomas Borrup, Executive Director
Mason Riddle, Visual Arts and Performance Curator

AWARD

Title: Jerome Foundation Installation Art Commissions
Purpose: To give emerging artists an opportunity to explore diverse artistic expression using new forms, mediums, and technologies for the purpose of creating an installation specifically for the Intermedia Arts gallery.
Categories of Support: New Genres, Sculpture
Type of Support: Project Grant
Year Established: 1986
Duration of Funding: Seven to eight months
Customary Month or Season of Deadline: March
Total Number of Applicants: 28
Total Number of Recipients: 3
Funding Amount: $2,000

APPLICATION PROCEDURE

Requirements: Application form, resume, slides (optional), sample of original work (optional), project description/statement, project budget
Restrictions: Applicant must be a Minnesota state resident, not currently enrolled in a degree-granting program. Grants limited to emerging artists only.
Time Between Application Deadline and Award Notification: Two months
Reapplication by Former Recipients: Information not provided

SELECTION PROCESS

Method: Peer Panel Review
Criteria: Quality of work is the primary criterion. Other factors include: resume, project description, appropriateness to guidelines, and ethnic background.

OTHER INFORMATION

Publications: Program Guidelines
Activities: See additional entries for this organization. Exhibition of recipient's work.

LAKE REGION ARTS COUNCIL, INC. (LRAC)

112 W. Washington Avenue
PO Box 661
Fergus Falls, MN 56538-0661
218-739-5780
Sonja Peterson, Program Coordinator

AWARD

Title: LRAC/McKnight Foundation Individual Artist Grant Program
Purpose: Developed by LRAC with McKnight Foundation funding to provide financial support to artists committed to advancing their careers. The program provides artists with critical grants for specific projects that contribute to their growth and development.
Categories of Support: Artists' Books, Crafts, Drawing, New Genres, Painting, Photography, Printmaking, Public Art, Sculpture
Type of Support: Project Grant
Year Established: 1989
Duration of Funding: One year
Customary Month or Season of Deadline: Fall
Total Number of Applicants: 13
Total Number of Recipients: 6
Funding Amount: $500

APPLICATION PROCEDURE

Requirements: Application form, resume, slides, sample of original work, project description/statement, financial statement
Restrictions: Applicant must be an area resident.
Time Between Application Deadline and Award Notification: Information not provided
Reapplication by Former Recipients: Allowed after three years

SELECTION PROCESS

Method: Staff Members, Board Members
Criteria: Quality of work is the primary criterion. Resume and project description are alsoconsidered.

OTHER INFORMATION:

Publications: Program Guidelines, Annual Report
Activities: Information not provided

MINNEAPOLIS COLLEGE OF ART AND DESIGN (MCAD)

Jerome Fellowship Program
2501 Stevens Avenue, South
Minneapolis, MN 55404
612-874-3785
John Slorp, President
Julie Yanson, Project Director, Jerome Foundation Fellowship Program

AWARD

Title: Jerome Foundation Visual Artist Fellowship
Purpose: Individual artist fellowships to emerging artists from the Minneapolis-St. Paul area.
Categories of Support: Artists' Books, Crafts, Drawing, New Genres, Painting, Photography, Printmaking, Sculpture
Type of Support: Unrestricted
Year Established: 1980
Duration of Funding: One year
Customary Month or Season of Deadline: May
Total Number of Applicants: 155
Total Number of Recipients: 5
Funding Amount: $6,000

APPLICATION PROCEDURE

Requirements: Resume, slides, project description/statement
Restrictions: Applicant must be a Minnesota state resident .
Time Between Application Deadline and Award Notification: Three months
Reapplication by Former Recipients: Allowed after three years

SELECTION PROCESS

Method: Peer Panel
Criteria: Quality of work is the primary criterion. Other factors include: financial need, resume, project description, geographic representation, and ethnic background.

OTHER INFORMATION

Publications: Program Guidelines, exhibition catalogues of former recipients, School Catalogue.
Activities: See additional entries for this organization.

MINNEAPOLIS COLLEGE OF ART AND DESIGN (MCAD)

McKnight Fellowship Program
2501 Stevens Avenue, South
Minneapolis, MN 55404
612-874-3785
John Slorp, President
Julie Yanson, Project Director, McKnight Foundation Fellowship Program

AWARD

Title: McKnight Foundation Visual Artist Fellowship
Purpose: Individual fellowships to established mid-career Minnesota artists.
Categories of Support: Crafts, Drawing, New Genres, Painting, Printmaking, Sculpture
Type of Support: Unrestricted
Year Established: 1981
Duration of Funding: One year
Customary Month or Season of Deadline: March
Total Number of Applicants: 250
Total Number of Recipients: 8
Funding Amount: $8,000

APPLICATION PROCEDURE

Requirements: Resume, slides
Restrictions: Applicant must be a Minnesota state resident.
Time Between Application Deadline and Award Notification: Three months
Reapplication by Former Recipients: Allowed after five years

SELECTION PROCESS

Method: Peer Panel
Criteria: Quality of work is the primary criterion. Other factors include: financial need, resume, geographic representation, and ethnic background.

OTHER INFORMATION:

Publications: Program Guidelines, Annual Report, exhibition catalogues of former recipients
Activities: See additional entries for this organization.

MINNESOTA STATE ARTS BOARD

432 Summit Avenue
St. Paul, MN 55102
612-297-2603
Sam W. Grabarski, Executive Director
Karen Mueller, Program Associate

AWARD

Title: Artist Assistance Fellowships
Purpose: To recognize, reward, and encourage outstanding artists throughout Minnesota.
Categories of Support: Artists' Books, Crafts, Drawing, New Genres, Painting, Photography, Printmaking, Public Art, Sculpture
Type of Support: Unrestricted
Year Established: 1983
Duration of Funding: One year
Customary Month or Season of Deadline: September
Total Number of Applicants: 248
Total Number of Recipients: 15
Funding Amount: $6,000

APPLICATION PROCEDURE

Requirements: Application form, resume, slides, project description/statement, description of submitted sample work
Restrictions: Applicant must be a Minnesota state resident 18 years of age or older.
Time Between Application Deadline and Award Notification: Four to five months
Reapplication by Former Recipients: Allowed after two years

SELECTION PROCESS

Method: Peer Panel, Staff Members, Board Members
Criteria: Quality of work is the primary criterion. Project description is also considered.

OTHER INFORMATION:

Publications: Program Guidelines, Annual Report
Activities: See additional entries for this organization.

MINNESOTA STATE ARTS BOARD

432 Summit Avenue
St. Paul, MN 55102
612-297-2603
Sam W. Grabarski, Executive Director
Karen Mueller, Program Associate

AWARD

Title: Career Opportunity Grants
Purpose: To help Minnesota artists at various stages of their careers to take advantage of impending, concrete opportunities that will significantly enhance their work or careers.
Categories of Support: Artists' Books, Crafts, Drawing, New Genres, Painting, Photography, Printmaking, Public Art, Sculpture
Type of Support: Project Grant
Year Established: 1985
Duration of Funding: Up to six months
Customary Month or Season of Deadline: Four deadlines per year
Total Number of Applicants: 64
Total Number of Recipients: 8
Funding Amount: $100-1,000

APPLICATION PROCEDURE

Requirements: Application form, resume, slides, artists' statement/project description, written confirmation of opportunity, description of submitted sample work
Restrictions: Applicant must be a Minnesota state resident 18 years of age or older.
Time Between Application Deadline and Award Notification: Six weeks
Reapplication by Former Recipients: Allowed immediately

SELECTION PROCESS

Method: Staff Members, Board Members
Criteria: Quality of work is the primary criterion. Project description is also considered.

OTHER INFORMATION

Publications: Program Guidelines, Annual Report
Activities: See additional entries for this organization.

MINNESOTA STATE ARTS BOARD

432 Summit Avenue
St. Paul, MN 55102
612-297-2603
Sam W. Grabarski, Executive Director
Karen Mueller, Program Associate

AWARD

Title: Headlands Residency Project
Purpose: To support Minnesota artists who wish to live and work at Headlands Center for the Arts, an interdisciplinary arts facility in the Marin Headlands near San Francisco.
Categories of Support: Artists' Books, Crafts, Drawing, New Genres, Painting, Photography, Printmaking, Public Art, Sculpture
Type of Support: Residency
Year Established: 1991
Duration of Funding: Three - five months
Customary Month or Season of Deadline: November
Total Number of Applicants: 16
Total Number of Recipients: 3
Funding Amount: Travel allowance, living stipend, housing and studio space for duration of residency

APPLICATION PROCEDURE

Requirements: Application form, resume, slides, artists' statement/project description, written description of submitted work
Restrictions: Applicant must be a Minnesota state resident 18 years of age or older.
Time Between Application Deadline and Award Notification: Six months
Reapplication by Former Recipients: Not allowed

SELECTION PROCESS

Method: Peer Panel Review, Staff Members, Board Members, final selection by Headlands Center for the Arts staff
Criteria: Quality of work is the primary criterion. Appropriateness to guidelines is also considered.

OTHER INFORMATION

Publications: Program Guidelines, Annual Report
Activities: See additional entries for this organization.

MISSISSIPPI ARTS COMMISSION

239 North Lamar Street, 2nd floor
Jackson, MI 39201
601-359-6030
Jane Crater Hiatt, Executive Director
Cindy Jetter, Program Administrator

AWARD

Title: Artist Fellowship
Purpose: To encourage and support the creation of new artwork
Categories of Support: Crafts, Drawing, Painting, Photography, Printmaking, Sculpture
Type of Support: Unrestricted
Year Established: 1986
Duration of Funding: One year
Customary Month or Season of Deadline: March
Total Number of Applicants: 25
Total Number of Recipients: 3
Funding Amount: $5,000

APPLICATION PROCEDURE

Requirements: Application form, resume, slides
Restrictions: Applicant must be a Mississippi state resident not currently enrolled in a degree-granting program.
Time Between Application Deadline and Award Notification: Three months
Reapplication by Former Recipients: Allowed after six years

SELECTION PROCESS

Method: Peer Panel, Staff Members, Board Members
Criteria: Quality of work is the primary criterion. Resume and ethnic background are also considered.

OTHER INFORMATION:

Publications: Program Guidelines, Annual Report
Activities: Information not provided

HELENA PRESENTS
9 Placer Street
Helena, MT 59601
406-443-0287
Arnie Malina, Executive Director

AWARD
Title: Individual Artist Grants
Purpose: Project grants to Lewis and Clark County resident artists in all media.
Categories of Support: Artists' Books, Crafts, Drawing, New Genres, Painting, Photography, Printmaking, Public Art, Sculpture
Type of Support: Project Grant
Year Established: 1980
Duration of Funding: One year
Customary Month or Season of Deadline: May
Total Number of Applicants: 25
Total Number of Recipients: 2
Funding Amount: $400-2,000

APPLICATION PROCEDURE
Requirements: Application form, resume, slides, project description/statement
Restrictions: Applicant must be a Lewis and Clark county (MT) resident.
Time Between Application Deadline and Award Notification: One month
Reapplication by Former Recipients: Allowed after one year

SELECTION PROCESS
Method: Peer Panel Review
Criteria: Quality of work is the primary criterion.

OTHER INFORMATION
Publications: Program Guidelines
Activities: See additional entries for this organization.

MONTANA ARTS COUNCIL
48 North Last Chance Gulch
Helena, MT 59620
406-444-6430
David E. Nelson, Executive Director
Julia A. C. Smith, Director of Artists Services

AWARD
Title: Individual Artist Fellowship
Purpose: Recognize, reward, and encourage outstanding visual artists in Montana.
Categories of Support: Artists' Books, Crafts, Drawing, New Genres, Painting, Photography, Printmaking, Sculpture
Type of Support: Unrestricted
Year Established: 1984
Duration of Funding: One year
Customary Month or Season of Deadline: May
Total Number of Applicants: 84
Total Number of Recipients: 5
Funding Amount: $2,000

APPLICATION PROCEDURE
Requirements: Application form, resume, slides, self-addressed stamped envelope
Restrictions: Applicant must be a Montana state resident not currently enrolled in a degree-granting program.
Time Between Application Deadline and Award Notification: Two months
Reapplication by Former Recipients: Not allowed

SELECTION PROCESS
Method: Peer Panel
Criteria: Quality of work is the primary criterion. Other factors include: financial need, resume, geographic representation, and ethnic background.

OTHER INFORMATION:
Publications: Program Guidelines
Activities: n/a

NEBRASKA ARTS COUNCIL (NAC)

1313 Farnam-on-the-Mall
Omaha, NE 68102-1873
402-595-2122
Jennifer Clark, Executive Director
Suzanne T. Wise, Visual Arts Coordinator

AWARD

Title: Individual Artist Fellowships
Purpose: Provides monetary awards to Nebraska artists in various disciplines.
Categories of Support: Artists' Books, Crafts, Drawing, New Genres, Painting, Photography, Printmaking, Sculpture
Type of Support: Unrestricted
Year Established: 1990
Duration of Funding: One year
Customary Month or Season of Deadline: November
Total Number of Applicants: 73
Total Number of Recipients: 5
Funding Amount: $2,000-4,000

APPLICATION PROCEDURE

Requirements: Application form, slides, project description/statement
Restrictions: Applicant must be a Nebraska state resident (two years); not currently enrolled in a degree-granting program.
Time Between Application Deadline and Award Notification: Three months
Reapplication by Former Recipients: Information not provided

SELECTION PROCESS

Method: Peer Panel, Board Members
Criteria: Quality of work is the primary criterion.

OTHER INFORMATION:

Publications: Program Guidelines
Activities: *Exhibits Nebraska* Touring Program, Technical Assistance Program

NEVADA STATE COUNCIL ON THE ARTS

329 Flint Street
Reno, NV 89501
702-688-1225
Kirk Robertson, Director, Individual and Community Programs

AWARD

Title: Fellowships
Purpose: To support and encourage outstanding Nevada artists and to increase public awareness and recognition of state artists.
Categories of Support: Artists' Books, Crafts, Drawing, Painting, Photography, Printmaking, Sculpture, New Genres
Type of Support: Unrestricted
Year Established: 1988
Duration Of Funding: One year
Customary Month or Season of Deadline: May
Total Number of Applicants: 75
Total Number of Recipients: 4
Funding Amount: $2,000-10,000

APPLICATION PROCEDURE

Requirements: Application form, resume, slides, samples of original work, project description/statement
Restrictions: Applicant must be a Nevada state resident. Students must provide proof of their status as a practicing professional artist.
Time Between Application Deadline and Award Notification: Two months
Reapplication by Former Recipients: Allowed after three years

SELECTION PROCESS

Method: Peer panel
Criteria: Quality of work is the primary criterion.

OTHER INFORMATION

Publications: Program Guidelines
Activities: Artists in Residence Program, Arts-in-Education Program

SIERRA ARTS FOUNDATION

200 Flint Street
Reno, NV 89501
702-329-1324
Virginia Keeney, Executive Director
Stephanie Sparks, Program Director

AWARD

Title: Grants in Aid
Purpose: Supports innovative individual artists and arts organizations. Initial personal contact from applicant is strongly advised.
Categories of Support: Artists' Books, Crafts, Drawing, New Genres, Painting, Photography, Printmaking, Public Art, Sculpture
Type of Support: Project Grant
Year Established: 1986
Duration of Funding: One year
Customary Month or Season of Deadline: Three deadlines per year. Contact Sierra Arts foundation for current deadlines.
Total Number of Applicants: 75
Total Number of Recipients: 30
Funding Amount: $2,000

APPLICATION PROCEDURE

Requirements: Resume, slides, project description/statement, letter of recommendation
Restrictions: Applicant must be a resident of northern Nevada not currently enrolled in a degree-granting program.
Restrictions: Two months
Reapplication by Former Recipients: Allowed after one year

SELECTION PROCESS

Method: Peer Panel
Criteria: Quality of work is the primary criterion.

OTHER INFORMATION

Publications: Newsletters, brochure
Activities: See additional entries for this organization. Art in Education Program

NEW HAMPSHIRE COUNCIL ON THE ARTS

40 North Main Street
Concord, NH 03301
603-271-2789
Susan B. Bonaiuto, Executive Director
Audrey V. Sylvester, Visual Arts Coordinator

AWARD

Title: Individual Artists' Fellowships
Purpose: Unrestricted fellowships to enhance the career development of New Hampshire visual artists.
Categories of Support: Artists' Books, Crafts, Drawing, New Genres, Painting, Photography, Printmaking, Sculpture
Type of Support: Unrestricted
Year Established: 1981
Duration of Funding: One year
Customary Month or Season of Deadline: Spring
Total Number of Applicants: 122
Total Number of Recipients: 3
Funding Amount: $3,000

APPLICATION PROCEDURE

Requirements: Application form, resume, slides
Restrictions: Applicant must be a New Hampshire state resident 18 years of age or older.
Time Between Application Deadline and Award Notification: Six months
Reapplication by Former Recipients: Allowed after one year

SELECTION PROCESS

Method: Peer Panel
Criteria: Quality of work is the primary criterion. Resume is also considered.

OTHER INFORMATION:

Publications: Press support
Activities: Public presentation by grant recipient, Touring Program, Project Assistance Grants, Technical Assistance

NEW JERSEY STATE COUNCIL ON THE ARTS
CN 306
Trenton, NJ 08625
609-292-6130
VOICE/TDD: 609-633-1186
Barbara F. Russo, Executive Director
Antonio Torres/Steve Runk, Program Coordinators-Grants

AWARD
Title: Fellowships
Purpose: Grants are awarded to professional New Jersey artists to enable them to pursue their artistic goals. Fellowships are granted to artists in recognition of their outstanding work and to allow the artist to work more freely and to obtain the time and space necessary for creative expression.
Categories of Support: Artists' Books, Crafts, Drawing, New Genres, Painting, Photography, Printmaking, Sculpture
Type of Support: Unrestricted
Year Established: 1970
Duration of Funding: One year
Customary Month or Season of Deadline: March
Total Number of Applicants: 1,052
Total Number of Recipients: 74
Funding Amount: $5,000-12,000

APPLICATION PROCEDURE
Requirements: Application form, resume, slides, slide list
Restrictions: Applicant must be a New Jersey state resident, not currently enrolled in a degree-granting program.
Time Between Application Deadline and Award Notification: Five - six months
Reapplication by Former Recipients: Allowed after one year

SELECTION PROCESS
Method: Peer Panel, Standing Committee
Criteria: Quality of work is the primary criterion. Resume is also considered.

OTHER INFORMATION
Publications: Program Guidelines
Activites: Slide registry

NEW MEXICO COUNCIL ON PHOTOGRAPHY

PO Box 1283
Santa Fe, NM 87504
505-988-3240
Gil Hitchcock, Executive Director
Austin Lamont, Coordinator

AWARD

Title: The Willard Van Dyke Annual Fellowship
Purpose: To support New Mexico Photographers.
Categories of Support: Photography
Type of Support: Unrestricted
Year Established: 1987
Duration of Funding: One year
Customary Month or Season of Deadline: April
Total Number of Applicants: 125
Total Number of Recipients: 1
Funding Amount: $2,000

APPLICATION PROCEDURE

Requirements: Application form, slides, project description/statement
Restrictions: Applicant must be a New Mexico state resident not currently enrolled in a degree-granting program.
Time Between Application Deadline and Award Notification: Three months
Reapplication by Former Recipients: Allowed immediately

SELECTION PROCESS

Method: Peer Panel, Board Members
Criteria: Quality of work is the primary criterion.

OTHER INFORMATION:

Publications: Program Guidelines
Activities: See additional entries for this organization. Exhibition of recipient's work.

ARTS COUNCIL FOR CHAUTAUQUA COUNTY

116 East 3rd Street
Jamestown, NY 14701
716-664-2465
Philip Morris, Executive Director
Patrice Turner, Associate Director

AWARD

Title: Fund for the Arts Project Pool Awards
Purpose: To support Cautauqua County artists. Both unrestricted and project awards.
Categories of Support: Artists' Books, Crafts, Drawing, New Genres, Painting, Photography, Printmaking, Sculpture
Type of Support: Unrestricted
Year Established: 1985
Duration of Funding: One year
Customary Month or Season of Deadline: Information not provided
Total Number of Applicants: 33
Total Number of Recipients: 12
Funding Amount: Up to $3,000

APPLICATION PROCEDURE

Requirements: Application form, resume, slides, sample of original work, project description/statement, project budget
Restrictions: Applicant must be a Chautauqua County (NY) resident.
Time Between Application Deadline and Award Notification: Three months
Reapplication by Former Recipients: Allowed immediately (may recieve a fellowship two out of three years)

SELECTION PROCESS

Method: Peer Panel
Criteria: Quality of work is the primary criterion. Other factors include: financial need, resume, project description, gender, and ethnic background.

OTHER INFORMATION

Publications: Program Guidelines, *Artifacts*
Activities: Arts in education, artist's insurance, technical assistance, Artists-in-residence

BRONX COUNCIL ON THE ARTS (BCA)
1738 Hone Avenue
Bronx, NY 10461
212-931-9500
Bill Aquado, Executive Director
Fred Wilson, Curator

AWARD

Title: BRIO (Bronx Recognizes Its Own)
Purpose: Direct grants to outstanding Bronx artists in all disciplines.
Categories of Support: Artists' Books, Crafts, Drawing, New Genres, Painting, Photography, Printmaking, Public Art, Sculpture
Type of Support: Unrestricted
Year Established: 1988
Duration of Funding: One year
Customary Month or Season of Deadline: Fall
Total Number of Applicants: 122
Total Number of Recipients: 18
Funding Amount: $1,500

APPLICATION PROCEDURE

Requirements: Application form, resume, slides
Restrictions: Applicant must be a resident of the Bronx 18 years of age or older. May not be currently enrolled in a degree-granting program.
Time Between Application Deadline and Award Notification: Five months
Reapplication by Former Recipients: Allowed after one year

SELECTION PROCESS

Method: Peer Panel
Criteria: Quality of work is the primary criterion.

OTHER INFORMATION

Publications: Program Guidelines
Activities: See additional entries for this organization

CENTER FOR PHOTOGRAPHY AT WOODSTOCK

59 Tinker Street
Woodstock, NY 12498
914-679-9957
Kathleen Kenyon, Executive Director
Colleen Kenyon, Associate Director

AWARD

Title: Photographers' Fund
Purpose: Provides money for the creation of visual objects.
Categories of Support: Photography
Type of Support: Unrestricted
Year Established: 1980
Duration of Funding: One year
Customary Month or Season of Deadline: May
Total Number of Applicants: Information not provided
Total Number of Recipients: 3
Funding Amount: $1,000

APPLICATION PROCEDURE

Requirements: Samples of original work, resume (optional), statement (optional)
Restrictions: Applicant must be a resident of Albany, Clinton, Columbia, Delaware, Dutchess, Essex, Fulton, Greene, Hamilton, Montgomery, Orange, Ostego, Rensselaer, Saratoga, Schenectady, Schoharie, Sullivan, Ulster, Warren, or Washington counties (NY). May not be currently enrolled in a degree-granting program.
Time Between Application Deadline and Award Notification: Information not provided
Reapplication by Former Recipients: Not allowed

SELECTION PROCESS

Method: Peer panel
Criteria: Quality of work is the primary criterion.

OTHER INFORMATION

Publications: Program Guidelines
Activities: Information not provided

DUTCHESS COUNTY ARTS COUNCIL

39 Market Street
Poughkeepsie, NY 12601
914-454-3222
Sherre Wesley, Executive Director

AWARD

Title: Dutchess Arts Fund (DAF) Individual Artists Fellowship
Purpose: Established to provide support to individuals living in Dutchess County (NY) who are in the developmental phase of their career as a creative artist.
Categories of Support: Artists' Books, Crafts, Drawing, New Genres, Painting, Photography, Printmaking, Sculpture
Type of Support: Unrestricted
Year Established: Information not provided
Duration of Funding: One year
Customary Month or Season of Deadline: June
Total Number of Applicants: Information not provided
Total Number of Recipients: 3
Funding Amount: $3,000

APPLICATION PROCEDURE

Requirements: Application form, resume, slides, project description/statement, attendance at grant application workshop
Restrictions: Applicant must be a Dutchess county (NY) resident 18 years of age or older, not currently enrolled in a degree-granting program.
Time Between Application Deadline and Award Notification: One month
Reapplication by Former Recipients: Not allowed

SELECTION PROCESS

Method: Peer Panel
Criteria: Quality of work is the primary criterion. Resume and project description are also considered.

OTHER INFORMATION

Publications: Program Guidelines
Activities: See additional entries for this organization. Grant application workshops.

LOWER MANHATTAN CULTURAL COUNCIL (LMCC)

1 World Trade Center, Suite 1717
New York, NY 10048
212-432-0900
Jane Dixon, Executive Director
Greta Gundersen, Artistic Director

AWARD

Title: Manhattan Community Arts Fund
Purpose: To support community-based arts organizations that do not yet have access to other government funding. Our goal is to provide small grants for arts projects that provide service to the Manhattan community. Individuals apply through a sponsoring non-profit organization.
Categories of Support: Artists' Books, Crafts, Drawing, Painting, New Genres, Photography, Printmaking, Public Art, Sculpture
Type of Support: Project Grant
Year Established: 1985
Duration of Funding: One year
Customary Month or Season of Deadline: January
Total Number of Applicants: 135
Total Number of Recipients: 76
Funding Amount: $300-1,500

APPLICATION PROCEDURE

Requirements: Application through a sponsoring non-profit art organization only.
Restrictions: Applicant must be a resident of Manhattan Borough, New York City.
Time Between Application Deadline and Award Notification: Four months
Reapplication by Former Recipients: Allowed immediately. Reapplication discouraged after three consecutive awards.

SELECTION PROCESS

Method: Peer Panel, Staff members
Criteria: Quality of work is the primary criterion. Other factors include: ethnic background, financial need, project description, geographic representation, and appropriateness to guidelines.

OTHER INFORMATION

Publications: Program Guidelines, Annual Report
Activities: Information not provided

NEW YORK FOUNDATION FOR THE ARTS (NYFA)

8 Beekman Street, Suite 600
New York, NY 10038
212-233-3900
Theodore S. Berger, Executive Director
Penelope Dannenberg, Director, Artists' Fellowship Program

AWARD

Title: Artists' Fellowships
Purpose: To direct funds given to individual artists to be used at their discretion.
Categories of Support: Artists' Books, Crafts, Drawing, New Genres, Painting, Photography, Printmaking, Sculpture. Supported media alternate on a yearly basis.
Type of Support: Unrestricted
Year Established: 1984
Duration of Funding: One year
Customary Month or Season of Deadline: January
Total Number of Applicants: 8,000
Total Number of Recipients: 230
Funding Amount: $7,000

APPLICATION PROCEDURE

Requirements: Application form, resume, slides, other documention depending on discipline, self-addressed stamped envelope
Restrictions: Applicant must be a New York state resident 18 years of age or older, not currently enrolled in a degree-granting program.
Time Between Application Deadline and Award Notification: Seven months
Reapplication by Former Recipients: Allowed after three years

SELECTION PROCESS

Method: Peer Panel
Criteria: Quality of work is the primary criterion. Resume is also considered.

OTHER INFORMATION

Publications: Program Guidelines
Activities: Artists-in-Residence, Artists in New Works

NEW YORK STATE COUNCIL ON THE ARTS (NYSCA)
915 Broadway
New York, NY 10010
212-387-7000
Elizabeth Merena, Visual Arts Coordinator

AWARD
Title: Project Residencies
Purpose: Provides support to artists for the creation, presentation, and development of new work. All applications to this program must be through one of the sponsoring organizations listed below (each organization sponsors one medium).
Categories of Support: Artists' Books, Crafts, Drawing, Painting, Photography, Printmaking, Sculpture
Type of Support: Project Grant
Year Established: 1965
Duration of Funding: One year
Customary Month or Season of Deadline: March
Total Number of Applicants: Information not provided
Total Number of Recipients: Information not provided
Funding Amount: Up to $10,000

APPLICATION PROCEDURE
Requirements: Application form, resume, slides, project budget
Restrictions: Applicant must be a New York state resident.
Time Between Application Deadline and Award Notification: Four to six months
Reapplication by Former Recipients: Allowed immediately

SELECTION PROCESS
Method: Peer Panel, Board Members
Criteria: Quality of work is the primary criterion. Resume and appropriateness to guidelines are also considered.

OTHER INFORMATION
Publications: Program Guidelines, Annual Report
Activities: Folk Arts Program, training and professional support, Architecture and Design Program, Arts in Education Program, Electronic Media and Film Program, institutional support

Sponsoring organizations:
Millwood Art Museum/516-299-2788 (Painting, Drawing, Printmaking)
Sculpture Space/315-724-8381 (Sculpture)
Lightwork/315-443-1300 (Photography)
Empire State Crafts Alliance/518-584-1819 (Crafts)

ARTS COUNCIL OF WINSTON-SALEM/FORSYTH COUNTY

305 West 4th Street
Winston-Salem, NC 27101
919-722-2585
David C. Hudson, President and CEO
Michael Lowder, Vice President for Development

AWARD

Title: Emerging Artists Fellowship Program
Purpose: To recognize and to provide financial support for committed, talented artists in their formative years, thereby enabling them to develop professionally and creatively.
Categories of Support: Artists' Books, Crafts, Drawing, New Genres, Painting, Photography, Printmaking, Public Art, Sculpture
Type of Support: Unrestricted
Year Established: 1988
Duration of Funding: One year
Customary Month or Season of Deadline: Information not provided
Total Number of Applicants: 17
Total Number of Recipients: 7
Funding Amount: $500-1,500

APPLICATION PROCEDURE

Requirements: Application form, resume, slides, sample of original work, financial statement
Restrictions: Applicant must be a Forsyth County (NC) resident
Time Between Application Deadline and Award Notification: Two months
Reapplication by Former Recipients: Allowed immediately

SELECTION PROCESS

Method: Peer Panel, Board Members
Criteria: Quality of work is the primary criterion. Other factors include: financial need, project description, and appropriateness to guidelines.

OTHER INFORMATION

Publications: Program Guidelines, Annual Report
Activities: Exhibition of recipient's work

NORTH CAROLINA ARTS COUNCIL
Department of Cultural Resources
Raleigh, NC 27601-2807
919-733-2111
Mary B. Regan, Executive Director
Jean W. McLaughlin, Visual Arts Director

AWARD

Title: Visual Artist Projects
Purpose: To encourage significant development in the work of individual artists and in the medium within which they work, to support the realization of specific artistic ideas, and to recognize further the central contribution professional artists make to the creative environment of the state.
Categories of Support: Artists' Books, Crafts, Drawing, New Genres, Painting, Photography, Printmaking, Public Art, Sculpture
Type of Support: Project Grant
Year Established: 1988
Duration of Funding: One year
Customary Month or Season of Deadline: February
Total Number of Applicants: 100
Total Number of Recipients: 5
Funding Amount: Up to $5,000

APPLICATION PROCEDURE

Requirements: Application form, resume, slides, other forms of documentation depending on medium, project description/statement
Restrictions: Applicant must be a North Carolina state resident not currently enrolled in a degree-granting program.
Time Between Application Deadline and Award Notification: Six months
Reapplication by Former Recipients: Allowed after three years

SELECTION PROCESS

Method: Peer Panel
Criteria: Quality of work is the primary criterion. Resume and project description are also considered.

OTHER INFORMATION

Publications: Program Guidelines, Annual Report, *NCArts*
Activities: See additional entries for this organization.

NORTH CAROLINA ARTS COUNCIL

Department of Cultural Resources
Raleigh, NC 27601-2807
919-733-2111
Mary B. Regan, Executive Director
Jean W. McLaughlin, Visual Arts Director

AWARD

Title: Visual Artist Fellowships
Purpose: To encourage the continued development of North Carolina's finest artists and to recognize the central contribution professional artists make to the creative environment of the state. Intended to allow artists to set aside time to work.
Categories of Support: Artists' Books, Crafts, Drawing, New Genres, Painting, Photography, Printmaking, Public Art, Sculpture, Film/Video
Type of Support: Unrestricted
Year Established: 1980
Duration of Funding: One year
Customary Month or Season of Deadline: February
Total Number of Applicants: 200
Total Number of Recipients: 8
Funding Amount: $8,000

APPLICATION PROCEDURE

Requirements: Application form, resume, slides, self-addressed stamped envelope
Restrictions: Applicant must be a North Carolina state resident not currently enrolled in a degree-granting program.
Time Between Application Deadline and Award Notification: Six months
Reapplication by Former Recipients: Allowed after three years

SELECTION PROCESS

Method: Peer Panel Review
Criteria: Quality of work is the primary criterion. Resume is also considered.

OTHER INFORMATION

Publications: Program Guidelines, Annual Report, *NCArts*
Activities: See additional entries for this organization.

NORTH CAROLINA ARTS COUNCIL

Department of Cultural Resources
Raleigh, NC 27601-2807
919-733-2111
Mary B. Regan, Executive Director
Jean W. McLaughlin, Visual Arts Director

AWARD

Title: Emerging Artists Program
Purpose: This program is intended to support exceptionally talented visual artists who already have a strong record of accomplishment but have yet to firmly establish their careers as professionals. Applications are submitted through local and county arts councils (see list on the following page).
Categories of Support: Artists' Books, Crafts, Drawing, New Genres, Painting, Photography, Printmaking, Public Art, Sculpture
Type of Support: Project Grant
Year Established: 1980
Duration of Funding: One year
Customary Month or Season of Deadline: Information not provided
Total Number of Applicants: Information not provided
Total Number of Recipients: Information not provided
Funding Amount: $250-1,000

APPLICATION PROCEDURE

Requirements: Application form, resume, slides, sample of original work, artists' statement/project description. Applications are submitted through local/county arts councils (see list on the following page).
Restrictions: Applicant must be a North Carolina state resident 18 years of age or older, not currently enrolled in a degree-granting program.
Time Between Application Deadline and Award Notification: Information not provided
Reapplication by Former Recipients: Allowed immediately

SELECTION PROCESS

Method: Peer Panel Review, Staff Members, Board Members
Criteria: Quality of work is the primary criterion. Other factors include: financial need, resume, geographic representation, ethnic background, and project description.

OTHER INFORMATION

Publications: Program Guidelines, Annual Report, exhibition catalogues of Former Recipients
Activities: See additional entries for this organization.

Local agencies participating in North Carolina's Emerging Artists' Program:

Arts and Science Council of Charlotte
704-372-9667

Arts Council of Fayetteville/Cumberland County
919-323-1776

Arts Council of Lower Cape Fear
919-763-2787

Arts Council of Winston-Salem/Forsyth County
919-722-2585

Caldwell Arts Council
704-754-2486

Catawba County Council for the Arts
704-324-4906

City of Raleigh Arts Commission
919-722-2585

Community Arts Council of Western NC
704-258-0710

Durham Arts Council
919-560-2709

Rutherford County Arts Council
704-245-4000

The Arts Council (Raleigh)
919-831-6234

Transylvania County Arts Council
704-884-2787

United Arts Council of Greensboro
919-333-7440

UNITED ARTS COUNCIL OF GREENSBORO, INC. (UAC)

Greensboro Cultural Center
PO Box 869
Greensboro, NC 27402
919-333-7440
Helen E. Snow, President
Judith K. Ray, Community Development Director

AWARD

Title: Emerging Artists Program
Purpose: To provide funding to individual artists in all disciplines that will help to further their artistic careers.
Categories of Support: Artists' Books, Drawing, New Genres, Painting, Photography, Printmaking, Public Art, Sculpture
Type of Support: Project Grant
Year Established: 1988
Duration of Funding: One year
Customary Month or Season of Deadline: Spring
Total Number of Applicants: 54
Total Number of Recipients: 27
Funding Amount: $150-750

APPLICATION PROCEDURE

Requirements: Application form, resume, slides, sample of original work, project description/statement, financial statement, recommendations
Restrictions: Applicant must be a Guilford County resident not currently enrolled in a degree-granting program.
Time Between Application Deadline and Award Notification: Two months
Reapplication by Former Recipients: Allowed immediately

SELECTION PROCESS

Method: Peer Panel, Staff Members, Board Members
Criteria: Quality of work is the primary criterion. Other factors include: financial need, resume, geographic representation, project description, and ethnic background.

OTHER INFORMATION

Publications: Program Guidelines, Annual Report
Activities: Information not provided

NORTH DAKOTA COUNCIL ON THE ARTS (NDCA)

Black Building, Suite 606
Fargo, ND 58102
701-239-7150
Vern Goodin, Executive Director
Lila L. Hague, AIE Coordinator

AWARD

Title: Visual Arts Fellowship and Media Fellowship
Purpose: To assist visual and media artists of outstanding ability at a critical point in their development. For new works, works in progress, or professional development. Visual artists apply every three years.
Categories of Support: Drawing, New Genres, Painting, Photography, Printmaking, Public Art, Sculpture
Type of Support: Unrestricted
Year Established: 1984
Duration of Funding: One year
Customary Month or Season of Deadline: February
Total Number of Applicants: 20
Total Number of Recipients: 4
Funding Amount: $2,500-5,000

APPLICATION PROCEDURE

Requirements: Application form, resume, slides, sample of original work, cover letter, project description/statement
Restrictions: Applicant must be a North Dakota state resident not currently enrolled in a degree-granting program
Time Between Application Deadline and Award Notification: Three months
Reapplication by Former Recipients: Not allowed

SELECTION PROCESS

Method: Peer Panel
Criteria: Quality of work is the primary criterion. Project description and resume are also considered.

OTHER INFORMATION

Publications: Program Guidelines
Activities: Artist-in-Residence, Touring Program

GREATER COLUMBUS ARTS COUNCIL

55 East State Street
Columbus, OH 43215
614-224-2606
Raymond J. Hanley, Executive Director
Diane Nance Lloyd, Grants Officer

AWARD

Title: Individual Artists' Fellowship
Purpose: Offers unrestricted fellowships to individual artists. Visual artists apply for funding in even-numbered years only.
Categories of Support: Artists' Books, Crafts, Drawing, New Genres, Painting, Photography, Printmaking, Sculpture
Type of Support: Unrestricted
Year Established: 1986
Duration of Funding: One year
Customary Month or Season of Deadline: July
Total Number of Applicants: 150
Total Number of Recipients: 6
Funding Amount: $5,000

APPLICATION PROCEDURE

Requirements: Application form, resume, slides, project description/statement
Restrictions: Applicant must be a Franklin county (OH) resident.
Time Between Application Deadline and Award Notification: Four months
Reapplication by Former Recipients: Allowed after five years

SELECTION PROCESS

Method: Peer Panel
Criteria: Quality of work is the primary criterion. Resume and geographic representation are also considered.

OTHER INFORMATION

Publications: Program Guidelines, Annual Report, exhibition catalogues of former recipients
Activities: Exhibition of recipient's work

OHIO ARTS COUNCIL (OAC)

727 East Main Street
Columbus, OH 43205-1796
614-466-2613
Wayne P. Lawson, Executive Director
Susan Dickson, Coordinator, Individual Artists Program

AWARD

Title: Individual Artists Fellowship Program
Purpose: To recognize outstanding work being produced in Ohio. Funds are intended to assist artists in the creation of new works, thus supporting the artists' efforts to advance their careers.
Categories of Support: Artists' Books, Crafts, Drawing, New Genres, Painting, Photography, Printmaking, Public Art, Sculpture
Type of Support: Unrestricted
Year Established: 1978
Duration of Funding: One year
Customary Month or Season of Deadline: January
Total Number of Applicants: 802
Total Number of Recipients: 96
Funding Amount: $5,000-10,000

APPLICATION PROCEDURE

Requirements: Application form, slides
Restrictions: Applicant must be an Ohio state resident.
Time Between Application Deadline and Award Notification: Six months
Reapplication by Former Recipients: Allowed after two years

SELECTION PROCESS

Method: Peer Panel
Criteria: Quality of work is the primary criterion. Appropriateness to guidelines is also considered.

OTHER INFORMATION

Publications: Program Guidelines
Activities: See additional entries for this organization. Slide registry.

OHIO ARTS COUNCIL (OAC)

727 East Main Street
Columbus, OH 43205-1796
614-466-2613
Wayne P. Lawson, Executive Director
Susan Dickson, Coordinator, Individual Artists Program

AWARD

Title: Major Fellowship Program
Purpose: To support artists of extraordinary talent and achievement who have contributed substantially to Ohio's artistic vitality and have demonstrated achievement within their art form.
Categories of Support: Artists' Books, Crafts, Drawing, New Genres, Painting, Photography, Printmaking, Public Art, Sculpture
Type of Support: Unrestricted
Year Established: 1987
Duration of Funding: Two years
Customary Month or Season of Deadline: January
Total Number of Applicants: 134
Total Number of Recipients: 5
Funding Amount: $50,000 ($25,000 per year)

APPLICATION PROCEDURE

Requirements: Application form, resume, slides, project description/statement
Restrictions: Applicant must be an Ohio state resident .
Time Between Application Deadline and Award Notification: Six months
Reapplication by Former Recipients: Not allowed

SELECTION PROCESS

Method: Peer Panel
Criteria: Quality of work is the primary criterion. Resume and appropriateness to guidelines are also considered.

OTHER INFORMATION

Publications: Program Guidelines
Activities: See additional entries for this organization. Slide registry.

SUMMERFAIR INC.

PO Box 8287
Cincinnati, OH 45208
513-821-2367
Kathleen K. Horowitz, Managing Director

AWARD

Title: Aid to Individual Artists
Purpose: To promote, stimulate, and provide a forum for local artists living in Cincinnati.
Categories of Support: Artists' Books, Crafts, Drawing, Painting, Photography, Printmaking, Sculpture
Type of Support: Unrestricted
Year Established: 1983
Duration of Funding: One year
Customary Month or Season of Deadline: August
Total Number of Applicants: 130
Total Number of Recipients: 3
Funding Amount: $3,000

APPLICATION PROCEDURE

Requirements: Application form, resume, slides, project desrcription/statement
Restrictions: Applicant must live within a 40 mile radius of Cincinnati, student status
Time Between Application Deadline and Award Notification: Two months
Reapplication by Former Recipients: Allowed after one year

SELECTION PROCESS

Method: Peer Panel
Criteria: Quality of work is the primary criterion. Other factors include: financial need, resume, and project description.

OTHER INFORMATION

Publications: Information not provided
Activities: Exhibition of recipient's work.

ARTS AND HUMANITIES COUNCIL OF TULSA
2210 South Main Street
Tulsa, OK 74114
918-584-3333
John L. Everitt, Executive Director
Georgia Williams, Director, Artists in the Schools

AWARD

Title: Individual Artist Grant
Purpose: The Arts and Humanities Council of Tulsa encourages the artistic development of individuals working in all artistic disciplines. Project grants are intended to foster artistic career and growth.
Categories of Support: Crafts, Drawing, New Genres, Painting, Photography, Printmaking, Public Art, Sculpture
Type of Support: Project Grant
Year Established: Information not provided
Duration of Funding: One year
Customary Month or Season of Deadline: April
Total Number of Applicants: 50
Total Number of Recipients: 11
Funding Amount: $300-1,000

APPLICATION PROCEDURE

Requirements: Application form, resume, slides, project description/statement, financial statement
Restrictions: Applicant must be a resident of the Tulsa metro area, not currently enrolled in a degree-granting program.
Time Between Application Deadline and Award Notification: Two months
Reapplication by Former Recipients: Allowed immediately

SELECTION PROCESS

Method: Board Members
Criteria: Quality of work is the primary criterion.

OTHER INFORMATION

Publications: Program Guidelines
Activities: Information not provided

OKLAHOMA VISUAL ARTS COALITION (OVAC)

PO Box 54416
Oklahoma City, OK 73154
405-842-6991
John McNeese, Director

AWARD

Title: OVAC Grant and Award Program
Purpose: To provide funds to Oklahoma artists through an awards program and sudden opportunity grants.
Categories of Support: Crafts, Drawing, Painting, Photography, Printmaking, Public Art, Sculpture
Type of Support: Unrestricted
Year Established: 1989
Duration of Funding: Varies with project
Customary Month or Season of Deadline: Continuing
Total Number of Applicants: 110
Total Number of Recipients: 15
Funding Amount: $250-1,500

APPLICATION PROCEDURE

Requirements: Application form, resume, samples of original work, slides
Restrictions: Applicant must be an Oklahoma state resident.
Time Between Application Deadline and Award Notification: Three weeks
Reapplication by Former Recipients: Allowed after one year

SELECTION PROCESS

Method: Peer panel
Criteria: Quality of work is the primary criterion. Project description and appropriateness to guidelines are also considered.

OTHER INFORMATION

Publications: Program guidelines
Activities: Exhibition of recipients' work, slide registry

METROPOLITAN ARTS COMMISSION (MAC)

1120 SW 5th Avenue, Room 518
Portland, OR 97204
503-796-5111
Bill Bulick, Executive Director
Eloise MacMurray, Public Art Manager

AWARD

Title: Technical Assistance Grant
Purpose: Professional development for artists and arts organizations.
Categories of Support: Drawing, Painting, Photography, Printmaking, Sculpture
Type of Support: Project Grant, Training Subsidy
Year Established: 1990
Duration of Funding: Varies with project
Customary Month or Season of Deadline: Continuing
Total Number of Applicants: 77
Total Number of Recipients: 64
Funding Amount: $500-1,000

APPLICATION PROCEDURE

Requirements: Application form, resume, slides, sample of original work, artists' statement/project description, financial statement
Restrictions: Applicant must be a county resident not currently enrolled in a degree-granting program.
Time Between Application Deadline and Award Notification: Information not provided
Reapplication by Former Recipients: Not allowed

SELECTION PROCESS

Method: Staff Members, Board Members
Criteria: Quality of work is the primary criterion. Other factors include: financial need, resume, project description, and appropriateness to guidelines.

OTHER INFORMATION

Publications: Program Guidelines
Activities: See additional entries for this organization.

OREGON ARTS COMMISSION (OAC)

835 Summer Street, NE
Salem, OR 97301
503-378-3625
Leslie Tuomi, Exective Director
Vncent Dunn, Fellowship Coordinator

AWARD

Title: Individual Artist Fellowships
Purpose: To assist individual Oregon artists in their professional acheivement. Visual artists may apply for funding in odd-numbered years only.
Categories of Support: Crafts, Painting, Photography, New Genres
Type of Support: Unrestricted
Year Established: 1977
Duration of Funding: One year
Customary Month or Season of Deadline: April
Total Number of Applicants: 175
Total Number of Recipients: 8 (Fellowships) 1 (Master's Fellowship)
Funding Amount: $3,000 (Fellowships); $8,000 (Master's Fellowship)

APPLICATION PROCEDURE

Requirements: Application form, resume, slides, sample of original work, project description/statement, project budget, self-addressed stamped envelope
Restrictions: Applicant must be an Oregon state resident.
Time Between Application Deadline and Award Notification: Two months
Reapplication by Former Recipients: Not allowed

SELECTION PROCESS

Method: Peer Panel, Board Members
Criteria: Quality of work is the primary criterion. Project description and resume are also considered.

OTHER INFORMATION

Publications: Program Guidelines, OAC Newsletter
Activities: See additional entries for this organization.

PENNSYLVANIA COUNCIL ON THE ARTS

Finance Building, Room 216
Harrisburg, PA 17120
717-787-6883
Derek Gordon, Executive Director
David Stephens, Program Director, Visual Arts

AWARD

Title: Visual Artist Fellowships
Purpose: Visual artist fellowships help to support the work of visual artists whose work has achieved or is coalescing into a distinctive personal statement.
Categories of Support: Artists' Books, Drawing, Painting, Photography, Printmaking, Sculpture
Type of Support: Unrestricted
Year Established: 1974
Duration of Funding: One year
Customary Month or Season of Deadline: October
Total Number of Applicants: Information not provided
Total Number of Recipients: Information not provided
Funding Amount: $5,000-10,000

APPLICATION PROCEDURE

Requirements: Application form, resume, slides, project description/statement
Restrictions: Applicant must be a Pennsylvania state resident not currently enrolled in a degree-granting program.
Time Between Application Deadline and Award Notification: Three months
Reapplication by Former Recipients: Allowed after two years

SELECTION PROCESS

Method: Peer Panel
Criteria: Quality of work is the primary criterion.

OTHER INFORMATION:

Publications: Program Guidelines
Activities: See additional entries for this organization. Media Fellowships, Folklife Fellowships, Art Criticism Fellowships

PENNSYLVANIA COUNCIL ON THE ARTS

Finance Building, Room 216
Harrisburg, PA 17120
717-787-6883
Derek Gordon, Executive Director
David Stephens, Program Director, Visual Arts

AWARD

Title: Interdisciplinary Arts Fellowships
Purpose: The program supports the work of a single artist working in two or more different disciplines.
Categories of Support: New Genres/Multi Media
Type of Support: Unrestricted
Year Established: 1974
Duration of Funding: One year
Customary Month or Season of Deadline: October
Total Number of Applicants: Information not provided
Total Number of Recipients: Information not provided
Funding Amount: Up to $5,000

APPLICATION PROCEDURE

Requirements: Application form, resume, slides, project description/statement, other supporting material dependent on media, project budget
Restrictions: Applicant must be a Pennsylvania state resident not currently enrolled in a degree-granting program.
Time Between Application Deadline and Award Notification: Three months
Reapplication by Former Recipients: Allowed after two years

SELECTION PROCESS

Method: Peer Panel
Criteria: Quality of work is the primary criterion. Project description and appropriateness to guidelines are also considered.

OTHER INFORMATION

Publications: Program Guidelines
Activities: See additional entries for this organization.

PENNSYLVANIA COUNCIL ON THE ARTS
Finance Building, Room 216
Harrisburg, PA 17120
717-787-6883
Derek Gordon, Executive Director
David Stephens, Program Director, Visual Arts

AWARD

Title: Crafts Fellowships
Purpose: Crafts fellowships help to support the work of both traditional and contemporary craftspeople, creating either functional or non-functional art.
Categories of Support: Crafts
Type of Support: Unrestricted
Year Established: 1974
Duration of Funding: One year
Customary Month or Season of Deadline: October
Total Number of Applicants: Information not provided
Total Number of Recipients: Information not provided
Funding Amount: $5,000 - maximum $10,000

APPLICATION PROCEDURE

Requirements: Application form, resume, slides
Restrictions: Applicant must be a Pennsylvania state resident not currently enrolled in a degree-granting program.
Time Between Application Deadline and Award Notification: Three months
Reapplication by Former Recipients: Allowed after two years

SELECTION PROCESS

Method: Peer Panel Review
Criteria: Quality of work is the primary criterion.

OTHER INFORMATION

Publications: Program Guidelines
Activities: See additional entries for this organization.

PEW CHARITABLE TRUSTS

The University of the Arts
250 South Broad Street, Suite 400
Phildelphia, PA 19102
215-875-2285
Ella King Torrey, Executive Director
Melissa Franklin, Administrative Assistant

AWARD

Title: Pew Fellowships in the Arts
Purpose: Pew Fellowships in the Arts was established to provide financial support directly to artists to afford the opportunity to dedicate themslves wholly to their art.
Categories of Support: Crafts, Drawing, New Genres, Painting, Photography, Printmaking, Sculpture. Supported media alternate on a yearly basis.
Type of Support: Unrestricted
Year Established: 1991
Duration of Funding: One and two year fellowships
Customary Month or Season of Deadline: Winter
Total Number of Applicants: Information not provided
Total Number of Recipients: 16 (all disciplines)
Funding Amount: $50,000 for each year of Fellowship

APPLICATION PROCEDURE

Requirements: Application form, resume, slides, project description/statement
Restrictions: Applicant must be a resident of Bucks, Chester, Delaware, Montgomery, or Philadelphia counties (PA), 25 years of age or older, not currently enrolled in a degree-granting program.
Time Between Application Deadline and Award Notification: Six months
Reapplication by Former Recipients: Allowed immediately - not encouraged

SELECTION PROCESS

Method: Peer Panel
Criteria: Quality of work is the primary criterion. Resume is also considered.

OTHER INFORMATION

Publications: Program Guidelines, Annual Report, exhibition catalogues of former recipients
Activities: technical assistance, discount health insurance, professional referral service for grant recipients

RHODE ISLAND STATE COUNCIL ON THE ARTS (RISCA)

96 Cedar Street, Suite 103
Providence, RI 02903
401-277-3880
Iona Dobbins, Executive Director

AWARD

Title: Individual Artist Fellowships
Purpose: To encourage the creative development of professional artists by enabling them to pursue work and career goals and to provide funds for the purchase of supplies and materials.
Categories of Support: 1993: Photography, Crafts, Sculpture, Film/Video, Folk Arts. 1994: New Genres, Painting, Drawing, Printmaking, Design
Type of Support: Unrestricted
Year Established: 1973
Duration of Funding: One year
Customary Month or Season of Deadline: April
Total Number of Applicants: 161
Total Number of Recipients: 6
Funding Amount: $6,000 (one award per discipline)

APPLICATION PROCEDURE

Requirements: Application form, resume, slides
Restrictions: Applicant must be a Rhode Island state resident 18 years of age or older, not currently enrolled in a degree-granting program.
Time Between Application Deadline and Award Notification: Three months
Reapplication by Former Recipients: Allowed after three years

SELECTION PROCESS

Method: Peer Panel, Out-of-State Judge
Criteria: Quality of work is the primary criterion.

OTHER INFORMATION

Publications: Program Guidelines, Annual Report, *Guide to the Rhode Island State Council on the Arts*
Activities: See additional entries for this organization. Exhibition of recipient's work, slide registry.

RHODE ISLAND STATE COUNCIL ON THE ARTS (RISCA)

96 Cedar Street, Suite 103
Providence, RI 02903
401-277-3880
Iona Dobbins, Executive Director
Edward Holgate, Director, Individual Artist Programs

AWARD

Title: Artist Projects
Purpose: Artist Projects grants enable an artist to create new work and/or complete works-in-progress by providing direct financial assistance for a specific project.
Categories of Support: Artists' Books, Crafts, Drawing, New Genres, Painting, Photography, Printmaking, Sculpture
Type of Support: Project Grant
Year Established: 1989
Duration of Funding: 18 months
Customary Month or Season of Deadline: October
Total Number of Applicants: 31
Total Number of Recipients: 8
Funding Amount: $2,000-5,000

APPLICATION PROCEDURE

Requirements: Application form, resume, slides, project description, project budget, public presentation plan
Restrictions: Applicant must be a Rhode Island state resident 18 years of age or older, not currently enrolled in a degree-granting program.
Restrictions: Three months
Reapplication by Former Recipients: Allowed after one year

SELECTION PROCESS

Method: Peer Panel Review
Criteria: Quality of work is the primary criterion. Project description, appropriatenes to guidelines, and feasibility of project are also considered.

OTHER INFORMATION

Publications: Program Guidelines, Annual Report, *Guide to the Rhode Island State Council on the Arts*
Activities: See additional entries for this organization. Slide registry.

SOUTH CAROLINA ARTS COMMISSION

1800 Gervais Street
Columbia, SC 29201
803-734-8696
Scott Sanders, Executive Director
Julia Jones, Fellowships Coodinator

AWARD

Title: Artist Fellowships
Purpose: Unrestricted non-matching funds awarded to outstanding resident artists.
Categories of Support: Artists' Books, Crafts, Drawing, New Genres, Painting, Photography, Printmaking, Sculpture
Type of Support: Unrestricted
Year Established: 1976
Duration of Funding: One year
Customary Month or Season of Deadline: September
Total Number of Applicants: 130
Total Number of Recipients: 2
Funding Amount: $5,000

APPLICATION PROCEDURE

Requirements: Application form, slides
Restrictions: Applicant must be a South Carolina state resident not currently enrolled in a degree-granting program.
Restrictions: Three months
Reapplication by Former Recipients: Allowed after five years

SELECTION PROCESS

Method: Peer Panel
Criteria: Quality of work is the primary criterion.

OTHER INFORMATION

Publications: Program Guidelines
Activities: Visual Artist Development, State Art Collection, Percent for Art Program

SOUTH DAKOTA ARTS COUNCIL (SDAC)

108 West 11th Street
Souix Falls, SD 57104-0788
605-339-6646
Denis Holub, Executive Director
Shirley Snere, Assistant Director

AWARD

Title: Artist Fellowship Grant
Purpose: To recognize individual artists for significant contribution to higher standards in the arts.
Categories of Support: Artists' Books, Crafts, Drawing, New Genres, Painting, Photography, Printmaking, Public Art, Sculpture
Type of Support: Unrestricted
Year Established: 1976
Duration of Funding: One year
Customary Month or Season of Deadline: February
Total Number of Applicants: 31
Total Number of Recipients: 4
Funding Amount: $5,000

APPLICATION PROCEDURE

Requirements: Application form, resume, slides, project description/statement (optional)
Restrictions: Applicant must be a South Dakota state resident not currently enrolled in a degree-granting program.
Restrictions: Three months
Reapplication by Former Recipients: Allowed after two years

SELECTION PROCESS

Method: Peer Panel, Board Members
Criteria: Quality of work is the primary criterion. Resume and ethnic background are also considered.

OTHER INFORMATION

Publications: Program Guidelines
Activities: See additional entries for this organization.

SOUTH DAKOTA ARTS COUNCIL (SDAC)
108 West 11th Street
Souix Falls, SD 57104-0788
605-339-6646
Denis Holub, Executive Director
Shirley Snere, Assistant Director

AWARD
Title: Emerging Artist Grant
Purpose: Recognizes an individual's potential for growth and contribution to higher standards for the arts at an early point in their career.
Categories of Support: Artists' Books, Crafts, Drawing, New Genres, Painting, Photography, Printmaking, Public Art, Sculpture
Type of Support: Unrestricted
Year Established: 1990
Duration of Funding: One year
Customary Month or Season of Deadline: February
Total Number of Applicants: 40
Total Number of Recipients: 10
Funding Amount: $1,000

APPLICATION PROCEDURE
Requirements: Application form, resume, slides, project description/statement (optional)
Restrictions: Applicant must be a South Dakota state resident.
Restrictions: Three months
Reapplication by Former Recipients: Allowed after three years

SELECTION PROCESS
Method: Peer Panel Review, Board Members
Criteria: Quality of work is the primary criterion. Resume and ethnic background are also considered.

OTHER INFORMATION
Publications: Program Guidelines
Activities: See additional entries for this organization.

SOUTH DAKOTA ARTS COUNCIL (SDAC)

108 West 11th Street
Souix Falls, SD 57102
605-339-6646
Denis Holub, Executive Director
Shirley Snere, Assistant Director

AWARD

Title: Individual Artist Project Grant
Purpose: Assists artists in the presentation of a project for the general public or for an activity which meets the specific needs of the applicant artist.
Categories of Support: Artists' Books, Crafts, Drawing, New Genres, Painting, Photography, Printmaking, Public Art, Sculpture
Type of Support: Project Grant
Year Established: 1976
Duration of Funding: One year
Customary Month or Season of Deadline: February
Total Number of Applicants: 4
Total Number of Recipients: 2
Funding Amount: $500-2,000 (up to 50% of total project cost)

APPLICATION PROCEDURE

Requirements: Application form, resume, slides, project description/statement, project budget
Restrictions: Applicant must be a South Dakota state resident.
Restrictions: Three months
Reapplication by Former Recipients: Allowed immediately

SELECTION PROCESS

Method: Peer Panel Review
Criteria: Quality of work is the primary criterion. Other factors include: resume, geographic representation, ethnic background, appropriateness to guidelines and project description.

OTHER INFORMATION

Publications: Program Guidelines
Activities: See additional entries for this organization.

MEMPHIS ARTS COUNCIL (MAC)

2714 Union Avenue Extended, Suite 601
Memphis, TN 38112
901-452-2787
Babs Feibelman, Executive Director
Minna Glenn or Eva Watson, Directors, Special Grants

AWARD

Title: Special Grants
Purpose: For use by established non-profit arts organizations in special projects. Groups may direct funds to individual artists under the organization's umbrella.
Categories of Support: Artists' Books, Crafts, Drawing, New Genres, Painting, Photography, Printmaking, Public Art, Sculpture
Type of Support: Project Grant
Year Established: 1982
Duration of Funding: Varies with project
Customary Month or Season of Deadline: Continuing
Total Number of Applicants: 20
Total Number of Recipients: 16
Funding Amount: $600-3,500 average - $10,000 maximum

APPLICATION PROCEDURE

Requirements: Application form, resume, slides, project description/statement, financial statement. Application through a sponsoring arts organization only.
Restrictions: Applicant must be a resident of the Memphis, TN area.
Time Between Application Deadline and Award Notification: Two months
Reapplication by Former Recipients: Allowed immediately

SELECTION PROCESS

Method: Peer Panel, Staff Members, Board Members
Criteria: Quality of work is the primary criterion. Other factors include: resume, appropriateness to guidelines, and project description.

OTHER INFORMATION:

Publications: Program Guidelines
Activities: See additional entries for this organization.

MEMPHIS ARTS COUNCIL (MAC)
2714 Union Avenue Extended, Suite 601
Memphis, TN 38112
901-452-2787
Babs Feibelman, Executive Director
Minna Glenn or Eva Watson, Directors, Special Grants

AWARD

Title: Innervisions
Purpose: Grass roots program for non-profit organizations in underserved communities, also for projects. Groups may direct funds to individual artists under the organization's umbrella.
Categories of Support: Artists' Books, Crafts, Drawing, New Genres, Painting, Photography, Printmaking, Public Art, Sculpture.
Type of Support: Project Grant
Year Established: 1984
Duration of Funding: Varies with project.
Customary Month or Season of Deadline: Continuing
Total Number of Applicants: 20
Total Number of Recipients: 16
Funding Amount: $600-3,500 average - maximum $10,000

APPLICATION PROCEDURE

Requirements: Application form, resume, project description/statement, financial statement
Restrictions: Applicant must be a resident of the Memphis, TN area.
Time Between Application Deadline and Award Notification: Two months
Reapplication by Former Recipients: Allowed immediately.

SELECTION PROCESS

Method: Peer Panel Review, Staff Members, Board Members.
Criteria: Quality of work is the primary criterion. Other factors include: resume, appropriateness to guidelines, and project description.

OTHER INFORMATION

Publications: Program Guidelines, Annual Report
Activities: See additional entries for this organization.

TENNESSEE ARTS COMMISSION

320 6th Avenue, North, Suite 100
Nashville, TN 37219
615-741-1701
Bennett Tarleton, Executive Director
Victoria Bonne, Director of Visual Arts

AWARD

Title: Individual Visual Arts Fellowship
Purpose: To promote practicing professional artists living in Tennessee.
Categories of Support: Crafts, Drawing, Painting, Photography, Printmaking, Sculpture
Type of Support: Unrestricted
Year Established: 1967
Duration of Funding: One year
Customary Month or Season of Deadline: January
Total Number of Applicants: 34
Total Number of Recipients: 3
Funding Amount: $2,500

APPLICATION PROCEDURE

Requirements: Application form, resume, slides, project description/statement
Restrictions: Applicant must be a Tennessee state residen .
Time Between Application Deadline and Award Notification: Six months
Reapplication by Former Recipients: Allowed immediately

SELECTION PROCESS

Method: Out-of-State Juror
Criteria: Quality of work is the primary criterion. Other factors include: financial need, resume, geographic representation, and ethnic background.

OTHER INFORMATION

Publications: Program Guidelines, newsletter
Activities: n/a

CULTURAL ARTS COUNCIL OF HOUSTON

1964 West Gray, Suite 224
Houston, TX 77019-4808
713-527-9330
Mary Ann Piacentini, Executive Director

AWARD

Title: Creative Artist Program
Purpose: Awards are intended to support the development of Houston artists by enabling them to set aside time to create new work, complete works in progress, or pursue new avenues of creative expression.
Categories of Support: Drawing, New Genres, Painting, Printmaking, Sculpture
Type of Support: Unrestricted
Year Established: 1986
Duration of Funding: One year
Customary Month or Season of Deadline: November
Total Number of Applicants: 200
Total Number of Recipients: 6
Funding Amount: $4,000

APPLICATION PROCEDURE

Requirements: Application form, resume, slides, other support material dependent on media
Restrictions: Applicant must be a Houston resident. US citizenship.
Time Between Application Deadline and Award Notification: Three months
Reapplication by Former Recipients: Allowed after three years

SELECTION PROCESS

Method: Peer Panel
Criteria: Quality of work is the primary criterion. Resume is also considered.

OTHER INFORMATION

Publications: Program Guidelines
Activities: Public service related to work completed during grant period.

DALLAS MUSEUM OF ART

Anne Giles Kimbrough Awards
1717 North Harwood
Dallas, TX 75201
214-922-1234
Debra Wittrup, Director, Awards to Artists

AWARD

Title: Anne Giles Kimbrough Awards
Purpose: Recognize exceptional talent and promise in young artists.
Categories of Support: Artists' Books, Crafts, Drawing, New Genres, Painting, Photography, Printmaking, Sculpture
Type of Support: Unrestricted
Year Established: 1980
Duration of Funding: One year
Customary Month or Season of Deadline: March
Total Number of Applicants: 75
Total Number of Recipients: 5
Funding Amount: Up to $3,500

APPLICATION PROCEDURE

Requirements: Resume, slides, project description/statement, project budget, two letters of recommendation
Restrictions: Applicant must be a Texas state resident under 30 years old.
Time Between Application Deadline and Award Notification: Three months
Reapplication by Former Recipients: Not allowed

SELECTION PROCESS

Method: Board Members
Criteria: Quality of work is the primary criterion.

OTHER INFORMATION

Publications: Program Guidelines
Activities: See additional entries for this organization.

DALLAS MUSEUM OF ART
Otis and Velma Davis Dozier Travel Grant
1717 North Harwood
Dallas, TX 75201
214-922-1234
Debra Wittrup, Executive Director

AWARD

Title: Otis and Velma Davis Dozier Travel Grant
Purpose: To recognize exceptional talent in professional artists who wish to expand their artistic horizons through travel.
Categories of Support: Artists' Books, Crafts, Drawing, New Genres, Painting, Photography, Printmaking, Sculpture
Type of Support: Travel Grant
Year Established: 1990
Duration of Funding: One year
Customary Month or Season of Deadline: March
Total Number of Applicants: 145
Total Number of Recipients: 1
Funding Amount: Up to $6,000

APPLICATION PROCEDURE

Requirements: Resume, slides, project description/statement, travel budget
Restrictions: Applicant must be a Texas state resident 30 years of age or older.
Time Between Application Deadline and Award Notification: Three months
Reapplication by Former Recipients: Not allowed

SELECTION PROCESS

Method: Peer Panel Review
Criteria: Quality of work is the primary criterion.

OTHER INFORMATION

Publications: Program Guidelines
Activities: See additional entries for this organization.

SAN ANTONIO DEPARTMENT OF ARTS AND CULTURAL AFFAIRS (DACA)

PO Box 839966
San Antonio, TX 78283-3966
512-222-2787
Eduardo Diaz, Executive Director
Kate Martin, Project Management Specialist

AWARD

Title: Individual Artist Grants
Purpose: Direct financial assistance to individual artists is designed to: a) assist both emerging and established artists by supporting work of artistic merit; b) encourage innovative projects; c) bring San Antonio based artists to greater public attention; d) support projects by individuals who do not have institutional support.
Categories of Support: Artists' Books, Crafts, Drawing, New Genres, Painting, Photography, Printmaking, Sculpture
Type of Support: Project Grant
Year Established: 1990
Duration of Funding: One year
Customary Month or Season of Deadline: February
Total Number of Applicants: 47
Total Number of Recipients: 16
Funding Amount: $1,500-3,000

APPLICATION PROCEDURE

Requirements: Application form, resume, slides, project description/statement , project budget
Restrictions: Applicant must be a Bexar county (TX) resident not currently enrolled in a degree-granting program. US citizenship.
Restrictions: Information not provided
Reapplication by Former Recipients: Allowed after one year

SELECTION PROCESS

Method: Peer Panel, Board Members
Criteria: Quality of work is the primary criterion. Other factors include: resume, geographic representation, project description, and ethnic background.

OTHER INFORMATION

Publications: Program Guidelines
Activities: Information not provided

UTAH ARTS COUNCIL

617 East South Temple Street
Salt Lake City, UT 84102
801-533-5895
Bonnie Stephens, Executive Director
Sherrill Sandberg, Visual Arts Coordinator

AWARD

Title: Visual Artist Fellowships
Purpose: To support and encourage artists from Utah who demonstrate quality and professionalism in their work and career.
Categories of Support: Artists' Books, Crafts, Drawing, New Genres, Painting, Photography, Printmaking, Public Art, Sculpture
Type of Support: Unrestricted
Year Established: 1985
Duration of Funding: One year
Customary Month or Season of Deadline: December
Total Number of Applicants: 50
Total Number of Recipients: 2
Funding Amount: $5,000

APPLICATION PROCEDURE

Requirements: Application form, resume, slides, project description/statement, three references
Restrictions: Applicant must be a Utah state resident not currently enrolled in a degree-granting program.
Time Between Application Deadline and Award Notification: Six months
Reapplication by Former Recipients: Allowed after three years

SELECTION PROCESS

Method: Out-of-State Juror
Criteria: Quality of work is the primary criterion. Resume and project description are also considered.

OTHER INFORMATION

Publications: Program Guidelines, Visual Arts Bulletin
Activities: Exhibition of recipient's work with catalog, Slide registry, Art in Education Program

VERMONT COUNCIL ON THE ARTS (VCA)

136 State Street
Montpelier, VT 05602
802-828-3291
Joanne Chow Winship, Executive Director
Cornelia Cary, Grants Officer

AWARD

Title: Fellowship
Purpose: Creative development for professional artists.
Categories of Support: Artists' Books, Crafts, Drawing, New Genres, Painting, Photography, Printmaking, Public Art, Sculpture
Type of Support: Unrestricted
Year Established: 1971
Duration of Funding: One year
Customary Month or Season of Deadline: Spring
Total Number of Applicants: 170
Total Number of Recipients: 8
Funding Amount: $500-3,500

APPLICATION PROCEDURE

Requirements: Application form, resume, slides
Restrictions: Applicant must be a Vermont state resident 18 years of age or older, not currently enrolled in a degree-granting program. US Citizenship
Time Between Application Deadline and Award Notification: Six months
Reapplication by Former Recipients: Allowed immediately. Fellows may recieve an award two out of every five years.

SELECTION PROCESS

Method: Peer Panel
Criteria: Quality of work is the primary criterion.

OTHER INFORMATION

Publications: Program Guidelines, Annual Report, Artists' Register
Activities: Slide registry, grants to organizations, Artists in Education, Touring Artist Program

VIRGINIA COMMISSION FOR THE ARTS

101 North 14th Street, 17th Floor
Richmond, VA 23219
804-225-3132
Peggey J. Baggett, Executive Director
Susan Fitzpatrick, Program Coordinator

AWARD

Title: Project Grants
Purpose: To support and encourage the Commonwealth's best artists through grants for work in progress or planned projects. Designed to recognize the central contribution of artists to the creative environment of the Commonwealth.
Categories of Support: Artists' Books, Crafts, Drawing, New Genres, Painting, Photography, Printmaking, Sculpture
Type of Support: Project Grant
Year Established: 1990
Duration of Funding: One year
Customary Month or Season of Deadline: April
Total Number of Applicants: Information not provided
Total Number of Recipients: Information not provided
Funding Amount: Up to $5,000

APPLICATION PROCEDURE

Requirements: Resume, slides, project description/statement, project budget
Restrictions: Applicant must be a Commonwealth of Virginia resident.
Time Between Application Deadline and Award Notification: Three months
Reapplication by Former Recipients: Not allowed

SELECTION PROCESS

Method: Peer Panel, Commission Review
Criteria: Quality of work is the primary criterion. Project description and project budget are also considered.

OTHER INFORMATION

Publications: Program Guidelines
Activities: Information not provided

VIRGINIA MUSEUM OF FINE ARTS

2800 Grove Avenue
Richmond, VA 23221-2466
804-367-0844
Fax: 804-367-9393
Paul N. Perrot, Executive Director
Susan F. Ferrell, Fellowship Program Coordinator

AWARD

Title: Virginia Musuem of Fine Arts Fellowship Program
Purpose: To support artists' work and studies. Professionals and full-time graduate and undergraduate students may apply.
Categories of Support: Crafts, Drawing, Painting, Photography, Printmaking, Sculpture
Type of Support: Unrestricted
Year Established: 1940
Duration of Funding: Ten months
Customary Month or Season of Deadline: March
Total Number of Applicants: 525
Total Number of Recipients: 13
Funding Amount: $8,000 Professional; $5,000 Graduate; $4,000 Undergraduate

APPLICATION PROCEDURE

Requirements: Application form, resume, slides, academic transcript(s) (students only), two letters of recommendation
Restrictions: Applicant must be a Commonwealth of Virginia resident.
Time Between Application Deadline and Award Notification: Two months
Reapplication by Former Recipients: Allowed immediately (students); Allowed after three years (professionals)

SELECTION PROCESS

Method: Nationally known juror (professionals); Panel review (students)
Criteria: Quality of work is the primary criterion.

OTHER INFORMATION

Publications: Program Guidelines
Activities: Graduate Art History Fellowships, Graduate and Undergraduate Internships, Statewide Artist Workshop Program, museum workshops, exhibitions

ALLIED ARTS FOUNDATION (AAF)

1001 Fourth Avenue, Suite 2200
Seattle, WA 98154
206-624-0432
Richard Mann, Executive Director

AWARD

Title: Project Grants
Purpose: To support generative works by individuals or unincorporated arts organizations and/or provide umbrella sponsorship. Both awards and sponsorship restricted to Puget Sound and are for any arts discipline.
Categories of Support: Artists' Books, Drawing, New Genres, Painting, Photography, Public Art, Sculpture
Type of Support: Project Grant
Year Established:1968
Duration of Funding: Six months
Customary Month or Season of Deadline: Information not provided
Total Number of Applicants: 37
Total Number of Recipients: 4
Funding Amount: $1,800

APPLICATION PROCEDURE

Requirements: Application form, project description
Restrictions: Applicant must be a Puget Sound region resident.
Time Between Application Deadline and Award Notification: Varies with project
Reapplication by Former Recipients: Allowed after one year

SELECTION PROCESS

Method: Staff Members, Board Members
Criteria: Quality of work is the primary criterion. Project description and appropriateness to guidelines are also considered.

OTHER INFORMATION

Publications: Program Guidelines, Annual Report
Activities: Sponsorship

ARTIST TRUST

512 Jones Building
1331 3rd Avenue
Seattle, WA 98101
206-467-8734
David Mendoza, Executive Director
Gabrielle Dean, Office Manager

AWARD

Title: Fellowships
Purpose: Recognizes quality of work and dedication to an artistic discipline. The fellowship is not to be viewed as project support.
Categories of Support: Artists' Books, Crafts, Drawing, New Genres, Painting, Photography, Printmaking, Sculpture
Type of Support: Fellowship
Year Established: 1987
Duration of Funding: One year
Customary Month or Season of Deadline: Summer
Total Number of Applicants: Information not provided
Total Number of Recipients: 7
Funding Amount: $5,000

APPLICATION PROCEDURE

Requirements: Application form, resume, slides
Restrictions: Applicant must be a Washington state resident, 18 years of age or older, not currently enrolled in a degree-granting program.
Time Between Application Deadline and Award Notification: Three months
Reapplication by Former Recipients: Allowed immediately

SELECTION PROCESS

Method: Peer Panel
Criteria: Quality of work is the primary criterion. Resume and geographic representation are also considered.

OTHER INFORMATION

Publications: Program Guidelines, *Artist Trust* (quarterly journal)
Activities: *GAP* Artists' Project Grants, Information services, access to health care, artists' registry, arts advocacy

KING COUNTY ARTS COMMISSION

1115 Smith Tower
506 Second Avenue
Seattle, WA 98104
206-296-7580
Mayumi Tsutukawa, Manager, Cultural Resources Division

AWARD

Title: New Works Projects
Purpose: The New Works Projects Program encourages experimentation and supports the creation and presentation of new works in literary, visual, media, performing, and interdisciplinary arts.
Categories of Support: New Genres, Public Art
Type of Support: Project Grant
Year Established: 1967
Duration of Funding: Eight months
Customary Month or Season of Deadline: January
Total Number of Applicants: Information not provided
Total Number of Recipients: Information not provided
Funding Amount: $1,000-5,000

APPLICATION PROCEDURE

Requirements: Application form, resume, slides, project proposal
Restrictions: Applicant must be a resident of western Washington state.
Time Between Application Deadline and Award Notification: Varies with project
Reapplication by Former Recipients: Allowed after one year

SELECTION PROCESS

Method: Peer Panel
Criteria: Quality of work is the primary criterion. Resume and project proposals are also considered.

OTHER INFORMATION:

Publications: Program Guidelines
Activities: Exhibition of recipient's work. Gallery Program, Percent for Art Program, King County Immediate Response Reserve

STATE OF WASHINGTON ARTS COMMISSION

110 9th and Columbia Building
Olympia, WA 98504-4111
206-753-3860
John W. Forman, Executive Director
Mary L. Frye, Awards Program Manager

AWARD

Title: Artist Fellowship
Purpose: For practicing professional artists of exceptional talent with at least five years professional experience.
Categories of Support: Crafts, Drawing, Painting, Photography, Printmaking, Sculpture
Type of Support: Unrestricted
Year Established: 1978
Duration of Funding: One year
Customary Month or Season of Deadline: Information not provided
Total Number of Applicants: 211
Total Number of Recipients: 2
Funding Amount: $5,000

APPLICATION PROCEDURE

Requirements: Application form, resume, slides, project description/statement
Restrictions: Applicant must be a Washington state resident. US citizenship.
Restrictions: Five months
Reapplication by Former Recipients: Allowed after five years

SELECTION PROCESS

Method: Peer Panel
Criteria: Quality of work is the primary criterion. Project description is also considered.

OTHER INFORMATION

Publications: Program Guidelines, Fellowship Brochure
Activities: Art in Public Places, Artists-in-Residence, Governor's Arts Awards, Institutional Support, Partnership

DANE COUNTY CULTURAL AFFAIRS COMMISSION
City-Council Building, Room 421
210 Martin Luther King, Jr. Blvd.
Madison, WI 53709
608-266-5915
Lynn Eich, Executive Director

AWARD

Title: Fellowships
Purpose: Recognizes and encourages Dane County (WI) visual artists.
Categories of Support: Artists' Books, Crafts, Drawing, New Genres, Painting, Photography, Printmaking, Sculpture
Type of Support: Unrestricted
Year Established: 1978
Duration of Funding: One year
Customary Month or Season of Deadline: September
Total Number of Applicants: 75
Total Number of Recipients: 2
Funding Amount: $5,000

APPLICATION PROCEDURE

Requirements: Application form, resume, slides
Restrictions: Applicant must be a Dane county (WI) resident.
Time Between Application Deadline and Award Notification: Three months
Reapplication by Former Recipients: Not allowed

SELECTION PROCESS

Method: Peer Panel
Criteria: Quality of work is the primary criterion.

OTHER INFORMATION

Publications: Program Guidelines
Activities: See additional entries for this organization.

DANE COUNTY CULTURAL AFFAIRS COMMISSION

City-Council Building, Room 421
210 Martin Luther King, Jr. Blvd.
Madison, WI 53709
608-266-5915
Lynn Eich, Executive Director

AWARD

Title: Project Grants
Purpose: Assists Dane County artists through provision of funds for completion of a specific work or body of work.
Categories of Support: Artists' Books, Crafts, Drawing, New Genres, Painting, Photography, Printmaking, Sculpture
Type of Support: Project Grant
Year Established: 1987
Duration of Funding: Varies with project
Customary Month or Season of Deadline: September
Total Number of Applicants: 60
Total Number of Recipients: 2
Funding Amount: Varies with project

APPLICATION PROCEDURE

Requirements: Application form, resume, slides, project description/statement
Restrictions: Applicant must be a Dane county (WI) resident.
Time Between Application Deadline and Award Notification: Varies with project
Reapplication by Former Recipients: Not allowed

SELECTION PROCESS

Method: Peer Panel
Criteria: Quality of work is the primary criterion. Project description is also considered.

OTHER INFORMATION

Publications: Program Guidelines
Activities: See additional entries for this organization.

MILWAUKEE ARTS BOARD (MAB)
809 North Broadway
PO Box 324
Milwaukee, WI 53212
414-223-5790
Pam Garvey, Cultural Affairs Officer

AWARD

Title: Neighborhood Arts Program (NAP)
Purpose: NAP is designed to help neighborhood-based organizations in the city of Milwaukee strengthen their capacity to work with local artists and to provide local arts programming.
Categories of Support: Artists' Books, Crafts, Drawing, New Genres, Painting, Photography, Printmaking, Public Art, Sculpture
Type of Support: Project Grant
Year Established: 1991
Duration of Funding: One year
Customary Month or Season of Deadline: Spring
Total Number of Applicants: 25
Total Number of Recipients: 10
Funding Amount: $1,750-5,000

APPLICATION PROCEDURE

Requirements: Application through a sponsoring organization only.
Restrictions: Applicant must be a Milwaukee resident.
Time Between Application Deadline and Award Notification: Two months
Reapplication by Former Recipients: Allowed immediately

SELECTION PROCESS

Method: Peer Panel
Criteria: Quality of work is the primary criterion. Project description and geographic representation are also considered.

OTHER INFORMATION:

Publications: Program Guidelines
Activities: See additional entries for this organization.

WISCONSIN ARTS BOARD
131 West Wilson, Suite 301
Madison, WI 53703
608-266-0190
Elizabeth Malner, Percent for Art Coordinator

AWARD
Title: Individual Artist Program
Purpose: Financial awards to individual artists.
Categories of Support: Artists' Books, Crafts, Drawing, New Genres, Painting, Photography, Printmaking, Sculpture
Type of Support: Unrestricted
Year Established: 1989
Duration of Funding: One year
Customary Month or Season of Deadline: September
Total Number of Applicants: 500
Total Number of Recipients: 45
Funding Amount: $1,000-5,000

APPLICATION PROCEDURE
Requirements: Application form, resume, project description/statement, slides
Restrictions: Applicant must be a Wisconsin state resident not currently enrolled in a degree-granting program.
Time Between Application Deadline and Award Notification: Five months
Reapplication by Former Recipients: Allowed immediately

SELECTION PROCESS
Method: Peer Panel
Criteria: Quality of work is the primary criterion.

OTHER INFORMATION
Publications: Program Guidelines, Annual Report
Activities: Percent for Art Program, Folk Arts Apprenticeship Program

WYOMING ARTS COUNCIL
2320 Capital Avenue
Cheyenne, WY 82002
307-777-7742
Joy Thompson, Executive Director
Lilianne Francuz, Visual Arts Program Manager

AWARD
Title: Visual Arts Fellowships
Purpose: To encourage the creative development of the state's professional artists with direct financial support. To encourage the creation of art and the advancement of artists' careers.
Categories of Support: Artists' Books, Crafts, Drawing, Painting, Photography, Printmaking, Public Art, Sculpture
Type of Support: Unrestricted
Year Established: 1986
Duration of Funding: One year
Customary Month or Season of Deadline: August
Total Number of Applicants: 70
Total Number of Recipients: 4
Funding Amount: $2,500

APPLICATION PROCEDURE
Requirements: Application form, resume, slides, project description/statement
Restrictions: Applicant must be a Wyoming state resident. US citizenship.
Time Between Application Deadline and Award Notification: One month
Reapplication by Former Recipients: Allowed after five years

SELECTION PROCESS
Method: Out-of State Jury
Criteria: Quality of work is the primary criterion.

OTHER INFORMATION
Publications: Exhibition Catalogues of former recipients
Activities: Exhibition of recipient's work

EMERGENCY GRANTS

ARTISTS FELLOWSHIP INC.

c/o Salmagundi Club
47 Fifth Avenue
New York, NY 10003
Richard Plonk, Executive Director

AWARD

Title: Emergency Aid
Purpose: Financial assistance for professional fine artists in the event of serious illness, distress, and bereavement.
Categories of Support: Drawing, Painting, Printmaking, Sculpture
Customary Month or Season of Deadline: Continuing
Funding Amount: Varies with situation

APPLICATION PROCEDURE-SELECTION PROCESS

Requirements: Application form, resume, slides, documentation of need
Time Between Application Deadline and Award Notification: Varies with situation
Method: Peer Panel
Criteria: Quality of work is the primary criterion. Financial need is also considered.

CHANGE INC.

P.O. Box #705,Cooper Station
New York, NY 10276
212-473-3742
Robert Rauschenberg, President
Denise LeBeau, Administrative Manager

AWARD

Title: Emergency Grants
Purpose: To give emergency aid to artists.
Categories of Support: Crafts, Drawing, New Genres, Painting, Photography, Printmaking
Customary Month or Season of Deadline: Continuing
Total Number of Applicants: 15
Total Number of Recipients: 8
Funding Amount: $100-500

APPLICATION PROCEDURE-SELECTION PROCESS

Requirements: Resume, slides, statement, financial statement
Time Between Application Deadline and Award Notification: One week
Method: Board Members
Criteria: Financial need is the primary criterion. Resume and appropriateness to guidelines are also considered.

CRAFT EMERGENCY RELIEF FUND

1000 Connecticut Avenue, Suite 9
Washington, DC 20036
413-625-9672
Lois Ahrens, Director

AWARD

Title: Emergency Loan
Purpose: Last resort loans for craftspersons working full-time who have experienced an emergency situation which interrupts their work.
Categories of Support: Crafts
Type of Support: Interest-free loan with no specified repayment schedule.
Total Number of Applicants: Information not provided
Total Number of Recipients: Information not provided
Funding Amount: $200-450

APPLICATION PROCEDURE-SELECTION PROCESS

Requirements: Application form, references
Time Between Application Deadline and Award Notification: One week
Method: Board Members
Criteria: Financial need is the primary criterion.

ADOLPH AND ESTHER GOTTLIEB FOUNDATION

380 West Broadway
New York, NY 10012
212-226-0581
Sanford Hirsch, Executive Director

AWARD

Title: Emergency Grant
Purpose: Financial assistance to mature, creative painters and sculptors who are beset by a current emergency situation, such as fire, flood, medical, or other unexpected, catastrophic events. Artists must demonstrate at least 10 years in mature phase of work. Recipients may not reapply for the same emergency. See p. 45 for a more detailed description of this program.
Categories of Support: Drawing, Painting, Printmaking,Sculpture
Total Number of Applicants: 86
Total Number of Recipients: 24
Funding Amount: $10,000

APPLICATION PROCEDURE-SELECTION PROCESS

Requirements: Application form, resume, referenes, documentation of emergeny
Time Between Application Deadline and Award Notification: Six weeks
Method: Board Members
Criteria: Nature of emergency is the primary criterion.

TEXAS FINE ARTS ASSOCIATION

3908-B West 35th Street
Austin, TX 78703
512-453-5312
Sandra Gregor, Executive Director

AWARD

Title: Disaster Relief for Texas Artists
Purpose: Emergency grants designed to assist artists in the event of a natural disaster. The program is aimed at getting artists back in their studios and is limited to *Texas state resident artists only.*
Categories of Support: Artists' Books, Crafts, Drawing, New Genres, Painting, Photography, Printmaking, Public Art, Sculpture
Type of Support: Emergency Grant
Funding Amount: Varies with nature of emergency

APPLICATION PROCEDURE-SELECTION PROCESS

Requirements: Information not provided
Time Between Application Deadline and Award Notification: Information not provided
Method: Information not provided
Criteria: Information not provided

AWARDS BY NOMINATION

The organizations in this section are provided for informational purposes only. They do not accept unsolicited applications. To be considered by these organizations, artists must be nominated by a third party, normally a curator, historian, academic, or other arts professional with broad knowledge in the field and specific knowledge of the nominee's work.

AMERICAN ACADEMY AND INSTITUTE OF ARTS AND LETTERS
633 West 155th Street
New York, NY 10032
212-368-5900
Virginia Dajani, Executive Director
Larry Landon, Art Program Coordinator

AWARD
Title: Academy-Institute Awards in Art; Jimmy Ernst Award in Art; Louise Nevelson Award In Art; Richard and Hinda Rosenthal Award in Art
Purpose: To honor and encourage individual artists in their creative work.
Categories of Support: Drawing, Painting, Printmaking, Sculpture (Awards in Art); Painting, Sculpture (Ernst Award); Painting, Sculpture, Printmaking (Nevelson Award); Painting (Rosenthal Award)
Type of Support: Unrestricted
Duration of Funding: One year
Total Number of Recipients: Five (Awards in Art), one recipient for all others.
Funding Amount: $5,000-7,500

ARTS FOUNDATION OF MICHIGAN
Creative Artists' Grants Program
1553 Woodward Avenue,Suite 1553
Detroit, MI 48228
313-964-2244
Kimberly Adams, Executive Director

AWARD
Title: Creative Artists' Grants
Purpose: For individuals to create new and significant projects with a strong public interaction element.
Categories of Support: Artists'Books, Crafts, Drawing, New Genres, Painting, Photography, Printmaking, Public Art, Sculpture
Type of Support: Unrestricted
Duration of Funding: One year
Funding Amount: up to $10,000

ISAAC W. BERNHEIM FOUNDATION

536 Starks Building
455 South Fourth Street
Louisville, KY 40202
502-543-2451
Charles K. McClure III, Executive Director

AWARD

Title: Bernheim Arboretum and Research Forest Art Fellowship
Purpose: Residential fellowship for visual artists in the Bernheim Arboretum and Research Forest, outside of Louisville, Kentucky.
Categories of Support: Drawing, Painting, Photography
Type of Support: Residency
Duration of Funding: Up to four months
Funding Amount: Up to $1,500 plus housing

HENRI CARTIER-BRESSON AWARD

American Express Company
American Express Tower, World Financial Center
New York, NY 10285-4800
Susan S. Bloom, Vice President, Cultural Affairs

AWARD

Title: Henri Cartier-Bresson Award
Purpose: Presented by the Centre National de la Photographie, the HCB Award is a prize to stimulate a photographer's creativity by offering the opportunity to carry out a project that would be otherwise difficult to achieve. The prize is by nomination only and is intended to award photgraphers who have already created a significant body of work.
Categories of Support: Photography (photojournalism and reportage)
Type of Support: Unrestricted
Year Established: 1989
Duration of Funding: Two years
Total Number of Recipients: 1
Funding Amount: ff250,000 (approx. $45,000)

DEUTSCHER AKADEMISCHER AUSTAUSCHDIENST (DAAD)

(German Academic Exchange Service)
New York Office
950 Third Avenue, 19th Floor
New York, NY 10022
212-758-3223

AWARD

Title: Artists-in-Berlin Program (DAAD Residency)
Purpose: To promote the exchange of artists' experiences and the concern for current cultural issues in othe countries. Visual artists are nominated by a third party while filmmakers, composers, and writers may apply directly to the program.
Categories of Support: Artists' Books, Drawing, New Genres, Painting, Photography, Printmaking, Sculpture
Type of Support: Unrestricted
Duration of Funding: One year
Total Number of Recipients: 15-20
Funding Amount: Stipend, room and board, studio, travel expenses, fabrication/ technical assistance for duration of residency

---

GEORGE A. AND ELIZA GARDNER HOWARD FOUNDATION

Box 867
Brown University
Providence, RI 02912
401-863-2640
Donald G. Rohr, Executive Director

AWARD

Title: Howard Foundation Fellowships
Purpose: To support younger people in the crucial early stages of their careers whose work to date is evidence of their promise. Intended to augment paid sabbatical leaves and other financial support. The award is by nomination only and categories rotate irregularly, with visual arts offered about once every five years.
Categories of Support: Painting, Photography, Sculpture
Type of Support: Unrestricted
Duration of Funding: One year
Total Number of Recipients: 8
Funding Amount: $18,000

LYNDHURST FOUNDATION
701 Tallen Building
Chattanooga, TN 37402
615-756-0767
Jack Murrah, Executive Director
Susan Barclift Probasco, Program Associate

AWARD
Title: Lyndhurst Prize
Purpose: Awards past achievements in various educational, cultural, and charitable fields of endeavor. Marked preference is given to residents of the Southeastern US with an emphasis on residents of Chattanooga, TN.
Categories of Support: Artists' Books, Crafts, Drawing, New Genres, Painting, Photography, Printmaking, Public Art, Sculpture
Type of Support: Unrestricted
Duration of Funding: Three years
Total Number of Recipients: 79 (all disciplines)
Funding Amount: $25,000-40,000

MACARTHUR FOUNDATION
140 South Dearborn Street, Suite 700
Chicago, IL 60603
312-726-8000
Kenneth W. Hope, Director, MacArthur Fellows Program

AWARD
Title: MacArthur Foundation Fellows Program
Purpose: The MacArthur Fellows Program provides unrestricted fellowships to exceptionally talented and promising individuals who have shown evidence of originality, dedication to creative pursuits, and capacity for self-direction.
Categories of Support: Artists' Books, Crafts, Drawing, New Genres, Painting, Photography, Printmaking, Public Art, Sculpture
Type of Support: Unrestricted
Duration of Funding: Five years
Total Number of Recipients: 4 (visual artists)
Funding Amount: $30,000-75,000

NATIONAL ENDOWMENT FOR THE ARTS-INTERNATIONAL PROGRAM

The Fund for US Artists at International Exhibitions
1100 Pennsylvania Avenue, NW
Washington, DC 20506
202-682-5422

AWARD

Title: The Fund for US Artists at International Exhibitions
Purpose: To support US participation at major international exhibitions and in areas of the world where US art is rarely seen. Artists apply with a sponsoring institution or independent curator.
Categories of Support: Artists' Books, Drawing, New Genres, Painting, Photography, Printmaking, Public Art, Sculpture
Type of Support: Project Grant
Duration of Funding: Varies with project
Total Number of Recipients: Information not provided
Funding Amount: Varies with project

NATIONAL FOUNDATION FOR ADVANCEMENT IN THE ARTS (NFAA)

3915 Biscayne Boulevard, 4th Floor
Miami, FL 33137
305-573-0490
William H. Banchs, President
Sherry Thompson, Programs Officer

AWARD

Title: Career Advancement of Visual Artists
Purpose: To assist artists in the early stages of their careers by providing time and space to work.
Categories of Support: Drawing, New Genres, Painting, Photography, Sculpture
Type of Support: Residency
Duration of Funding: Four months
Total Number of Recipients: 3
Funding Amount: $5,000-15,000 plus housing and transportation

PENNY MCCALL FOUNDATION

c/o McCaffrey and McCall
575 Lexington Avenue
New York, NY 10022
212-350-1777
Joan McCall, President

AWARD

Title: Artists' Fellowships
Purpose: Awards Grants for the Promotion of Artistic Development
Categories of Support: Artists' Books, Drawing, New Genres, Painting, Photography, Printmaking, Sculpture
Type of Support: Unrestricted
Duration of Funding: One year
Total Number of Recipients: 16
Funding Amount: $2,000-15,000

NEW MEXICO COUNCIL ON PHOTOGRAPHY

PO Box 1283
Santa Fe, NM 87504
505-988-3240
Gil Hitchcock, Executive Director
Austin Lamont, Coordinator

AWARD

Title: Eliot Porter Grant
Purpose: To Complete an ongoing project
Categories of Support: Photography
Type of Support: Project Grant
Duration of Funding: One year
Total Number of Recipients: 1
Funding Amount: $5,000

PILCHUCK GLASS SCHOOL

Artists-in Residence Program
107 South main Street, Suite 324
Seattle, WA 98104
206-621-8422
Marjorie Levy, Executive Director

AWARD

Title: Summer Artist -in-Residence Program
Purpose: To provide visual artists the opportunity to work in glass with technical assistants and excellent facilities and supplies.
Categories of Support: Crafts, New Genres, Sculpture
Type of Support: Residency
Duration of Funding: Four Months (May-August)
Total Number of Recipients: 10
Funding Amount: $500

LOUIS COMFORT TIFFANY FOUNDATION

PO Box 480, Canal Street Station
New York, NY 10013
212-431-3685
Angela Westwater, President

AWARD

Title: Artist's Award
Purpose: Fellowship program for outstanding visual artists
Categories of Support: Crafts, Painting, Photography, Printmaking, Sculpture
Type of Support: Unrestricted
Total Number of Recipients: 20
Funding Amount: $20,000

WATERSHED CENTER FOR THE CERAMIC ARTS

RR 1, Box 845
Cochran Road
North Edgecomb, ME 04556
207-882-6075
Holly Walker, Director

AWARD

Title: Guest Artist
Purpose: Watershed brings one to two artists for two, six week residency periods each session during the summer months. Artists are given a studio, materials, equipment, food and housing as well as an honorarium for a public lecture.
Categories of Support: Crafts, New Genres, Painting, Public Art, Sculpture
Type of Support: Residency
Duration of Funding: Two - three weeks
Total Number of Recipients: 5
Funding Amount: Free housing, studio, materials, and equipment, plus $100 honorarium

---

WEXNER CENTER FOR THE ARTS (WCA)

North High Street at 15th Avenue
Columbus, OH 43210
614-292-0330
Robert Stearns, Executive Director
Sarah Rogers-Lafferty, Senior Curator of Exhibitions

AWARD

Title: Wexner Center Residency Awards
Purpose: Annual awards in the areas of visual, media, and performing arts. The purpose of the Wexner Center Residency Awards is to foster the creation or completion of of new works and to encourage an artist to explore new directions.
Categories of Support: New Genres
Type of Support: Residency
Funding Amount: Information not provided (new program)

APPENDIX AND BIBLIOGRAPHY

Public Art Organizations - Supplementary List

The following organizations supplement more detailed entries listed in the main sections of the book. Write to these organizations to receive current guidelines.

Alaska

MUNICIPALITY OF ANCHORAGE • 21 West 7th Avenue, P.O. Box 196650, Anchorage, AK 99519-6650

Arizona

CITY OF CHANDLER • Percent for Art Program, 125 E. Commonwealth, Chandler, AZ 85225

GLENDALE ARTS COMMISSION • 5127 W. Northern Avenue, Glendale, AZ 85301

PHOENIX ARTS COMMISSION • 2 North Central Avenue, Suite 125, Phoenix, AZ 85004

California

ART IN PUBLIC PLACES • City of Thousand Oaks, 2150 West Hillcrest Drive, Thousand Oaks, CA 91320

ARTS COMMISSION OF SAN FRANCISCO • 25 Van Ness Avenue, Suite 240, San Francisco, CA 94102

BERKELEY CIVIC ARTS COMMISSION • 2180 Milivia Street, Berkeley, CA 94704

CITY OF VENTURA • Percent for Art Program, P.O. Box 99, Ventura, CA 93002

FOUNDATION FOR ART RESOURCES • P.O. Box 38145, Los Angeles, CA 90038

INTER-ARTS OF MARIN • 1000 Sir Francis Drake Boulevard, San Anselmo, CA 94960

PALM DESERT CIVIC ARTS COMMITTEE • 73-510 Fred Waring Drive, PalmDesert, CA 92260

PUBLIC ART ADVISORY COUNCIL • 555 Overland Avenue, Building 2 Room 135, San Diego, CA 92123

PUBLIC ART WORKS • Falkirk Cultural Center, P.O. Box 150435, San Rafael CA 94915-0435

SACRAMENTO METROPOLITAN ARTS COMMISSION • 800 10th Street, Suite 2 Sacramento, CA 95814

SAN JOSE OFFICE OF CULTURAL AFFAIRS • 291 South Market, Street San Jose, CA 95113

SAN LUIS OBISPO COUNTY ARTS COUNCIL • P.O. Box 1710, San Luis Obispo, CA 93406

SANTA BARBARA COUNTY ARTS COMMISSION • 112 West Cabrillo Boulevard, Santa Barbara, CA 93101

STANFORD UNIVERSITY ART DEPARTMENT • Panel on Outdoor Art, Crown Quadrangle, Stanford, CA 94305

Colorado

COMMISSION ON CULTURAL AFFAIRS • 303 South Colfax, Suite 1600, Denver, CO 80204

Connecticut

NEW HAVEN DEPARTMENT OF CULTURAL AFFAIRS • 770 Chapel Street, New Haven, CT 06510

District of Columbia

INTERNATIONAL SCULPTURE CENTER • 1050 Potomac Street, Washington, DC 20007

Florida

BROWARD CULTURAL AFFAIRS COUNCIL • 100 South Andrews Avenue, Fort Lauderdale, FL 33301

HILLSBOROUGH COUNTY PUBLIC ART COMMITTEE • 505 East Jackson Street #207, Tampa, FL 33602

PALM BEACH COUNTY ARTS COUNCIL • 1555 Palm Beach Lakes Boulevard # 206, West Palm Beach, FL 33401

PASCO FINES ARTS COUNCIL • 2011 Moog Road Holiday, FL 33590

Iowa

CEDAR RAPIDS/MARION ARTS COUNCIL • P.O. Drawer 4860, Cedar Rapids, IA 52407

Louisiana

ARTS COUNCIL OF NEW ORLEANS • Percent for Arts, 821 Gravier Street, Suite 600, New Orleans, LA 70112

Massachusetts

CAMBRIDGE ARTS COUNCIL/ARTS ON THE LINE • Slide Registry, 57 Inman Street Cambridge, MA 02139

CONTEMPORARY SCULPTURE AT CHESTERWOOD • P.O. Box, Stockbridge, MA 01262

MASSACHUSETTS CULTURAL COUNCIL • 80 Boylston Street, Boston, MA 02116

OFFICE OF THE ARTS AND HUMANITIES • City Hall, Room 720, Boston, MA 02201

TEMPORARY SCULPTURE • A Brush with History, 256 Market Street, Lowell, MA 01852

Maryland

CIVIC DESIGN COMMISSION • Wolman Building, Room 9, Holiday and Lexington Streets, Baltimore,MD 21202

MAYOR'S ADVISORY COMMITTEE ON ART AND CULTURE • 21 South Eutaw Street, Baltimore, MD 21201

Michigan

COMMISSION ON ART IN PUBLIC PLACES • 1200 6th Avenue, Suite P-120, Detroit, MI 48226

CULTURAL ARTS DIVISION • Parks and Recreation Department, 26000 Evergreen, Southfield, MI 48037

MICHIGAN COMMISSION ON ART IN PUBLIC PLACES • 1200 6th Avenue, P-120, Detroit, MI 48226

Minnesota

DULUTH PUBLIC ARTS COMMISSION • 400 City Hall, Duluth, MN 55802-119

Missouri

KANSAS CITY MUNICIPAL ARTS COMMISSION • City Hall, 26th Floor, Kansas City, MO 64106

LAUMEIER SCULPTURE PARK • 12580 Rott Road, St. Louis, MO 63127

MUNICIPAL ART COMMISSION • City Hall, 17th Floor, 414 East 12th Street, Kansas City, MO 64106-2798

REGIONAL ARTS COMMISSION • 329 North Euclid Street, St. Louis, MO 63108

North Carolina

CITY OF RALEIGH ARTS COMMISSION • 305 South Bount Street, Raleigh, NC 27601

COMMITTEE FOR PUBLIC ART • P.O. Box 1004, Hickory, NC 28603-1004

Nebraska

METRO ARTS • P.O. Box 1077 DTS, Omaha, NE 68101

New Hampshire

CITY OF MANCHESTER • Department of Recreation, 635 Mammoth Road, Manchester, NH 03104

New Jersey

ATLANTIC COUNTY OFFICE OF CULTURAL AFFAIRS • 1333 Atlantic Avenue, 7th Floor, Atlantic City, NJ 08401

CITY WITHOUT WALLS • One Gateway Center, Plaza Level, Newark NJ 07102-5311

New Mexico

CITY OF ALBUQUERQUE • Cultural Affairs 423 Central Avenue, NW, Albuquerque, NM 87102

LOS ALAMOS COUNTY • Art in Public Places Program, P.O. Box 30, Los Alamos, NM 87544

SANTA FE COUNCIL FOR THE ARTS • 109 Washington Avenue, Santa Fe, NM 87501

New York

ART IN PUBLIC PLACES COMMITTEE • Rockland County, 22 South Madison Avenue, Spring Valley, NY 10977

ARTS COUNCIL OF ROCKLAND • Rockland County Health CenterBuilding A, Room 201, Pomona, NY 10970

BATTERY PARK CITY REDEVELOPMENT AUTHORITY • 1 World Financial Center, 18th Floor, New York, NY 10281

BUFFALO ARTS COMMISSION • 920 City Hall, Buffalo, NY 14620

NEW YORK CITY DEPARTMENT OF CULTURAL AFFAIRS • 2 Columbus Circle, New York, NY 10019

NIAGARA COUNCIL OF THE ARTS • Box 937, Falls Station, Niagara Falls, NY 14303

SOCRATES SCULPTURE PARK • Broadway and Mt. Vernon Boulevard, P.O. Box 6259, Long Island City, NY 11106

STATEN ISLAND COUNCIL ON THE ARTS • Pouch Terminal, Staten Island, NY 10305

STORM KING ART CENTER • Old Pleasant Hill Road, Mountainville, NY 10953

WESTCHESTER PUBLIC ART • 271 North Avenue, New Rochelle, NY 10804

Ohio

ARTS COMMISSION OF GREATER TOLEDO • 618 North Michigan Street, Toledo, OH 43624

MIAMI VALLEY ARTS COUNCIL • P.O. Box 95, Dayton, OH 45402

Oklahoma

OKLAHOMA CITY ARTS COMMISSION • 400 West California, Oklahoma City, OK 73102

ULSA ARTS COMMISSION • 2210 South Main Street, Tulsa, OK 74114

Oregon

ART IN PUBLIC PLACES • 511 NW Drake Road, Bend, OR 97701

ARTS COUNCIL OF SOUTHERN OREGON • 33 North Central Avenue, Suite 308, Medford, OR 97501

CITY OF EUGENE • Department of Parks, Recreation, and Cultural Services, 1 Eugene Centre, Eugene, OR 97401

EUGENE ART IN PUBLIC PLACES PROGRAM • Public Works Department, 855 Pearl, Eugene, OR 97401

SPRINGFIELD ARTS COMMISSION • 225 North 5th, Springfield, OR 97477

Pennsylvania

CITY OF PITTSBURGH ART COMMISSION • Public Safety Building, Pittsburgh, PA 15219

MATTRESS FACTORY • 500 Sampsonia Way, Pittsburgh, PA 15212

PERCENT FOR ART PROGRAM • Municipal Services Building, Room 1680, Philadelphia, PA 19102-1684

PHILDELPHIA PERCENT FOR ART PROGRAM • Department of Cultural Affairs, 100 Municipal Services Building 15th and JFK Boulevard, Philadelphia, PA 19102-1684

PHILDELPHIA REDEVELOPMENT AUTHORITY • 1234 Market Street, 8th Floor, Phikdelphia, PA 19107

Texas

ARTS COUNCIL OF BRAZOS VALLEY • 111 University, Suite 217, College Station, TX 77840

CITY OF AUSTIN - ART IN PUBLIC PLACES • Parks and Recreation Department, P.O. Box 1088, Austin, TX 78767

CITY OF CORPUS CHRISTI • Parks and Recreation Department, 1581 North Chaparral, Corpus Christi, TX 78401

DART ARTS BANK • Dallas Area Rapid Transit, 601 Pacific Avenue, Suite 300, Dallas, TX 75202

NAVARRO COUNCIL OF THE ARTS • P.O. Box 2224, 119 West 6th Avenue, Corsicana, TX 75110

TEXAS COMMISSION ON THE ARTS • P. O. Box 13406, Austin TX. 78711-3406

Virginia

CITY OF VIRGINIA BEACH • Arts and Humanities Commission, Municipal Center, Virginia Beach, VA 23456-9002

PORTSMOUTH MUSEUM • Civic Arts Program, P.O. Box 850, Portsmouth, VA 23705

Washington

BELLEVUE ARTS COMMISSION • P. O. Box 1768, Bellevue, WA 98009

CITY OF SEATTLE DEPARTMENT OF CONSTRUCTION AND LAND USE • 400 Municipal Bldg., Seattle, WA 98104

EDMONDS ARTS COMMISSION • 700 Main Street, Edmonds, WA 98020

EVERETT CULTURAL COMMISSION • 3002 Westmore, Everett, WA 98201

RENTON MUNICIPAL ARTS COMMISSION • 200 Mill Avenue, Renton, WA 98055

WENATCHEE ARTS COMMISSION • P.O. Box 2111, Wenatchee, WA 98801

WESTERN WASHINGTON UNIVERSITY • Bellingham, WA 98225

Wisconsin

MADISON COMMITTEEE FOR THE ARTS • 215 Monona Avenue, Room 120, Madison, WI 53710

Resource Organizations for Artists

The following national organizations provide services to visual artists. Additional lists of resources are to be found in *How to Survive and Prosper as an artist* and *Supporting Yourself as an Artist* (please see the Selected Bibliography preceding this list)..

AMERICAN COUNCIL FOR THE ARTS (ACA)
1285 Avenue ofthe Americas, 3rd Floor
New York, NY 10019
212-245-4510
• In cooperation with the Marie Walsh Sharpe Art Foundation, ACA offers a nation-wide, toll-free information hotline for American visual artists. Artists can call 1-800-232-2789 to reach the Art Resource Consortium Library at the ACA. Library staff will match the specific needs of callers with a databae of information resources for visual artists. The Information Hotline's hours of operation are Monday through Friday, 2 - 5 pm, Eastern Standard Time.
•Publishes reference materials and periodicals on funding, management, distribution, and policy issues.

AMERICAN CRAFT COUNCIL (ACC)
40 West 53rd Street
New York, NY 10019
212-956-3535
•Reference library; publishes *American Craft*

ARTS EXTENSION SERVICE
Division of Continuing Education
604 Goodell Building
University of Massachussetts
Amherst, MA 01003
413-545-2360
•Technical assistance on public art management; programs to serve management needs of artists in business

ASSOCIATION OF HISPANIC ARTS (AHA)
200 East 87th Street, 2nd Floor
New York, NY 10028
212-369-7054
•Information on Hispanic arts activities; technical assistance; publishes *AHA Hispanic Arts News*

ASSOCIATION OF INDEPENDENT FILM AND VIDEO MAKERS
625 Broadway, 9th Floor
New York, NY 10012
212-473-3400
•Professional organization for independent film/video artists and producers

ATLATL
402 West Roosevelt
Phoenix, AZ 85003
602-253-2731
•Networking, resources, and technical assistance for Native American artists

DEAF ARTISTS OF AMERICA
PO Box 18190
Rochester, NY 14618
716-244-8697
•Services to hearing-impaired artists

THE FOUNDATION CENTER
79 5th Avenue
New York, NY 10003
212-620-4230
800-424-9836 (for Foundation Center collection in your area)
•National network of library reference collections on private philanthropic giving; publishes reference books and management guides

GRAPHIC ARTISTS GUILD
11 West 20th Street
New York, NY 10011
212-463-7730
•National union for professional graphic artists

NATIONAL ALLIANCE OF MEDIA ARTS CENTERS (NAMAC)
1212 Broadway, Suite 816
Oakland, CA 94612
510-451-2717
•Services to media organizations and artists, including publications, technical assistance grants,workshops, and an annual conference

NATIONAL ASSEMBLY OF LOCAL ARTS AGENCIES (NALAA)
1420 K Street, NW, Suite 204
Washington, DC 20005
202-371-2830
•Information on programs of support for artists at local arts agencies around the country

NATIONAL ASSEMBLY OF STATE ARTS AGENCIES (NASAA)
1010 Vermont Avenue, NW, Suite 920
Washington, DC 20005
202-347-6352
•Information on state arts agencies across the country, most of which have residencies, public art programs, and other programs of support for visual artists

NATIONAL ASSOCIATION OF ARTISTS' ORGANIZATIONS (NAAO)
918 F Street, NW
Washington, DC 20004
202-347-6350
•Services to and information on artists' organizations that provide residencies, project grants, and/or other direct support for artists; publishes *NAAO Bulletin*, *Flash*, and the *NAAO Directory of Artists' Organizations*

NATIONAL CENTER ON THE ARTS AND AGING
National Council on the Aging
409 3rd Street, SW, Suite 200
Washington, DC 20024
202-479-1200
•Clearinghouse on programs for the aging that involve art and artists

NATIONAL ENDOWMENT FOR THE ARTS (NEA)
1100 Pennsylvania Avenue, NW
Washington, DC 20506
202-682-5400 (general information number)
202-682-5448 (Visual Arts Program)
•Publishes various guides and program guidelines including *A Guide to the National Endowment for the Arts*

SOCIETY FOR PHOTOGRAPHIC EDUCATION
University of Colorado, Campus Box 318
Boulder, CO 80309
303-492-0588
•National association for professional photography educators

VISUAL AIDS
131 West 24th Street, 3rd Floor
New York, NY 10011
212-206-6758
•Information on AIDS awareness in the visual arts

BOOKS THAT LIST GRANTS TO VISUAL ARTISTS

Cruikshank, Jeffrey L., and Korza, Pam. *Going Public: A Field Guide to Developments in Art in Public Places.* Amherst, MA: Arts Extension Service and the National Endowment for the Arts, 1988.

Fandel, Nancy A. *The National Directory of Grants and Aid to Individuals in the Arts, International.* 6th ed. Washington, DC: Washington International Arts Letter, 1987.

Haile, Suzanne W., ed. *Foundation Grants to Individuals.* 7th ed. New York, NY: The Foundation Center, 1991.

Niemeyer, Suzanne, ed. *Money for Visual Artists.* New York, NY: ACA Books, 1991.

Press, Jaques Cattell, ed. *American Art Directory.* 52nd ed. New York, NY: R.R. Bowker Company, 1990.

PERIODICALS THAT LIST GRANTS TO VISUAL ARTISTS

Afterimage. Visual Studies Workshop. 31 Prince Street. Rochester, NY 14607. Published monthly.

ArtCalendar. 1032 Springvale Road. Great Falls, VA 22066. Published eleven times a year.

ArtPaper. Visual Arts Information Service. 2402 University Avenue, Suite 206, St. Paul, MN, 55114. Published eleven times per year.

ArtPapers. Atlanta ArtPapers, Inc. 28 Sixteenth Street, NW. Atlanta, GA 30309. Published six times a year.

ArtWeek. ArtWeek, Inc. 1628 Telegraph. Oakland, CA 94612. Published forty-four times a year.

The Crafts Report. The Crafts Report Publishing Company. 700 Orange Street. Wilmington, DE 19801. Published eleven times a year.

FYI. New York Foundation for the Arts. 5 Beekman Street, Suite 600. New York, NY 10038. Published quarterly.

National Arts Placement-Affirmative Action Arts Newsletter. National Art Education Association. 1916 Association Drive,.Reston, VA 22091-1590. Published nine times per year.
Reflex. 105 South Main Street, Suite 204, Seattle, WA, 98104..

Sculpture. International Sculpture Center. 1050 Potomac Street, NW. Washington, DC 20007. Published six times a year.

New Art Examiner. The New Art Association. 230 East Ohio. Chicago, IL 60611. Published ten times a year.

HELPFUL BOOKS FOR VISUAL ARTISTS

Hoover, Deborah A. *Supporting Yourself as an Artist: A Practical Guide.* New York and Oxford: Oxford University Press, 1989.

Michels, Caroll. *How to Survive and Prosper as an Artist: A Complete Guide to Career Management.* 2nd ed. New York, NY: Henry Holt and Company, 1991.

Murphy, Charlotte R., ed.. NAAO Directory of Artists' Organizations. Washington, DC: National Association of Artists' Organizations, 1992

INDEX

Geographic Eligibility/Media Index

RES=*Residency*	**A**=*Artists' Books*	**F**=*Photography*
PRO=*Project Grant*	**B**=*Crafts*	**G**=*Printmaking*
EMG=*Emergency Grant*	**C**=*Drawing*	**H**=*Public Art*
PUB=*Public Art Purchase/Commission*	**D**=*New Genres*	**I**=*Sculpture*
HON=*Honoraria/Exhibition Fee*	**E**=*Painting*	**J**=*Other*
FEL=*Fellowship*		
TRV=*Travel Grant*		

National Organizations

State, Local, and Regional Sources *see the key on p. 304*

Award | Organization | Media

Alphabetical Index